L·A

Aug 2

`Wicked` Content Day

Shoot.

VIEWFINDER

RANDOM HOUSE

NEW YORK

VIEWFINDER

. . .

A MEMOIR OF

SEEING

AND BEING

SEEN

. . .

JON M. CHU

AND

JEREMY McCARTER

GLINDA: All you do is follow the yellow brick road.

DOROTHY: But what happens if I—

Glinda cuts her off.

GLINDA: Just follow the yellow brick road.

—THE WIZARD OF OZ
(1939)

VIEWFINDER

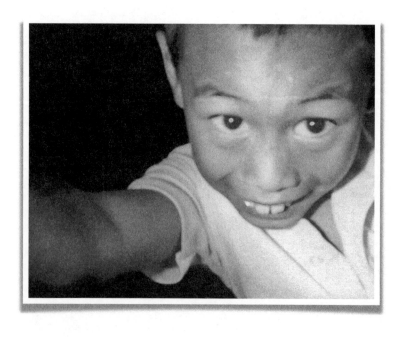

PROLOGUE

I grew up in the future.

All around me, in places like Palo Alto, Cupertino, and Sunnyvale, I saw people reaching. In offices and laboratories, they pushed the limits of what seemed possible. They made wild ideas become real.

The future manifested in our little corner of the world because of the engineers who lived there, many thousands of them. Stanford University was just up the road, with its bustling Research Park. So were the offices of NASA, HP, Apple, and Intel. Tech companies sponsored the local Boy Scout troop and our boxcar races. Their logos were on the soccer teams' jerseys. It would've felt like living in *Wired,* except the magazine didn't exist yet.

When I'd get homesick during sleepovers at my friend Jared's house, his dad would drive me home in the middle of the night. I knew that his job had something to do with satellites and something to do with maps. It didn't sound more impressive than what a lot of my other friends' dads were doing. Then I saw his face on the cover of a magazine, hailed as the father of GPS navigation.

———

WHEN I SAY THAT I grew up in the future, I'm mainly saying that I grew up in Silicon Valley. That I spent the '80s and '90s riding a wave of technological change, getting to see the world as it was going to exist in a few years' time.

But when I say that I grew up in the future, I also mean it in another, more personal way: It was the future that my parents had imagined for themselves many years before.

In 1964, Lawrence Chu glided under the Golden Gate Bridge on a steamship bound for San Francisco. Three years later, Ruth Ho looked out an airplane window and saw California rise into view. Before they met, my mom and dad already shared a vision of what life was going to be: more fulfilling and offering more possibilities than the places they'd left behind (Taiwan for her; Chongqing, Hong Kong, and Taiwan for him).

They tried to realize their dream by opening a restaurant: a lunch counter in a nothing-special strip mall in Los Altos, a little town on the peninsula south of San Francisco. By the time I was born—in 1979, the same year as the Apple II Plus—Chef Chu's had grown to become a local institution. For Mom and Dad, as for so many of their immigrant friends and neighbors, the fact that hard work led to security and prosperity seemed like fulfillment of the American promise that had drawn them across the ocean. Main Street, USA, really might be what Walt Disney and Ronald Reagan told them it was.

But security and prosperity were only part of the future that my parents and their friends had dreamed about. They imagined that one day, their as-yet-unborn children would get to enjoy the full bounty of American life. They'd be able to go anywhere, to do anything. They wouldn't just live here—they'd *belong* here.

But when you get right down to it, how does a kid actually do that, especially a kid whose parents might have arrived not too long ago from Taipei? Or New Delhi, or Manila, or Seoul, or a hundred other cities across the sea? In the '80s and '90s, the surest way for my brothers and sisters and me to do it seemed to be assimilating into the mainstream American culture that we saw on our TV. With Mom and Dad's encouragement, we dressed the part, acted the part, even, to the extent we could manage it, *looked* the part.

In family photos from those years, the seven members of the Chu family look clean-cut, sharply dressed, and smiling. Like Asian Kennedys. Like *Americans*.

No question, it made a pretty picture.

WHEN YOU GROW UP in the future, in either of the senses I've just described, you tend to become an optimist. You find yourself assuming that tomorrow will be brighter than today. Thinking that way can put you at odds with skeptics and doubters, the people who fail to see the promise of every new upgrade or beta release that comes along.

"Just wait," you say. "Just wait."

I found myself saying that all the time when I moved to Los Angeles to make movies. Hollywood, around the turn of the millennium, was traditional, nostalgic, and overwhelmingly analog—the opposite of the place I'd left behind. The change was so abrupt it felt like a form of time travel.

I figured out fast that my Silicon Valley origins gave me an advantage, and I pressed it for all it was worth. The tools I used, the projects I chose: All of it was shaped by my desire to use technology as an aid to storytelling, a belief—derived from my hero, Steve Jobs—that technology could be the best friend that creativity ever had.

For more than a decade, I watched as Silicon Valley products and systems opened up new possibilities for Hollywood's creators. When I directed *Crazy Rich Asians,* I had the sensation that I was riding that wave, drawing on the strengths of both places, making good on so much of the promise I'd foreseen in my childhood.

But in the years since 2018, something has changed. Actually, almost everything has changed.

The relationship between my old home, Silicon Valley, and my new one, Hollywood, has gone from mutual benefit to something more like a demolition derby. Bay Area companies like Netflix, which is based a few miles from Chef Chu's, have disrupted moviegoing traditions that stretched back decades, much as they've done with music, media, and other industries. For somebody like me, who fell in love with movies because of big-screen communal spectacles—the kind that Steven Spielberg makes—this has been painful to watch. And it has put me in a deeply unfamiliar situation. I'm not used to regretting the changes that technology has brought or feeling nostalgic for the way things used to be.

When you grow up in the future, you never expect to be one of the horse-and-buggy people.

But the collapse of Hollywood is only one of the dislocations that have upset my world—and everybody else's. The 2020s have seen the rise of forces that a lot of us never thought possible: the pandemic, broad social unrest, threats directed at Asian Americans. The more dangerous the country gets for us, the more I question the belief in the place that I inherited from my parents. Is this still where we belong?

I get the sense that a lot of people have been asking questions like these. Maybe, like me, you feel that you were given a set of directions to steer you through life and promises about what you would find along the way, only to discover that the landscape has changed. The map no longer works. And now you don't know where to turn.

At a moment when I've never felt less certain about the future, I have the most urgent need to understand it. I have four young children. They are beautiful brave curious explorers who come to me every day with questions about this world they're beginning to discover. The most important thing in my life is keeping them safe and self-assured, so I want to give them the right answers. I want to prepare them for whatever might be coming.

What do I do now that I'm no longer sure what to say?

IF I WAS FEELING this confused on a film set, I'd know just what to do: I'd grab my viewfinder. It's one of the most useful tools in a director's toolbox. When you're lost, it helps you find your way.

Here's how.

When I'm on set, amid the confusion and mayhem and noise, everybody looks to me to decide how we should film a scene. How should we frame the shot? Where do we put the camera? I walk to a spot that seems promising. Then I raise a black metal cylinder—like a pirate's spyglass, only fancier—to my eye and look through it.

Immediately, like a switch being thrown, the noise and

commotion around me go away. I'm alone in the dark with a tiny rectangle of light. It lets me see, amid all the chaos, a possible shot. And it allows me to answer some crucial questions: Does what I'm seeing tell a story clearly? Will it mean what I want it to mean?

The answer is almost always no. But that's okay. Because I can apply what I learned and try again. Maybe I need to change my position, so I can see the scene from a different angle. Or maybe I should stand a little taller, to change the height of the horizon. More likely, I need to look at the scene through a different lens. You wouldn't believe the power of those curved pieces of glass. A few millimeters more or less can transform how a scene looks, even how it feels.

I need in my life what a viewfinder can supply in my work: a way to see myself and my place in this convulsing world more clearly. Unfortunately there's no way to turn a viewfinder around and point the lens at myself. Viewfinders don't work like that.

But books do.

THIS BOOK IS THE story of the journey that has brought me here and my search for where I will go next. And while I'm sure that your journey hasn't been the same as mine, I offer mine to you in the hope that it might help as you seek your own path as a storyteller, a parent, a friend, or just a citizen in these perplexing times.

I've been lucky to pick up lessons along the way—from other people, from things I've tried, sometimes from mistakes I've made. As the story unfolds, in sidebars throughout the text, I'll call attention to some of those lessons. They are tools too, just as surely as a viewfinder is. The most important lesson I've learned, the one that informs all the others, is that feeling brave isn't a minor consideration—it's the main thing. Each of us has a courage engine, and we're responsible for keeping it running.

One of the best uses for that courage is telling other people how the world looks through your eyes. In a society as big and diverse as ours, that's the only way to form a complete picture of the life we share—a mosaic made up of the infinite variety of our hopes, fears, desires, ideals. If we share our perspectives, we contribute new chapters to the American story. We can help the next generation to understand this big experiment and to see its promise. The good news is that in spite of all the things that haven't turned out the way I imagined they would in my Silicon Valley boyhood, it's undeniable that more people have more powerful tools for telling their own stories than ever before. If you have a smartphone, you have a movie studio in your pocket.

You might feel that everything has been said and done, that there's nothing new to add. But once you've used a viewfinder, you discover that no two lenses are identical, no matter how similar they might seem. Each of them has its own fingerprint, the result of where the glass came from, how old it might be, and irregularities that have built up over time—tiny changes that you can feel when you hold it in your hand and see when light refracts through it. Nobody else can tell your story, because nobody else can see the world as you do.

You might also feel that telling your story doesn't matter. That in this huge, bewildering world, one more little story couldn't possibly make a difference. But of course it does. I tell stories for a living, but even in my case, before audiences get a chance to see one of them on a big screen, it's just a tiny image in my viewfinder, a secret known only to me.

The basketball players were like gods at my school. They were tall. They had swagger. My brother Larry wasn't the tallest player on the team—six-two according to him, six-one according to science—but he was definitely its leader. When I was in fifth grade, around the time that Larry and his varsity teammates were dominating the league, some of my friends admitted they hung out with me just so they could hang out with him. (Some of my friends still say that.)

I didn't blame them. Larry was more than a star athlete. He had a second distinction, one that would turn out to have a formative influence on his kid brother's later life and career: He was a movie star.

Before big games, the whole school would pile into the gym to watch highlight reels of the team's exploits: hitting clutch shots, hustling on defense, and generally showing their superpowers—all with flashy titles and a sick soundtrack. Today, anyone with a smartphone can make more sophisticated movies than those. But in 1990, only a handful of people around our school had the necessary tools and skills to create such wonders. Even the basketball players regarded them with awe, bestowing on them the ultimate comparison for film-making greatness: *That's the next Steven Spielberg*.

Thanks in part to the popularity of the basketball rallies, a zeal for filmmaking swept the campus of Pinewood School. A few teachers even let us make videos instead of writing book reports. Larry was an enthusiastic adopter of this movies-for-homework scheme. It was fun in a way that writing a paper couldn't be, not for somebody as sociable as he was. Filmmaking did have one disadvantage compared to writing papers. You needed to lug around a heavy camcorder. In the VHS era, the battery alone was the size and weight of a brick. But Larry found a solution for that problem: his little brother.

One day, he was making a video for English class, on what might have been *The Canterbury Tales*. It would explain my memory of Larry and his friends roaming Los Altos dressed as medieval squires. As always, I brought up the rear, toting the camera. After a long day spent mostly goofing off and occasionally filming scenes, Larry called a wrap. He and his costars headed back to "base camp," meaning our living room. That's when things started getting interesting.

Larry commandeered our TV and VCR. Then he brought in *another* VCR from our parents' room. One of his friends—one of the savvy few who understood where videos came from—placed what I would later learn was a mixing board on our coffee table and, when that filled up, spread some other devices on the floor, patching everything together with a spiderweb of yellow, red, and white cords.

I gathered that all of this gear was required for "editing." I didn't know what that word meant, but I wasn't about to draw attention to myself by asking any questions. Not while my cool big brother, the golden child, was letting me hang out with him.

Eventually I figured out that "editing" meant cutting up the pictures and sounds we'd recorded, then sticking them back together. It sounds straightforward, but making even the simplest change turned out to be unbelievably complicated. The exact right buttons needed to be pushed in the exact right order. Pause, *record,* fast-forward, *record,* rewind, *record.* Slowly, cut by cut, splice by splice, the video started to improve. It gained energy and momentum, even some emotional moments. After an hour or two, a ragtag bunch of kids who had spent the day messing around started to look like committed performers, like people who actually cared about what they were doing.

But that wasn't good enough for Larry. He had a vision. He wanted to punch up the video by adding footage from *Monty Python and the Holy Grail:* God parting the clouds and talking to the people below. Only this time, the audio would be Larry's voice. In those clunky old analog days, mixing audio and video effects this way added a fearsome layer of complexity to the editing process. It meant pushing a bunch of buttons, spinning a bunch of dials, and adjusting a bunch of sliders *at the same time.* For Larry to achieve his big effect, everybody would need to help. Even me.

I got into my assigned position in front of our stereo. My fingertip hovered over the play button.

Three . . . two . . . one . . . *record!*

Fingers pushed. Dials spun. Tape began to roll.

It didn't work. Our timing needed to be perfect and it was not perfect. We had to try again. And try again. With each botched attempt, the pressure increased. When you work with videotape, or any other analog technology, the quality decreases every time you record onto it.

At last we thought we got it. When we watched the playback, we fell over laughing. It was ridiculous. It was *genius*.

Thirty-five years later, I still remember the wonder I felt at that moment—the life-altering insight that flashed across my mind.

Oh, I thought, *so this is how you make a movie.*

PINEWOOD'S WILLINGNESS TO LET us make videos for homework shouldn't be taken as a sign of some freewheeling, anything-goes approach to education. Though the school is officially nonsectarian, it was founded by a Mormon family and was influenced by Mormon values. Forget having booze or cigarettes or drugs on campus: We couldn't even have caffeine. Some kids probably felt suffocated by all the restrictions. I felt protected.

Though we were all pretty sheltered at Pinewood, I was more sheltered than most. In the six years that separated me and Larry, my parents added three whole children to the family: Christina, Howard, and Jennifer. By the time I was old enough to put on a Pinewood uniform, they had cleared a path for me. My teachers knew me before they'd even met me.

Getting the various Chu kids to and from school, plus our extracurricular activities, posed a constant challenge for my parents. It didn't help that my dad worked unbelievably long hours. As in, first-to-arrive-and-last-to-leave hours. As in, miss-the-family-vacation hours. (In a Chinese restaurant, he says, management *is* micromanagement.) So it fell to my mom to manage our mayhem. Knowing what she was up against, I didn't take it personally when she would occasionally forget to pick me up at the end of the day. To cover the embarrassment, I'd make the teachers think I was headed for her minivan, then hide in the bushes. When everyone was gone, I'd walk to my aunt's house a few blocks away.

On many Sundays during my childhood, though, there was no scattering. We moved as one. Mom would drive all five kids to San Francisco, where we had season tickets to just about everything: opera, ballet, the symphony. Because we'd been going for so many years, we eventually got great seats. At intermission, I'd wander down to the orchestra pit to check out the instruments. Eventually the conductor of the San Francisco Ballet Orchestra, Denis de Coteau, got to know me.

"One day you're going to be our first violin and sit right there, right?"

"Actually, I want *your* job."

When he finished laughing, he handed me his baton and told me to keep it. I loved that baton and did indeed keep it—until my dog ate it.

Mom had a sincere desire that we get to know our Beethoven and our Brahms. But as I look back on those outings now, they also seem like an act of storytelling. They were her chance to craft a narrative about our family, for an audience of everyone who happened to be nearby.

Mom was invested in the idea that we were an all-American dream family. That we were as smart and as cultured as anybody else. That we had access. That we were worthy. We didn't slouch our way through the lobby on those Sunday afternoons: She made sure we looked sharp, *in matching suits.*

This story wasn't merely by us or about us, it was *for* us. She wanted us to feel comfortable amid the codes and rituals of this unfamiliar place. She gave us a living example of how to move confidently through any situation. (My mother is a friendly, smiling presence until you cross her. We are almost all Scorpios, so it makes sense.) She wanted us to feel that we belonged here. That we belonged *anywhere*.

It went as planned. Sort of.

You might think that our years of concertgoing would've made the Chu kids rapt little aficionados. The people who had the bad luck to sit near us would tell you otherwise. Mom could insist that we go to shows, but there are limits to how much control any parent can exert over five small, overdressed kids. Sometimes we paid attention. Mostly we were kind of wild.

Inevitably we got dirty looks from our neighbors. We heard nasty whispers. Now you can see how this might pose a problem—maybe even a crisis. It ran counter to the story we were supposed to be telling everyone about our family and its sophistication. How could my mother, who was fully aware of the commotion, keep her story intact?

Her solution was inspired. Ingenious, really. She ignored the rebukes, the shushing, the tut-tutting, the glares: She let them glide right by her. When my siblings and I saw that they didn't matter to her, we decided they didn't matter to us. Without ever telling us she was doing it, she created a kind of bubble around the family, a force field within which we could nurture our sense of ourselves, insulated from the arrows of the outside world.

At times the aggrieved neighbors probably had a point. Maybe we could have toned down the jokes about the exposure of the guys in tights. But over the years, we invoked my mother's lesson much more often in situations where we'd done nothing wrong, and somebody had said or done something hurtful anyway. It amounted to a kind of family philosophy, never announced but always obeyed: When other people treat you badly, never complain.

Never complain.

IN THE STORY WE told about our exceptional family, each of us was supposed to be an exceptional individual. That's why, from an early age, Mom gave us opportunities to develop every conceivable gift, talent, skill, and inclination.

We had lessons and classes of every kind. We learned how to play a minuet, how to hit a drop shot while charging the net, how to chip onto a green. We even had etiquette lessons with a prim British lady who taught us the proper way to get the last sip out of a bowl of soup (which was not at all the boorish American way). It was like a training regimen for a social decathlon, Mom's intensive preparation for us to be able to walk into any room, chin high, and win people's respect.

Eventually we settled into distinct roles. Christina, for example, discovered and nurtured an extraordinary gift for ballet. She was welcome to that lane, as far as I was concerned. Dance was never my forte, not even after twelve years of tap classes (not much use for a kid, hugely helpful for a director of movie musicals). Jennifer excelled at both basketball and dance. I got tagged as "the creative one." Amid the chaos of my family, I made a safe world for myself with my imagination, especially when I had a colored pencil in my hand.

I loved to draw. I drew constantly. I'd dream up other-worldly creatures, then sketch them into existence. I wasn't the best artist in my classes, but nobody matched my joy. More generally, "creative one" was a euphemism for "weirdo." At school, protected by the presence of my siblings, I'd act out however I pleased. Today, a kid with my sometimes chaotic energy might get a clinical diagnosis, but not back then, and not at Pinewood. "That's just Jon being Jon," they'd say when, for example, I painted my face in the school colors like the WWF's Ultimate Warrior and acted crazy at basketball games.

Mom didn't just tolerate these antics—she encouraged them.

"Oh my gosh, you're so funny," she would say after some silly song or dance, like when I tried to do the moves I'd seen on my Michael Jackson *Moonwalker* tape (which I wore out more than once). "You're so talented."

I let her build me up. Why wouldn't I?

So in sixth grade, when Pinewood wanted to hold a haunted house to scare and amuse the students, but every-body—even the parents—was at a loss for how it should work, I piped right up with my big ideas. I had maps, plans, drawings. To my surprise and delight, kids and grown-ups alike got excited about making it real.

And when a friend told me that the San Jose Civic Light Opera was looking for an eleven-year-old actor for its next production, I thought I might have a chance at getting cast, especially when I found out it was looking specifically for an Asian actor. Even as a kid, I knew there weren't many of those.

Mom said she would drive me to the audition, but first I would need a résumé.

"What's a résumé?"

"It's where you write what you've done and what you can do."

Great, I can do that. Not knowing any better, I created a lavishly ornamented drawing of my name with illustrations of things I liked to do, such as "breakdancing" and juggling. On the day of the audition, I slipped it into a manila envelope, along with my most recent school photo (huge grin, big teeth, wide ears), and handed it to one of the casting directors.

She took it into the auditorium. Mom and I sat outside.

Moments later, a burst of laughter.

Was that good?

The casting director called me in, smiling. My résumé had been a big hit. I sang the song I'd picked out: "Think of Me" from *The Phantom of the Opera,* a show I was obsessed with. No one pointed out that singing a ballad directed to a past lover might be an odd choice for an eleven-year-old. All the same, I booked the gig.

The show turned out to be *Pacific Overtures,* Stephen Sondheim and John Weidman's musical about America's first contact with Japan. Which meant that I had the astonishing luck to make my professional debut in a company entirely of Asian descent.

The other actors were at least a decade older than me; all of them were bursting with spirit, energy, life. They had trained like crazy to sing and dance the way they could, showing a level of commitment that put my dabbling in tap and piano to shame. Best of all, the legendary Japanese American actor Mako played the lead, carrying a nobility through every rehearsal, every break, every performance.

I loved being part of that company, especially since I wasn't some anonymous member of a kiddie chorus. My job was to perform "Someone in a Tree," the number that Sondheim called his favorite of all the songs he'd written. Every night, I would climb up a fake trunk, perch on a fake branch, and sing about being a witness to history. A big orchestra played; a huge crowd watched.

During one show, I was up in my tree, singing my song, when I felt the energy around me shift. The conductor looked confused, maybe even angry. The other actors seemed rattled. Why was the music still playing even though I'd sung the last lyric? Then I realized: *I had skipped a verse!* My heart sank— I tried not to cry. My heroic castmates, being total pros, covered for me. If you weren't a Sondheim obsessive, you might not have noticed what I'd done. But I was horrified, ashamed of myself. I felt sick.

My mom was in the audience for that show. Busy as she was, she saw almost all of them. Afterward, sitting on the stairs of our house, she held me as I cried and cried. That was the same night that somebody on the production staff had brought in a review that said cruel things about my performance. The other actors had tried to keep me from seeing it, but I had seen it. I didn't want to finish the run—or go onstage ever again.

Mom hugged me close. In the midst of all that pain, she knew what to say. She told me that this was just another part of my story. I would look back on it as something I had overcome. Gradually, her words rebuilt the invisible shield that she'd spent years creating around all of us.

"You must finish," she said.

So I did.

ALTHOUGH AN ENDLESS STREAM of cool new gadgets was the birthright of Silicon Valley kids, my friends and I had the same monthly ritual as kids everywhere else in America: waiting for the new Sharper Image catalog to arrive. Each edition brought a fresh batch of gizmos that none of us really needed and all of us totally wanted. Night-vision goggles, an actual submarine: Even *we* thought that shit was cool.

In fifth grade or so, I was poring over the latest issue of this magical catalog when I spotted something familiar: a device just like the one that Larry's friends had used in our living room. The caption identified it as an AV mixing board, a console that could combine inputs from different audio and video machines. At least, that's what I'd watched them do. And if they could do it . . .

I called the restaurant, where my dad was working another late night. "Can I get an AV mixer from Sharper Image?" I asked him.

"A what?"

"A video-editing machine."

A pause on the phone. He had no idea what I was talking about. But he also had no time to chitchat. He cut to the chase. "How much does it cost?"

"Two hundred fifty dollars."

A longer pause. "That's really expensive."

"Well, I can make videos for you. For the restaurant," I said. "And I can put music to it. And I can . . ."

On and on I went with my pitch, my first high-stakes presentation to somebody who had something I needed. I've made thousands of pitches since then, in every corner of Hollywood and beyond, but this might have been the most important one of my life. I hadn't gone very far when Dad cut me off.

"Fine, fine, fine."

An eternity later, the mixer arrived. I borrowed my brother's VCR, figuring I would ask permission as soon as he complained. But how did the thing actually work? The instructions left me with as many questions as answers. My parents didn't know anything about AV equipment. Larry didn't know much more. I would have to figure it out for myself.

As the rest of the family drifted off to sleep that night, I kept working, sprawled on the floor in front of the TV. In retrospect, it wasn't all that complicated. But for someone who had no idea what the yellow and red and white plugs meant, it was like building with Legos in the dark. I pushed and pulled, plugged and unplugged, trying different combinations. At any moment, I expected to be electrocuted or blown sky-high by the electricity that I assumed was running through the cables. I kept going anyway. Eventually I got a clear picture—then sound!

At last, the sprawling apparatus began to make sense, but now a new puzzle arose: *What should I do with this?*

I found the answer lying right there in front of me, right next to our TV: stacks and stacks of VHS tapes. Our home videos.

We'd always taken our camcorder on family vacations, recording whatever we happened to be doing until the tape or the battery ran out. But like many (or maybe all) families, once we got home, we never bothered to sit through the endless hours of footage. All of a sudden, those shelf-fillers seemed rich with possibilities.

At the top of the pile was a tape from our latest trip to Boston. There was nothing special about it, but it would do.

I got to work.

Through a lot of trying things and trying again, I figured out how to pick moments that had energy, that were funny, or that were just in focus, then started stringing them together. God knows how, but I even figured out how to add music. There was no autosave feature in those analog days—no file backup at all. Your whole project relied on the quality of your damn pause button. Once the project started, you couldn't stop. You couldn't even go back.

The footage captured my parents, my siblings, and me exploring the usual Boston attractions. At least I *think* it did. The only image that comes back to me clearly after all these years is a face: my brother Howard. He's the middle child—the heart of our family in more ways than one.

Howard had been born two and a half months early. "No bigger than the palm of your hand," my parents would say. During his long hospitalization, the doctors became aware of some health complications. He would grow up and be physically healthy, but his mental development wouldn't keep pace with his body. His autism meant that he would require special care for his entire life.

My parents had no frame of reference for what they were hearing. With two little kids and a small business to run, the pressure on them was already huge. How could they take care of this child? What were they going to do?

My mom fell into despair. She stopped going to church. At last, *her* mother, whom we all called Bu Bu, found a way to make sure she didn't shatter completely. She told my mom that God must have had a soul ready to send to earth and knew of a family who would give that soul a loving home.

That spoke to my mom. From then on, she decided that Howard was a spiritual gift to all of us and that we would act accordingly. Except for not sending him to Pinewood—he went to a different school that could offer him more specialized lessons—she integrated Howard into every aspect of our lives. He and I shared a bedroom. When we went to all those plays and concerts and operas, he was always with us. My mom tried to buy aisle seats, so if he got restless, she could take him to the back of the theater—though to be honest, the rest of us tended to be antsier than he was. (I had near-permanent bruises on my thigh from Chrissy hitting me to make me stop fidgeting.)

Still, there were bad moments. If a show used bangs or flashes, like the gunshot in *Oklahoma!,* we had to go. If Howard got upset while we were waiting for a plane to take off, we had to leave, even if the cabin door was already closed—even if two hundred people shot daggers at this Chinese family as we stumbled up the aisle. I often felt like screaming, "Stop staring!" but I never did, just turned my eyes away from them. It taught me to be understanding of other people in distress: You have no idea what anyone else might be going through.

Mom refused to let us feel ashamed in those situations. If people scorned us, that was *their* problem, she believed. We never talked about those awkward departures—not while they were happening, not on the drive home, not ever. Those disruptions were just a fact of our emotional life, to be absorbed in silence like so many other things. We were trained to keep moving.

When I made my Boston video, I found a fresh reason to be glad that Howard was always with us. The footage consisted mainly of shaky, badly tilted shots showing my parents and siblings drifting in and out of the frame, oblivious to the camera. Only Howard noticed it. Always aware, always curious: He saw what others missed.

He'd walk right up to the lens. "Am I on TV?" he'd say.

Every time he did it, he made me laugh. And he did it a lot. In fact, the video became a kind of showcase for Howard. I didn't plan it that way, but I'm glad that's how it turned out. My only clear memory of my first night trying to make a movie is Howard's face on the screen, smiling back at mine.

When my parents came down for breakfast, they found me where they'd left me. I didn't feel tired—I was excited to share whatever mess I'd made with someone, *anyone*.

I asked them to sit on the couch. I sat to the side so I could watch their reactions.

I pressed play.

The music started: a song from an oldies tape that my mom had bought from an infomercial. She immediately smiled. When the first images of our family cut onto the screen, their eyes lit up. When funny things happened, they laughed. When they were surprised, like when somebody in the family tripped, their mouths opened in delight.

For the few minutes the video played, I had their undivided attention. That was a first for me. *And I liked it.*

When it ended, they clapped. They must have said kind things, but the message that came through most clearly was the tears in their eyes. I'd only wanted to make something fun, but I had moved them. They were proud of me, but not in the usual "oh, Jon, you're so creative" way. I'd done something that even my superhero parents couldn't do, and it earned me their respect.

I had made my first movie. I had held my first screening. I've had many premieres since that morning, but none that was so important to who I became or that meant so much. Because I'd shown my parents that our family story was true.

We had value. We were worthy. How could we not be? There we were, our lives on a screen.

EVERY TIME I PLAYED my Boston video for somebody, I felt a rush of pride, a new kind of satisfaction. I loved to watch people watching what I'd made. Lucky for me, I had plenty of chances.

Several nights a week, my parents hosted giant family dinners: aunts, uncles, grandparents, cousins—sometimes twenty of us or more. My mother's mother, Bu Bu, would lead the cooking, assisted by my mom and her sisters. As the baby of the family, I helped her fold the dumplings. My folds were always pretty terrible, especially compared with Bu Bu's; her hands moved like a jazz musician's. My memory of those simple, joyful afternoons with her is the reason I put a dumpling-folding scene in *Crazy Rich Asians*.

Amid the kitchen chaos, Bu Bu always took extra care of Howard. She'd make him a special soup with roots that she thought would help him grow. And she'd walk with him all the time, just the two of them. I remember how small her feet were—how impossibly, unnaturally small—another painful fact of our family story that was never mentioned, never discussed. We would just watch her and Howard walking up and down, up and down, one tiny step after the next.

There was always enough food, but there were never enough chairs. People would sit on couches or even the stairs, plates teetering on their knees. Conversation rang throughout the house, but never about what we might be feeling toward one another. Never about challenges or problems we might be facing. In our family, the food itself expressed our love, our frustrations, our hopes, our fears, our everything.

This was not like dinner at my friends' houses.

There, parents would return from their tech jobs in time for everyone to gather around the table. It was quiet; it was polite. People talked about their days. Much as I loved my family, I envied how "regular" everything seemed in those homes. *Why can't our house be like this?*

The irony is that my friends usually left my house saying the same thing. My mom made sure of that. She wanted our friends to like hanging out with us, so she kept drawers stocked with candy. Other families—especially other immigrant families—tended to have strict rules about things like watching TV or guzzling soda, but at our house, we could pretty much do what we pleased.

Still, nothing could prepare our friends for the moment they discovered *the pile.*

The pile lived in our garage. It was taller than my head and wider than it was tall. It had not formed all at once, but gradually, imperceptibly, whenever someone in my family wanted to get rid of something without throwing it away. Was it a product of my family's immigrant past? Was it some undiagnosed hoarding compulsion? I never knew—and still don't. Whatever created the pile, it had toys. Lots of toys. A blank photo album. Memorabilia from my dad's early days at the restaurant. The purse my mom had worn on their fourth date. Jen's papers from second grade.

My friends gawked at it, found it amazing, delightful. We'd scramble up the sides of it, burrow down into it. At the very bottom, if you could tunnel that far, was a 1979 Panther Lima:

a bright yellow roadster, like something out of *The Great Gatsby*. My dad had bought it for my mom, and my mom had loved it, but she hadn't wanted to drive it. Which was why, a decade later, my friends and I enjoyed scooting behind the wheel to honk its horn.

At some point my friends started making jokes about the pile, which added to the embarrassment I'd already been feeling. One day I decided this all had to stop. If nobody else was going to do it, then I'd make the pile go away. It would be my gift to my parents. I'd rid us of this messiness, this garbage, these ugly scraps of our history. One bulging trash bag at a time, I'd make us a little more like everybody else.

When my parents found out what I'd done, they weren't grateful—they were furious. I'd never seen them more emotionally distraught over things. I couldn't understand it, but I knew I had to stop. Just as it wasn't my place to pepper them with questions—about what their lives were like before I was around, or what an ordeal it must have been to start the restaurant, or the bigotry they had faced and were facing, or the pressure and confusion and fear and dread that must have gone along with raising a special-needs child, or any other factor that might have led them to spin their story around us—it also wasn't my place to dispose of their stuff.

We fought and fought over the pile. Finally they promised they'd deal with it when they were ready.

Thirty years later, it's still there.

PLENTY OF OUR FAMILY friends, even our aunts and uncles and cousins, were content to stay within the Asian American community. That wasn't hard to do in Silicon Valley: At Pine-wood, nearly a third of my class was Asian.

But that wasn't an option for my mom and dad. The restau-rant needed to cater to all kinds of people, which meant they had to welcome everybody. And sometimes they paid a price for it. I used to watch my dad chatting up customers, serving them food, leaning over with a smile on his face. Some of them would talk down to him or complain about something trivial, as if they weren't a guest in his home, as if he were a servant in theirs.

I heard the terrible things that my parents had to put up with. It made me defensive—angry even. But my parents didn't get mad. They didn't fight back. Instead they told me to be calm. The way they saw it, we might be the first Chinese family these customers have ever known. That made us am-bassadors for all the other Chinese families out there. If we stayed poised, if we showed class, maybe those obnoxious cus-tomers would see that a Chinese family could be anything. And then maybe they'd treat the next family better than they'd treated ours.

Did this hurt my parents? Did they want to lash out, in spite of everything they told me? They didn't say.

Never complain.

Beyond the restaurant, there was real boldness in the way they launched themselves into mainstream American life. They were community leaders and even celebrities. My dad published a cookbook and did a book tour. He was inter-viewed in newspapers and on television, including by a young Oprah Winfrey.

Through some combination of nature and nurture, my siblings picked up my parents' knack for stepping forward, for taking charge. *We were Chus. We were leaders.* So Larry wasn't just a star of the basketball team but also its captain. He'd graduate Pinewood as the student body president. Coming up behind him, I held my share of class offices too, always taking them more seriously than the other kids, pouring in more time and energy than were necessary or, in retrospect, reasonable.

"Okay, we gotta come in hard on class spirit day," I said during my tenure as freshman class president, something that no Pinewood freshman had probably ever said. When it was our turn to decorate the school, I rallied my constituents to make the place look, feel, and sound like *Jurassic Park*. Giant *Jurassic Park*–themed gates greeted students when they arrived, complete with flames and the movie's theme song booming away from hidden loudspeakers. There was a life-sized papier-mâché triceratops in front of the principal's office. It *breathed*.

But even this pales next to the over-the-top way I performed my duties as sports commissioner.

The whole spirit operation needed a reboot, I declared: School spirit wasn't going to flood Pinewood's gyms and fields and classrooms and hallways and parking lots by itself. Our games needed to be *shows*—as entertaining on the sidelines as on the court.

So we designed Pinewood-themed swag and gave it away. We organized contests along the sidelines of sporting events, with prizes for the winners. It seemed logistically impossible to realize my dream of having a DJ at our basketball games, given the tight confines of the gym, but then we figured out how to put the mixing board and speakers on wheels.

Only one thing thwarted my vision. Try as I might, I couldn't find anybody willing to be the school mascot. But it had to happen: None of my plans were going to work without a school mascot.

Which is how I became the school mascot.

The administration paid for the outfit: a full-body panther suit with a big round head, padded paws, and a long black tail. And it sent me to cheerleading camp, where I received specialized mascot training from the San Jose Shark: how to dance, how to mime, how to express yourself without words, how to handle tough situations, like when some jerk pulls your tail or kicks you in the balls. Camp was exhausting—I was a sweaty mess in that suit—but I loved every minute. It didn't hurt that out of hundreds of campers I was one of the only boys.

At last it was time to be the Pinewood Panther. At an actual game. In front of actual fans.

In spite of my training, the school's supportive atmosphere, and my mom's attempts to build a bubble of self-confidence around me, I was scared as hell. But there was no way out, not after I'd been zipped into most of the outfit. So I hoisted the panther head onto my shoulders. I took a deep breath. I stepped into the light.

Imagine my surprise: When the crowd's eyes turned in my direction, I didn't feel scared. I wasn't embarrassed. I felt *free*.

Even though everybody knew it was me in there, and I knew they knew, my insecurities were gone. I could dance ridiculously. I could pounce into a group of people, even sit on their laps, and they'd think it was hilarious. It was unbelievably empowering. I could do everything a regular fan wanted to do but couldn't. Or rather, *wouldn't*.

Everybody wanted to talk to me; everybody wanted to hang out with me. If a kid was crying, I could cheer him up. And if somebody didn't like it, who cared? I had the visibility

I'd craved without any vulnerability. In the suit, you could kick me, you could punch me, but you couldn't hurt me. But then nobody wanted to hurt me. Through my panther teeth, I could see the joy on people's faces. When I was in the suit, I was loved.

That night, I got lost in happiness—the total immersive happiness—of pouring all of myself into a creative act and having an audience see it. As soon as I took off the mask, I yearned to put it on again. Only later, in retrospect, would it seem bittersweet. For a few hours, I'd gotten to feel all the freedom, the confidence, and the sense of acceptance that my mother had wanted for me. I just had to stop being me to do it.

TWO SHITTY PATCHES

I was never a great Boy Scout, but the summer before eighth grade, I somehow got picked to attend the national jamboree. It meant spending three weeks in and around Washington, DC. On day two, homesickness knocked me flat. I was helpless, frantic, inconsolable. I called Mom and begged her to come get me. When she refused, it cracked my brain. To make myself feel better I squeezed rocks until my palms bled. Amid the pain, some tiny voice in my mind said: *No one's going to save you. If you're going to survive this, you have to do it yourself.* That's when I noticed the patches. When we'd arrived, the counselors had given us a handful of uniform patches representing our home region. Kids had started trading them. The Bay

Area patches were, alas, super shitty. Nobody wanted them. But I got an idea. I traded one of my patches for two *even shittier* patches. Then I found a kid willing to take those two terrible patches in exchange for one kind of good one. By the end of the day, I'd put together a decent selection. Even better, trading had kept my mind busy. It had given me a way to put one foot in front of the other. For the rest of camp, whenever I felt my homesickness creeping back, I'd skip our planned activities for more wheeling and dealing. Eventually I traded my way to one of the best collections of patches in the camp and made a bunch of new friends doing it. That summer put an end to my homesickness, but it changed me in other ways. I became less trusting in my relationships, less willing to be vulnerable. Mom carries some guilt about the whole ordeal, but she was right. I learned the lesson she wanted me to learn—one that we all have to learn: Left on my own, I could keep myself together. My mind figured out little tricks to survive. I would need those tricks more than once in my life—times when I'd lost my way, and needed help, and wouldn't even have patches to trade.

Where's your growth?

The question drives Silicon Valley. It unlocks doors. It makes gears turn. It causes dollars to flow—and to multiply. It comes first and last and everywhere in between.

When the investors on Sand Hill Road ask about growth, they're talking about future revenues. They'll write a check only if you can identify a market for your product—and other markets beyond that market, and so on, until your brave little start-up is a herd of unicorns, riding to a ten-digit market cap.

But a devotion to growth isn't just a business consideration, at least not in Silicon Valley. It's a worldview. It says that a plan intended only to preserve what you've already got, that *doesn't* lead to significant growth, is pretty much a waste of time. The only survival lies in expansion, in conquest, in *bigger,* in *more.*

Once you start thinking this way, any sign that you're growing begins to feel like an affirmation. If you're piling up wealth or fame or power, then you must be on the right path, right? And the quicker your growth, the righter your path. You don't get your name on a building at Stanford if your company is growing only 8 percent a year.

It's no wonder that Silicon Valley tends to be excited about the future. The way some people here see it—even if they never put it in these terms—tomorrow is bound to be better than today, because if it's not better than today, then there *is* no tomorrow.

AT NO POINT IN my childhood did I say *Where's your growth?* to my father, not in so many words. But I certainly asked him plenty of questions *like* that question. And not just once.

If you can imagine standing in a spot where you have Menlo Park and Stanford to your left, Mountain View and Cupertino to your right, and Los Altos Hills at your back, you'd be picturing the very center of Silicon Valley.

You'd also be standing in the parking lot of Chef Chu's.

Although the restaurant was only a decade old when I was born, it seemed like it had been there forever. My dad had started it as a simple lunch counter in a strip mall. But he spotted an opportunity. In the best Silicon Valley tradition, he pivoted to address an emerging market, turning Chef Chu's into a sit-down restaurant that catered primarily to families—people who wanted a comfortable, reliable spot for a meal. He started to grow. He took over the leases of the neighboring businesses: the salon next door, the accountant's office upstairs. Before long, he'd bought the building itself and expanded to fill every inch of it.

And then he stopped.

More than once, a prospective business partner approached him about opening another Chef Chu's location elsewhere in the Valley. My dad even bought real estate a couple of times, weighing whether to start franchising. But he always decided against it.

As a teenager during the '90s boom, I wasn't about to take that "no" for an answer. Dot-com money was flooding the Valley and spilling over its sides, creating fortunes throughout the towns that weren't going to be clusters of little ranch houses among apricot trees much longer. I pushed him to keep up with the times, to recognize the potential customer base that was changing all around him. Why not take the restaurant upmarket, to draw in the newly fancy neighbors who mostly sped by on San Antonio Road? If he didn't want Chef Chu's to grow, why not try to make it, you know, *cool*?

My dad is smooth: an incredible talker, a natural diplomat. But he's formidable when he needs to be. (And in that kitchen he usually needs to be. It's primal back there, all fire and ice and blood and steel.) By the time I was old enough to offer him unsolicited advice, Dad had plenty of scars from kitchen knife mishaps, the kind you get in a lifetime of deboning chickens at 6:00 a.m. He had burn marks from boiling oil. So he gave me the explanation he felt like giving me and nothing more.

He said he didn't want to spend more hours away from home than he already did. For some reason, never quite clear to me, he wouldn't scale up, not as long as there was only one of him to run the show. Though he refreshed the menu from time to time, he wasn't interested in doing a wall-to-wall re-decoration to make the place look sleek and new. Same old red door, same candle that long ago melted to a blob at the hostess stand. Nor would he change the restaurant's accounting system: namely my grandmother doing the books by hand every night, *with an abacus*. In a very un–Silicon Valley way, he was content with the business he already had and the success it had brought to his family. And my mother agreed with him.

To be fair, there are things to say in my dad's defense.

Whatever ordeals my siblings and I faced, we never worried about running out of money. Plenty of restaurants, including some "cool" restaurants, have come and gone, but Chef Chu's is still standing, pretty much the way it stood when I used to nag him about changing it.

So I recognize the irony in the story I'm telling: that I became a true son of Silicon Valley thanks in large part to a restaurant that has no use for most of what the Valley stands for.

I'm thinking of a startling day, toward the end of 1993, when a customer gave me a glimpse of the future that was extreme even by Silicon Valley standards. He invited me to his office to see a brand-new program he'd begun to use: Mosaic. He explained that this "web browser" (a term I'd never heard before) was going to link the world's information. As I clicked around, watching its little globe icon spin, I felt dizzy with the possibilities. Because if all of the world's information was connected, it meant all of the world's people would be connected, too. It meant that Silicon Valley was going to fulfill one of the highest aspirations of technology. It meant growth without bounds, with no limits. It'd be a revolution in our lives.

But I'm also thinking of the many, many afternoons before and after that momentous day, when the restaurant gave me what I really needed: tools that made me feel I was a part of that revolution—and helping to speed it along.

EATING IS THE MAIN activity at Chef Chu's, but talking has always run a very close second.

My parents long ago decided that to be a good host means to strike up a conversation with just about everybody who walks through the door. My dad has a nimble memory. He'll recall if you like your sweet-and-sour pork without bell peppers, and he'll ask about each of your kids by name. My mom could coax a mop into chatting with her, if the mop looked like it needed company. (She's also been known to walk customers past the hostess stand and seat them herself, to the consternation of the hostesses.) With all their talking and listening, asking and answering, the place isn't just a restaurant: It's a house of stories.

Tales about the Chu family children have been part of my parents' repertoire for as long as we've been around. The restaurant's regulars have come to expect it, like the tea-smoked duck or XO chili sauce. From my usual after-school spot on a banquette by the bar, I got used to seeing Mom or Dad guide a customer toward my table. The sight of me would add a visual element to whatever story they were telling. I didn't mind: A smile, a nod, and a wave seemed a small price to pay for an endless supply of Chef Chu's classic lava flows (a nonalcoholic wonder drink: a piña colada and strawberry daiquiri swirling volcanically in a glass).

As I grew up, customers were treated to a running account of my hobbies: drawing, then making home movies, then uniting those passions by learning the basics of stop-motion animation. In eighth grade, quite unexpectedly and totally implausibly, this stream of trivial chitchat changed my life. That's when my parents began telling their faithful clientele—who were, remember, a bunch of Silicon Valley engineers and their neighbors—that I'd developed an interest in . . . *computers*.

Specifically: I'd started using a Macintosh SE. Not because I was some kind of Apple obsessive. Not yet, anyway. I just had shitty handwriting.

My teachers had said that we could start doing our homework on word processors, the transitional devices between clackety old typewriters and sleek, modern laptops. The catch was that we needed to type fifty words per minute. My typing, unfortunately, was as terrible as my handwriting, and my handwriting was—is—atrocious. (I like to say I do it on purpose, so the things I write will be for my eyes only. The reality is my brain moves too chaotically for me to care about legibility.) So I devised a homebrew tutorial for myself: I traced a keyboard on the back cover of my French notebook, then pretended to type on it when my teachers talked.

Almost immediately, two things happened: I found out that you can't learn typing that way, and I remembered that Larry had successfully learned to type by using a computer. Nobody in my family had much use for electronics, but we also didn't throw things away, so I had a hunch it might still be around.

A little digging unearthed it in—where else?—the pile.

There was the Macintosh SE, a model so old that Apple had stopped making them years earlier. The tidy beige tower included a nine-inch monochrome display, giving it a vague resemblance to a friendly robot's head. After a couple of tries, it turned on, the fan making a satisfying whir, some mechanism in its brain skittering away. I was delighted. Although I had no idea what I was doing, it wasn't hard to figure out the basics. A couple of clicks on the chunky rectangular mouse revealed a drawing program. Best of all, as a whimsical little grace note, it had some built-in animation sequences—a first glimpse of what would happen if you used a computer to make a drawing *move*. All of it was fascinating. I might even have remembered the part about learning to type, too.

In the early '90s, in plenty of places, the news that a kid had started dabbling with a dusty old computer would probably evoke pity and a suggestion to go outside and play. But once word got around at Chef Chu's, it led to the opposite: *upgrades*.

One of the restaurant's regulars, Dave Smith, led a company that supplied high-end graphics cards to Apple and other tech companies. When my dad told him about my new computing inclinations, he offered me a laptop he no longer needed for work. The PowerBook Duo was Apple's subnotebook, miraculously tiny by the standards of its time, thick and blocky by the standards of ours (picture four iPads in a pile). My Duo wasn't going to set any records for high performance, and it was limited to a gloomy grayscale monitor, but it was a leap beyond the capabilities of my Mac SE.

More leaps kept coming.

A few months later, Dave gave me a docking station. It let me connect the Duo to one of his company's monitors. I plunged into a world of color, like Dorothy landing in Oz. The dock also had a state-of-the-art 28.8 kbps modem, which meant that I could plug in a phone line and, after waiting through a few seconds of screeching and crackling, gain access to the networked world. My friend Sean Perkins had recently used a program called FirstClass Client to set up a place for us to "chat"—a new term in those days—and to share files. We used it to trade pictures, so this would have been around puberty.

Dave came back to the restaurant a few months later for lobster yee mein (it's not on the menu, but my dad recommended it), and this time he left without a Macintosh Quadra 660AV. I couldn't believe what the thing could do. It was faster—*way* faster—than the Duo. And the "AV" in its name meant that it had audio and video inputs, a little advance that had gigantic consequences for me. Now I could plug my camera directly into the computer. It let me import sound and video from VHS tapes.

In other words: My filmmaking had gone digital.

Movie footage was no longer trapped on a ribbon of tape that could only go forward and backward. It had become bits and bytes, little clusters of 1's and 0's that could be chopped up, copied, shifted around, made to dance. I felt a rush of freedom. Even though I didn't have sophisticated software or any real idea what I was doing (my restaurant hand-me-downs generally came without instructions), I knew that digitization would be a revolution in how I edited videos. Just like that, my whole elaborate moviemaking setup, the one that depended on synchronizing VCRs and home stereos, with its tangle of cords and tedious button pushing, was gone forever.

What I didn't grasp right away—what would unfold over years, not just for me but for everybody—was that digitization also would lead to a revolution in *thinking*. In a digital world, things don't have to be linear. Experimentation is safe and cheap, because you try things out on a copy of a copy. Because so many tasks become quick and simple, you can accomplish a lot without getting mired in frustration or bogged down in the fear that one mistake will mean permanent failure—an immense value if you happen to be a kid whose brain throws out more ideas than he knows what to do with.

The Quadra didn't just provide an outlet for my teenage creativity. It incentivized me to be *more* creative, to keep exploring, to stretch my imagination as far as it could go. All these years later, I still have it—and still get excited every time I see it.

A cycle was beginning to spin—and just in time. Because a few months after I started using my Quadra, in the spring of 1995, I had a life-changing night at the movies.

I don't remember what my siblings and I had gone to see, but I do remember the location: the Century 16 in Mountain View. We were still getting used to the place. (For years, our go-to theater had been the Old Mill, a six-screen multiplex in a mall that had an indoor pond and spinning waterwheel. The place was as rinky-dink as it was amazing: a remnant of an earlier, quirkier time in Silicon Valley. Developers knocked it down to build condos.)

We took our seats, the lights dimmed, the trailers began. Up popped the logo of Walt Disney Pictures. My love of animation owed a lot to the Disney renaissance in the preceding few years, from *The Little Mermaid* to *Beauty and the Beast* to *Aladdin*. But those movies in no way prepared me for what I was about to see.

For the next three minutes I sat there slack-jawed, experiencing the most powerful "what the f&^%k" moment of my life. And I don't just mean up until that night. I mean up until *now*.

A narrator said it was a story about "a world where toys come to life."

Flashing across the screen: a cowboy, an astronaut, Little Bo Peep, a platoon of little green soldiers. They were unlike any characters I'd ever seen. And the toys were just the beginning. Snarling dogs, zooming cars, more and more and more—a whole dazzling world. It was, the narrator continued, "the first ever computer-animated motion picture."

A couple of years earlier, I would have thought this trailer was cool. But after my hands-on experience with the Quadra, with my new (if rudimentary) understanding of how computers and animation actually worked, I was overwhelmed. It was *crazy*. A whole movie made by computer animation!

How—*how*—had they done it?

We'd all seen computer graphics in movies by then: the liquid metal robot in *Terminator 2, Jurassic Park*'s dinosaurs, even a few moments in Disney animated films, like the ballroom scene in *Beauty and the Beast*. But this wasn't a moment—it was *a whole movie*. I felt like I was seeing the future of storytelling: the creative imagination set free, *completely free,* by computers.

In the months before the movie's premiere, I read everything I could find about *Toy Story*. Every profile, every feature, every technical explanation. All of it was a discovery to me. The names of the people involved were unfamiliar—except for one. A name I'd heard around my neighborhood.

A name I'd even heard around the restaurant.

GIVE MY PARENTS A CHANCE, and even now they'll tell you that Steve Jobs was one of their early customers. In Apple's start-up days, he'd drop by with his then girlfriend for almond chicken or chow mein.

By the time I was old enough to do my homework there, Steve had stopped coming around. (Rich people eat sushi, my dad explained.) But he continued to be a presence in our lives. Apple devotees have been known to make pilgrimages to the unassuming ranch house at 2066 Crist Drive in Los Altos. According to legend, that's where he and Steve Wozniak founded the company in his parents' garage.

We used to ride our bikes past that place all the time.

BEING LAST

Being the youngest, smallest kid in a big family has its downsides. Hand-me-down clothes, toys, you name it: I was the kid with the already-broken-in stuff. But that made stuff not very important to me, which helped me later. In fact, lots of aspects of being last did. By mostly ignoring me, my brothers and sisters trained me to fade into the background and simply observe, then find a way to get what I wanted without the drama. Making movies has been no different. Some leaders feel the need to flex their authority—such a firstborn-child move—but I give everyone room to speak, then make a decision based on the ideas and insights they've shared. So in spite of our culture's obsession with being first, don't be too shook if you end up being last: the last to speak, the last to find love, the last to land your dream job. In my experience, it means you'll be the one still standing at the end.

In 1995, conventional wisdom said that Steve's heroic days were over. He was a decade removed from leading Apple, having been ousted after losing an ugly power struggle. He'd started a new company, NeXT, which had developed sophisticated technology that hadn't gained much market share. The tech world of the '90s—of networks and browsers, of Netscape and Java—seemed to have left him behind.

Then *Toy Story* arrived. The movie had been created by a company called Pixar. And Pixar owed its existence to Steve.

A decade earlier, he'd spent $10 million of his own money to buy the computer division of Lucasfilm. He kept writing checks in the late '80s and early '90s so the company's ragtag bunch of engineers and animators could boost the capacity of their hardware and the sophistication of their storytelling. In interviews I read after seeing the *Toy Story* trailer, Steve said that at Pixar, computing and artistry had equal importance. The theory was that if both cultures were nurtured and allowed to grow, the combination would yield something astonishing.

The results of the experiment arrived on November 22, 1995. *Toy Story* was a revolution in animated storytelling comparable with *Snow White and the Seven Dwarfs*, Disney's first full-length animated feature (which was itself the product of a technological breakthrough: a multiplane camera). Anyway, that's how it seemed to me, stumbling out of the theater, blown away by what I'd seen. Lots of people who knew more than I did agreed with me. A week later, Pixar went public. The IPO made Steve a billionaire—an incredible payoff to his decade-long gamble.

I reveled in his success. Though I'd never met him, he felt like a kindred spirit. I admired Walt Disney, revered Steven Spielberg, and couldn't take my eyes off Michael Jackson, but Steve Jobs was different from my other idols. He and I breathed the same air. We walked the same sidewalks—maybe only hours apart. He was, quite literally, my hometown hero. I was ready to follow him wherever he might go next.

The answer turned out to be: home.

A year after *Toy Story*'s premiere, Apple announced that it was buying NeXT, a dramatic move intended to reverse its sorry decline. (Tech journalists had been calling Apple "takeover bait.") Ostensibly, Apple wanted NeXT for its programming language, but even I could see the true importance of the deal. Steve was coming back.

Outwardly, Steve's return to Apple was a story about corporate governance. But to me, it was an epic adventure, the tale of the old king returning to save his dying kingdom. I scoured *Wired, BusinessWeek,* and the web for the latest developments. I bored friends, family members, and my parents' customers with updates, like how Steve was technically an official adviser to Apple but was obviously its leader-in-waiting. By the time the inevitable happened, and Steve reclaimed the title of CEO, I was so invested in the story that it felt like I was living the experience with him.

Steve's detractors, and even many Apple fans, hated a lot of the changes he made, like when he killed off some of the company's most popular products. This made it all the sweeter—for both of us—when he turned out to be right. When you watch someone disassemble a company that had been left for dead and revive its fortunes, it has a profound effect on how you see the world. It provides a lesson in vision, persistence, guts. In other words, leadership.

Spending those years in the fire, defending Steve when other people kept saying he was wrong, gave me precious experience in how to confront naysayers. Two decades later, when I had to persuade people that *Crazy Rich Asians* would succeed only if we put it on the big screen, I was just flexing a muscle that I had started to build then.

———

THOUGH I ADORED STEVE, I was still very much a product of my environment. So I couldn't keep myself from asking the standard Silicon Valley questions: What's next for Apple? Where is it headed? *Where's your growth?*

The answers, we learned, would arrive on the night that *Toy Story* had its TV premiere. Steve fired Apple's ad agency—another corporate maneuver that I invested with breathless dramatic importance—and rehired Chiat/Day, which had created the famous "1984" ad that had introduced the Macintosh. (I was too young to have seen it when it aired but went back to watch it. *Many times.*) Now a new sixty-second commercial would introduce Steve's revitalized vision for Apple's future.

This was big. *Huge.* My friend Aaron Reitman and I made plans to watch it at his house. We commandeered his TV. We leaned in for every commercial break. Waiting. *Hoping.*

At last: a gentle swirl of music and the voice of—wait, is that *Richard Dreyfuss?*

"Here's to the crazy ones," he said. "The misfits. The rebels."

We saw clips of different historical figures: Albert Einstein, Bob Dylan, Martin Luther King Jr.

Dreyfuss kept talking. "The troublemakers. The round pegs in the square holes. The ones who see things differently. They're not fond of rules, and they have no respect for the status quo."

More historical figures: Mahatma Gandhi, Amelia Earhart, Pablo Picasso. Then Dreyfuss again: a few more lines of narration, coming at last to the big finish.

"While some see them as the crazy
Because the people who are crazy enough
change the world are the ones who do."

A little girl looked into the camera, then
the Apple logo over the words "Think differen.

I was confused.

The ad had nothing to do with computers: n new products, no technological breakthroughs. When the shock wore
off, the rationale for the ad started to become clear.

The point of the commercial—the point of Apple—wasn't
to sell a product line. It was to stand for an idea. To have a
purpose.

The world could change, but only if people broke the
rules. And Apple would provide the tools to help them do it,
to make their visions real. That was what the company had
stood for in its earliest days, when Steve was still my dad's customer, when he liked to declare, "We are inventing the future." The commercial was his way of saying that we just
needed to get back to that feeling.

I realize it's weird to use "we" when talking about
Apple—even a little cultlike. But my connection to the company and its message felt completely genuine. I *believed*. Its
declaration that the world could change was exactly what a
teenager wanted to hear, especially one from Silicon Valley.
It's hard to remember this now, but Apple was an underdog in
those days. I felt like an underdog, too. So did lots of creative
kids, all of us believing that we had more to offer than we'd yet
had the chance to show. The commercial was only restating
what I'd grown up believing, things that I knew to be true,
because Apple computers were even then helping me to find
my voice, to express myself.

a stage of life when kids get obsessed with a team or a _c_, I got obsessed with a commercial. I committed it to memory. When we needed to submit a message to run next to our pictures in the senior yearbook, I printed the script—every word of it. You can dismiss it as an adolescent enthusiasm, but youthful passions leave a mark. Sometimes something gets through to us on such a profound level that it fundamentally shapes the rest of our lives. There's a reason the final shot of _In the Heights_ is a little girl looking directly into the camera.

"We believe that creativity is the force that pushes the human race forward," Steve wrote in a booklet distributed to Apple employees after the commercial aired. (Of course I got my hands on one.) That was exactly how I saw the world in high school. It was the gospel of my hometown hero, borne out every day by my own experience.

The tools I'd acquired at the restaurant had always brought me joy. Thanks to Steve, they also made me feel that I was part of something bigger than myself. Wasn't I one of the creative spirits he'd been talking about, using Apple technology to bring something new into the world? There was no limit to what we could achieve. I just had to commit to my vision and keep finding ways to make it real.

I understood. And Steve understood. It didn't matter that nobody in my family understood.

Except, one ugly night, it did.

EACH YEAR IT GOT a little harder to sustain our story about being an all-American dream family. The arrows aimed at our bubble got sharper, and there were more of them.

My mother had always been the most poised person in my

world. Unshakable. Indomitable. But one day, when I was alone with her at home, she answered the phone, gasped, dropped the receiver—I'd been playing with the cord, my hands were all tangled up in it—and ran out of the room. I shouted for her to come back, then chased after her. She was lying facedown on the couch, screaming into a pillow. She'd just been told that my *ah na,* my mother's grandmother, had died suddenly. I was terrified by the sound she was making. My mom, the ultimate guarantor of our confidence, was lying there broken by grief—beyond consolation, beyond comfort—me standing unheeded by her side.

When we lost Bu Bu a few years later, it was even more traumatizing—for all of us. One night, I had a vivid dream that she was standing in a driveway and was struck by a car. It scared me so badly that my mom and I called her the next morning. She assured us that she was fine. A few hours later, while standing in her driveway, she suffered a massive brain aneurysm. She never woke up. All of us fell apart. She had just given me a trash can for Christmas (my special request—God knows why). I became convinced that if I talked into it, she would hear me. Howard walked in circles around a table in our house. He couldn't cope without her. None of us could. Our big family dinners ended that day and never resumed. Mom couldn't bear to host them without her.

By then, Larry had left for college. Christina soon followed, joining him at UCLA. Then Jennifer did, too. It meant the end of those Sunday afternoons at the symphony, when the five of us would show the world—and reassure ourselves—that we belonged anywhere. My parents said I could move into Larry's old room, but I stayed with Howard. We kept the same beds we'd always had and the same rainbow decals on the walls that

I'd picked out when I was three. I needed the pocket of security in our rapidly changing life.

Gradually, my computer turned into something more than a hobby and fascination: It became a refuge. My newest one, a Power Macintosh 7200, had more speed and functionality than my Quadra, but I added upgrades anyway. The ever-generous Dave Smith gave me a copy of Adobe Premiere, the first video-editing software intended for home use, which was still only a few years old. Suddenly I had a remarkably grown-up digital editing workstation, a rudimentary version of a setup that's still used in Hollywood today.

At school, I became known as the guy who specialized in making videos for homework. My real chance to shine was the annual class video competition. Though my friends treated it as an excuse to put on costumes and act goofy, I thought of it as an opportunity to experiment, to stretch, to grow. One year, we decided our video would be *Lifeless,* a redo of *Clueless* about a couple of computer nerds. It gave me a chance to try *everything:* experiments with color, a makeover scene, a fight scene, a montage edited to a pop song, even a full-blown musical number, nine of my classmates dancing around campus to "One" from *A Chorus Line.* (It also included a prophetic joke: At one point, a jock made fun of a nerd by telling him to go home and play with his computer. The nerd fired back that he *had his computer with him,* something that seemed impossibly dorky at the time. The fake computer he pulled out of his pocket looked like an iPhone 15 Plus.)

But the part of the class video I worked at the hardest, and was proudest of, was an animated sequence: some multicolored geometric shapes that danced around the title of the movie. It was only possible because my dad's customer Russell Brown—a Silicon Valley legend, one of the original Photoshop gurus—had given me After Effects, Adobe's brand-new and very sophisticated animation software. Nobody was going to confuse my efforts with *Toy Story,* but I was dreaming in that direction and using the tools at my disposal to start making those dreams real.

These projects took time. So much time. Time to figure out how to use the tools, since most of them still didn't come with instructions. When I was done, even more time to render the gigantic video files—that is, to convert them to a format that could be exported. It often took hours. Since there was still no autosave, it was disastrously easy to lose everything in a freeze or a hard drive crash. Which would mean yet *more* time, retracing my steps, sometimes starting over.

Lucky for me, I didn't need much sleep. And Howard slept through everything. So I got into a routine of saying good night to my family, then working until four in the morning, then crashing for a couple of hours before heading off to school.

That's why I was still at my desk very late one night when my mom appeared in our doorway.

"What are you doing up right now?" Before I could answer, she said, "You need to go to sleep, to get rest, otherwise you can't work hard at school."

"I'm editing, and this *is* work for school."

"No, this isn't. This is you tricking the teachers into letting you play."

She walked over to the wall, reached down, and—in what looked like extreme slow motion—pulled the plug out of the wall.

The screen went black. I froze, disbelieving.

Hours of work—just like that—*gone*.

"I'm calling school tomorrow and telling them you can't do this," she said. Then she went back to bed.

I wanted to argue. But my mom's a very strong woman. She rules.

I shut off the lights. Went to bed. Couldn't sleep.

It was devastating. My parents had supported me since I was a little kid, cheering me on, helping me to believe in myself. Now I'd reached the limit of that support. They saw my identity as "the creative one" as some kind of adolescent phase, one I'd abandon for the worthier, as-yet-unidentified tasks they expected me to do in the next part of my story. They failed to understand that I was more serious about my film work than anything else I'd done or could imagine doing.

With the benefit of hindsight, I can see how that kind of miscommunication is bound to happen in a family where people avoid digging into the depths of how they're feeling. But that night, staring at my ceiling, shaking with hurt and rage, I wasn't remotely capable of having that perspective.

No, I thought. *This is not okay.*

I stood up. Marched down the hall. Woke Mom and Dad. Launched into a speech.

(I'm pretty weepy here. It was very dramatic.)

"You've always told us to do what we love and to work hard at it. Well, this is what I love. It's not a joke to me. It's not a hobby. You can support me or you can fight me, but this is what I'm doing."

Then I turned around and went back to bed.

At breakfast the next day, nobody said a word about the

night before: the standard Chu family response to painful experiences. But that afternoon, when Mom picked me up from school, a stack of books was on the seat next to her.

"You want to be a filmmaker, read all of that," she said.

I looked closer. They were books about making movies.

From that day on, my parents backed off. I kept drawing pictures and looking for ways to animate them. I would run around with my friends and our video camera, then stay up half the night editing the results. Mom and Dad didn't love it, but they didn't get in my way.

Night after night, clicking away at some video or other, my dreams kept growing. They grew bigger than the bedroom I shared with my brother, even bigger than the restaurant that provided me with most of my tools. Could I become a real director and make movies like Steven Spielberg or George Lucas? I didn't know, but I decided that I was going to try.

However, since I was a Silicon Valley kid, even this vast Hollywood dream got supercharged. Enthralled by the gospel of Steve Jobs, it seemed to me that the way to do the most creative work—which also meant doing the most good for the world—was to build infrastructure for myself: a company. Somehow, to realize my dream of dreams, I needed to lead something like Pixar.

I know that sounds grandiose, maybe even deluded. But remember that I was very young, and it was Silicon Valley in the '90s—a place and time when the only mortal sin was thinking small.

LOVE CAN KISS MY F-ING
JANUARY '00 (Ex.1)
Film 2 / February '00
22:37 - Film 1 / JANUARY '00
HOMAGE TO BRITNEY
THE ONE - Film 4

The *Titanic* was sinking. The Atlantic was icy; the sky was black. Survivors clung to debris.

"I love you, Jack," said Kate Winslet, half frozen on a makeshift raft.

The camera cut to the man in the water next to her: *me.*

I explained that my name wasn't Jack, it was *Jon,* and I couldn't love her back, because I was already dating a great girl. So, pretending to shiver, I asked for a favor: that she would keep living and deliver a letter inviting my girl to the senior prom for me.

But wait, I continued, Lauren was so great that she was keeping me warm inside. She was keeping me alive!

"Screw this," I said. "I'm gonna swim the Atlantic and find her myself. Thanks anyway, Rose."

As the score of *Titanic* continued to play, I climbed out of what looked like the ocean (but was actually a freezing cold swimming pool), kissed the ground, and started running down a dark street, the camera tracking alongside me. I stopped to pull a bouquet out of some bushes, then stopped again to take a gigantic balloon and a bag with a goldfish in it from my friend Aaron, who was standing by.

The screen went blank, but the music kept playing. It set a mood of epic romance for the moment when—in real life, not on-screen—I rang the doorbell of the house where Lauren and some classmates were watching *Titanic*. Specifically, an advance screening copy of the movie that I'd borrowed from family friends and edited myself into, unbeknownst to Lauren and all but one of the girls watching it with her.

They opened the door. Standing on the porch, dripping wet (thanks to the garden hose I'd preset on the front yard), I offered her the bouquet, the balloon, the fish, and the letter.

After all the laughing and disbelief, she said yes.

So I was getting better at making movies.

BY THE TIME I was old enough to vote, I was well on my way to running a mini movie studio out of my bedroom. It was only a few years after Billy Crystal had delighted the Oscars audience by popping up in clips from nominated films, and here I was, alone at my computer, trying to match James Cameron cut for cut and camera angle for camera angle, stitching myself into *Titanic*.

As always, having the right tools made the difference. The arrival of MiniDV made every shot crisper. But the real leap forward—the last and greatest of my Silicon Valley youth—was the Media 100 video card. With that amazing device plugged into the internal SCSI drive of my Power Mac, I could edit in real time, which meant no more waiting around for clips to render. The extra freedom came at a price: The Media 100 was shockingly expensive. It wasn't even available at that time for consumers to buy, only businesses. I spent a year trying to convince my parents to help me pay for it, pleading, nagging, taping contracts to their bathroom mirror. I was lucky that they finally gave in and even luckier that the card gave me a way to start earning back the money I'd spent acquiring it: People would call me when they needed a wedding video, a memory video, any and every kind of video. With demand for my services growing, I set myself up as Chu Studios—an imposing name for a ragtag operation. I felt like I'd started to build the creative company of my dreams.

Since I didn't know what I was doing, and nobody was around to teach me, every project was a chance to learn. When I used footage from old home movies, like for a bar mitzvah video, I noticed that the image would have more grain, which made it feel nostalgic. Zooming in on newlyweds during their first dance made the moment more poignant. Add slow motion and a little Celine Dion, and it'd reliably draw some tears from the happy couple. It was like coding for emotions, and I was quickly learning the tricks of the trade.

Before long, I would show up at a wedding with a checklist in my head, ready to grab the shots I needed for the feeling that I wanted to capture for my clients.

"Oh man," they told me. "You're the next Steven Spielberg."

SO I ARRIVED AT film school feeling ready. I had a backpack full of tricks and couldn't wait to use them.

In 1998, when my Power Mac G3 and I moved to Los Angeles, USC was Top Gun for aspiring filmmakers: the proving ground for people who wanted to be the best of the best. It was the alma mater of George Lucas, John Singleton, and Robert Zemeckis. It's the place that offered young filmmakers the skills they would need to follow in the footsteps of these iconic filmmakers, or to break the rules and become Quentin Tarantino, which was why 90 percent of my classmates were there.

For many of my fellow freshmen, USC meant cutting loose from parental supervision, and in the heart of L.A., no less. Being a straitlaced kid, I didn't feel much of an urge to party the way college students were expected to. A serious case of Asian flush kept me away from booze; the memory of my mother smashing the marijuana pipe of a sibling who shall remain nameless sapped the appeal of drugs. I entertained myself in other ways.

My dorm had a LAN connection, a blazing-fast way to share files, especially photos and music. (Napster was a few months away—at this point, we could only do a direct download.) Since Macs were set to see one another on the network, I had a way to find other Apple users. We "Macolytes" thought of ourselves as creative rebels, though hardly anybody took their devotion as far as I did. My room was wallpapered, and I do mean *wallpapered,* in "Think different" posters.

I got the benefits of college life without giving up the benefits of home. Lauren was a year behind me, so I flew back a lot to see her during her senior year. (She was Pinewood's star athlete; I'd been the student body president—we felt like a Panther power couple.) Getting away from school on the weekends was a breeze because my film classes wouldn't start until my second year, which was also when Lauren would be joining me at USC.

Sophomore year. That's when my work and love would come together in sunny L.A.

Or so I thought.

It turned out I had a lot to learn. And sophomore year was when the universe forced me to learn it.

For example: that I didn't know anything and, in fact, had *never* known anything; that I couldn't do anything, at least not anything worth doing; that I was a nobody, a fake, a fraud; that I was going to die alone (she dumped me) without having amounted to anything in this life; that my mom had been doing me a favor when she'd unplugged my computer in the middle of that night; that on second thought, Jack was lucky when he went down with the damn ship.

THREE AND A HALF million people lived in Los Angeles. They didn't matter to me. I was alone, *truly* alone, for the first time in my life.

No more getting a pass from teachers who had taught my siblings. No more retreating to the restaurant that had been a safe harbor for my entire life. All my landmarks were gone, up to and including the mountains that framed the Valley.

Since I'd never created a new world for myself, the experience was bound to be painful. But at USC, it was excruciating. Even on that great big campus, there was a daily threat I'd run into my ex-girlfriend—who was also my first girlfriend— maybe with her new boyfriend, a football star.

Also, in L.A., I was Asian.

I'd always been Asian, obviously. But that meant one thing in the sheltered world of Silicon Valley, where so many of my classmates were Asian—where even the mayor had been Asian—and something very different in L.A. For the first time, I felt myself being judged at a glance because of how I looked—being treated, in all sorts of ways, as if I weren't supposed to be there. Eyeballs seemed to track me wherever I went. Briefly, and with laughable innocence, I thought this might be a case of mistaken identity. USC has a huge international population—it's one of the glories of the place—so maybe people assumed, in a harmless sort of way, that I'd just arrived in America.

Having people on the streets shout at me to go back where I came from would clear up my confusion about this. As would my sister Jen, across town at UCLA, telling me that she'd been spit on while crossing the street.

I wasn't in Los Altos anymore.

When I look back on it now, the only surprising thing about the hostility I faced was the fact that I was surprised. It was my first visceral and sustained encounter with what Asians have experienced since the Chinese built this country's railroads: the view that they have no business being here.

The feeling of all that animosity being aimed in my direction sent me running for cover, looking for my people.

But who were they?

In L.A., I had my first encounter with Asian Americans who were bitter toward non-Asians, who got angry about the way we were treated. I could understand that anger and often felt it, but I couldn't make a daily practice of stoking it. Especially when some of these Asian Americans told me that since I dressed like "them" and talked like "them," I could, in so many words, go fuck myself.

Now you might be thinking, *Three and a half million is a big number.* Among all those Angelenos, there must have been a few young Asian Americans who shared my predicament. Like me, they must have struggled to define their in-between identity, reconciling their Asian heritage with the broad American culture where they felt most at home. But I didn't go looking for those kindred spirits. I avoided them.

My surroundings might have been different in L.A., but I was the same kid I'd been in Los Altos. The one who would bury any aspect of my Asianness if I got the sense that somebody didn't like it. The one who would march off to school with a lunch box full of my parents' dumplings—which I loved and which people literally paid money to eat—and toss them in the bushes before anyone could make fun of the smell. If I were to hang around other Asians at USC, it would call attention to my Asianness. What if those kids didn't have my skill at code-switching, or my constant, urgent need to assimilate? All I wanted was *not* to be the Asian dude. I just wanted to be a dude. Like everyone else.

Every time an Asian kid got near a group of friends that I'd so carefully infiltrated, we'd share a look. It was mostly me silently saying, *I worked really hard to get here, so don't screw this up for me.* At least, that's how my predicament looks in retrospect. I wasn't conscious of my motivations at the time, and I sure never talked about them. Which was a big part of the problem. I felt so alone. If we had been open about what we were feeling, we could have helped each other. It would have been a lot healthier than competing for what we thought was the one available slot for the Asian friend.

So I kept on searching for my people. For a circle of friends where I'd feel safe and happy. For the sense of belonging I'd taken for granted back in Los Altos. For a place where I could *breathe*.

It did not go well.

Since fraternities were huge at USC, and Larry had been the president of UCLA's Sigma Nu chapter, I decided to give

Greek life a shot. The rush process had its upsides. Getting dragged out of your room in the middle of the night, being stuffed into a closet, being force-fed mayonnaise: All of these were welcome distractions from a stomped and bleeding heart. I stuck it out long enough to get into a fraternity, but I knew it was never going to be my scene. I drifted away.

I also tried to get God on my side, which is not as desperate as it might sound.

In my junior year at Pinewood, I'd heard somebody talking about a Bible study group. Nobody in my family went to church, so I was intrigued enough to check it out. We'd meet at a café early on Friday mornings to talk about Scripture and how it related to what was happening in our lives: a precious opportunity for me, since we didn't share our feelings at home. Before long, I was going to church every Sunday, going to camps—I even got baptized. My parents were supportive; my siblings were confused.

But being a young Christian, like being Asian, meant something very different when I got to L.A. Instead of the super-tolerant post-hippie spirituality of the Bay Area, the believers of USC came from all over the country, including places where Christianity had a hard-line fundamentalist edge. I found a "cool" church and started going to services. But the pastor liked to show videos with his sermons. They were indeed a revelation—but not in the way I expected. I didn't know much about Scripture, but I knew Adobe Premiere. While I appreciated the message they were trying to convey, I could spot all the tricks they were using, the subtle manipulations. If this were really the revealed Word of the Almighty, it shouldn't have needed the techniques I'd been using in my videos. It turned me off. So I drifted away from church, too.

When all my other attempts failed, one thing made me feel better: cigarettes. My new vice gave me a reason to take smoke breaks with people. Cigarettes eased my loss. They curbed my loneliness. They "worked," as long as you overlooked the toll they were taking on my body.

I was so desperate to find a community in L.A. that I was more than happy to poison myself to do it.

FILM CLASSES, I'D HOPED, would make me feel like myself again. Once I was reunited with my tools and back in the groove of making movies, I'd regain my sense of self. Instead, I felt even more lost than before.

I'd spent my adolescence mastering the latest digital film-making techniques. USC forbade all of them. The teachers expected us to use yesterday's technology: everything analog, everything manual. By 2000, the rest of the world was abandoning this stuff, and they knew it. Our orientation pamphlet said, "You can usually get a good deal [on a Super-8 camera] since no one uses Super-8 anymore."

Moving from digital filmmaking back to analog meant a painful shift from the realm of metaphor to the world of real stuff. My editing software called a snippet of footage a "clip." Once I started working with actual film, I discovered that we stored the frames we cut from our footage in Ziploc bags that we would "clip" onto the wall. "Bins" ceased to be the windows where I organized my files and became the all-too-real containers where I stuffed messy ribbons of film. We bled learning how these old tools worked, which is not a metaphor: We all got cuts on our fingers from splicing film together.

No matter how embarrassing the results might be, our

teachers expected us to start using these tools immediately, making five short films in a semester. The technical
elements—camera angles, T-stops—came more easily to me
than to some of my classmates. But in other ways, I was miles
behind them. In spite of my mother's best efforts to give us
cheat codes so we'd fit in anywhere, the other students were
better read, more knowledgeable about cinema, and way more
emotionally sophisticated than me. Especially the kids from
L.A., a bunch of savvy intimidators. We were the same age,
but somehow I always felt young and naive when they were
around.

The way to be taken seriously, I gathered, was to make dark,
brooding movies. Films that challenged the system. But I didn't
have dark and brooding in me. When a teacher told us to make
a video demonstrating what we'd learned about camera movement, my classmate Jason and I decided to create a full-on music
video, whirling down the hallways, jumping onto tables, performing an elaborate dance to Britney Spears's ". . . Baby One
More Time." We couldn't get the precision we needed from
our primitive analog tools, but I came up with a workaround,
which is a Silicon Valley–ish way of saying I found a loophole
and exploited it. I projected our raw footage onto my bedroom
wall, then filmed the projection with my MiniDV camera.
Then I transferred *that* footage to my Mac, where I worked out
exactly how the edits should go. With the digital version as a
guide, it was easy to cut the original footage to make it frame-
perfect—even to have sync sound from a CD player.

When we screened the video in class, all the oohing and
aahing and laughing (which might have been with us or might
have been at us—probably both) gave me two and a half minutes of feeling like my high school director self again. But the

rush didn't last. The most painful lesson I learned that semester was that the film work I'd done back in Los Altos, all the videos I'd been so proud to direct, didn't count as directing at all. My teachers made me see that I'd been reactive: shooting like an editor, not like a director. In fact, I'd tried so hard to duplicate the movies that inspired me that I was essentially just a copying machine.

Directors need a point of view, we were told. They make *choices*. Those choices might turn out to be wrong, but they're never safe or obvious, never down the middle of the road. The criterion for being a director isn't: *Can you make something that looks professional?* Almost anybody can do that. The challenge is: *Can you tell a story in a way that the audience never forgets it?*

The only craft that really matters, they taught us, is storytelling craft. Not clever angles, but emotional accessibility; not flashy edits, but dramatic momentum, where each scene has an emotional conflict that advances a character's development. They wanted us to spend less time reverse engineering the stylistic flourishes of Zemeckis or Tarantino and more time asking hard questions of ourselves.

Who are you? What's your perspective? *What are you trying to say?*

To develop as filmmakers—and to get passing grades—we needed to make our work personal, to tap into the raw material of our lives. My raw material continued to be very, very raw. Months after the fact, I still hadn't made peace with my breakup—my gut-churning, soul-crushing breakup. I poured those feelings into a short film titled *Love Can Kiss My Fucking Ass*. The protagonist, a college student going through a sudden breakup, argues with his girlfriend, burns her letters, then ends up crying alone on his couch. My big artistic swing was holding the shot of him sobbing for *two and a half minutes*. No music. No dialogue. Just the sound of him weeping and the crackling of the burning letters. It was unbelievably awkward for the audience, and I relished every second of it. I wanted them to swim in the pain as I was swimming in it.

My classmates were shocked. They weren't sure how I could be the same guy who made the funny Britney Spears thing. I couldn't answer that question, not when I was struggling to answer bigger questions of my own. Namely: If you took my friends, family, girlfriend, and tools away, what was left of me? Who was I?

Out here, in the real world, nobody cared that I was Larry's kid brother. Nobody was fooled by my tricks. If I made something I thought was good, it couldn't satisfy me, not after a lifetime of relying on other people's approval, of constantly seeking ways to be the center of attention—of being *encouraged* to seek it.

It all suddenly seemed so pathetic, so embarrassing: screwing up a Sondheim show, dancing around in a panther suit. It made me angry. It made me sad for the kid who'd been led astray, painfully unequipped for the challenges of real life.

I resented the bubble in which I'd been raised. Why had my mother spent all those years building up my hopes, encouraging me to be "the creative one," telling me I had talent that I plainly didn't have?

I even started resenting *her*. But then she got sick.

HERE'S ANOTHER VIDEO I made that year. Not for class.

My mother sits at our kitchen table. It is very late at night. She eats soup, talking quietly with me and my sister Jennifer.

CHECK THE PROJECTOR

I suffered enough technical mishaps in high school to learn that technology can be fickle. So at USC, when it was my turn to share dailies with my class, I got there early—*really* early, when hardly anybody was around. I would talk to the projectionist, who was usually some grad student who didn't want to be there. I'd give him cookies, then we'd string up my film and make sure it looked right. Usually I discovered that I needed to make a few adjustments. Once class started, and other students wrestled with dailies that were out of sync or blurry, mine always played right. I know this sounds trivial, but it gave me a sense of pride. And I needed to feel pride in my work, and in how it was presented, if I was going to expect anyone else to care about it. No one will tell you those extra steps are necessary. But to me, they are. In filmmaking or any other field, it's all about how you value your work. Making sure that every detail is exactly how you want it to be is well worth the time, the effort, and the dozen cookies from Albertsons.

In a few hours, she'll go to the hospital for a double mastectomy.

Her first breast cancer diagnosis had come when I was in high school. She'd received radiation at the time and seemed to be all better, but the monster returned in my sophomore year at USC—the worst of that year's horrors. As soon as my classes ended, I flew home for the summer, determined to help but not sure what I had to offer. So I brought the one thing I knew how to use that might normalize the situation: my camera. In the days leading up to her surgery, I filmed my parents and siblings, as I'd filmed them so many times before: going about their lives, eating and talking, preparing as best they could for what Mom was about to endure.

Sometimes I let the camera roll, quietly observing; sometimes I posed questions. That night in the kitchen, I asked Mom if she was scared of the pain—a question I couldn't imagine asking without a camera between us.

She said, characteristically, that she wasn't.

"I did my crying," she told me. "I did my screaming. It's all done. All past. Once you make the decision you're gonna do it, just do it. There's nothing you can do."

What did worry her, she said, was whether anybody was going to take out the garbage while she was gone. That was characteristic, too.

The reason for all my filming and prying, I told my parents and siblings, was that I might make a short documentary about my mother's sickness and recovery. But looking back now, I had a deeper motivation. Pointing a camera at my family was, quite literally, a way to put a frame around our fear and pain. If I was filming the story, then I must be, on some subconscious level, outside the story, with all its terrors. If I was watching it, I couldn't be living it. If this were a movie, it might turn out to have a happy ending.

The surgery took all day. More than ten hours. When it ended, my dad admitted (in the hospital waiting room, camera rolling) just how worried he'd been about her getting through that ordeal. But the hardship would continue. She faced another round of chemo. That's why, when the camera caught my reflection in a mirror or window, you can see that I'd already shaved my head in solidarity.

The upheaval in our family that summer, the close quarters we were forced to keep, the mortality suddenly crowding us—they created an opening for the conversation that my parents and I had been avoiding. It was my chance to ask them why they'd set me up the way they had, raising me in such a bubble. Why they'd given me a sense of my own ability that far exceeded what I was actually capable of doing. What happened before I came around that made them raise us the way they raised us—that had made them who they were?

But we didn't have that conversation. How could we? The only way to get into those questions would have been for me to tell them I'd been feeling lost in L.A. I wasn't about to say that, not after everything they'd taught me.

Never complain.

Though I couldn't talk about USC, I also couldn't stop thinking about the place. Before summer ended, I needed to come up with an idea for my junior-year project, a five-minute short film without sync sound, which meant no dialogue. I worked up one idea after another, but none of them seemed good enough. Certainly none of them showed any emotional availability, which was what my teachers really wanted. If anything, I seemed to be moving backward, using my camera to create distance for myself, not to delve into my deepest feelings or insecurities.

I was stuck. Until, all of a sudden, I wasn't.

One night that summer, I shot up in bed, a voice in my

head saying, *Write this down now, it might not make sense in the morning.*

I thought about how it felt to walk into stores in L.A., how different it felt from going into stores back home. Like I was being watched. Like people thought I was there to steal something. I wanted to say, *I'm not what you think I am.* But of course I never said a word. And I knew plenty of other people had been through much worse than me.

My sense of being an outsider—of being judged at a glance—reshaped itself as a dramatic scenario. I began to imagine an encounter in a little grocery store between a young Black man, an older white lady, and the Asian store owner. Each one misunderstood, and each one misunderstanding.

I'd always had a brain full of ideas, but this was something new: an idea that came from deep inside me, one so personal I was a little afraid to touch it. I couldn't talk with my parents about the alienation I'd felt in L.A., so the impulse found its way out through my imagination.

I kept scribbling late into the night, trying to pin my ideas down before they flew away. There would be plenty of chances later to slow down and organize them. There would be all the time in the world to be intimidated as hell about who was waiting for me back in L.A.

EVERETT LEWIS WAS THE least professorial of all my professors, a tall, tattooed artist who always wore a hat. Every year, Everett inherited a fresh batch of juniors like me, overachievers who were desperate to please. And every year, he told them to get over themselves. He wanted us to see that in spite of what the rest of the faculty would have us believe, sometimes wrong can be right: that the most memorable and effective thing a filmmaker can do is the one that flouts the rules, that's conspicuously strange.

I was fully prepared for Everett to hate me, a congenital people pleaser who would always struggle with his commandment to "Be weirder." (Even now, it haunts me.) I dreaded the day when it would be my turn to stand in front of his class and present my idea, especially since he had taken apart most of the students who preceded me. So I overprepared. I showed up to class with a board stocked with pictures and pitched my project as if my life depended on it.

When I finished, I turned to Everett, bracing for impact.

"This is how you're supposed to present, guys," he told the class. "You're a *storyteller*. Every time you walk into a room, you need to show people how you're a storyteller."

For the first time in a long time, somebody had given me a reason to think I might actually belong in film school. That mixture of joy and relief propelled me right into production, when I'd face challenges beyond anything I'd tried before.

I wanted the film to switch back and forth between two modes: the interactions among the three characters would be in color, and the stereotypes that each harbored about the others would be in black and white. We'd see that the young Black man had come to the store for water after a tap dance rehearsal. When I pitched the idea, my classmates pointed out that this could be an old and potentially ugly trope. I could see their point. But I wanted to get beyond the stereotype, to show the individuality of this person. The movie would contrast the other characters' prejudices with the reality of his life—for instance, that he'd been baptized, that he was taking care of his mother as she went through chemo. It was another way that this film was more personal than anything I'd made.

It was also more experimental. In the late '90s and early 2000s, groups like *NSYNC and Backstreet Boys dominated the charts. I felt like their songs followed a pattern, taking listeners on an emotional journey through a certain rhythm and structure. So I set myself a challenge: *Can you make a film in the form of a pop song?* When the young man arrives at the store, it's like the opening of a song: The energy builds. The verse is when he walks through the aisles, as the other two characters dart glances at him, their minds flashing to their preconceived notions of who he is—as he does the same to them. As he approaches the counter, the rhythm slows down the way a Max Martin–produced hit does. When he comes face-to-face with the store owner—the tension between them mounting, like a showdown in a western—the rhythm erupts again, like an out-chorus.

I'd decided early on that the sound of his tap rehearsal would be the soundtrack for the movie. (Since I couldn't use dialogue, there weren't many other options.) My tap teacher once told me that the most powerful beat in a song is the one you don't hear—the one you supply yourself. It gave me my title: *Silent Beats*.

At the end of the semester, we held a screening for our friends and families. Mom was there. She was making her way back to health, though she still had a shaved head. So did the mother of Antoine Grant, the lead actor—she was recovering from cancer, too. People seemed impressed and a little surprised that I had elevated a class project into something experimental, something poignant—something maybe even relevant. *Silent Beats* would go on to win some awards and earn me a couple of scholarships. The Anti-Defamation League designed a workbook around it.

Even Everett liked it.

A wordless five-and-a-half-minute video might not sound like much, but it changed everything for me. I still suspected that I might not be as smart or creative as a lot of my classmates, but I began to feel that my work had value anyway. Watching the audience react to it—watching them recognize that all of us judge other people and are judged—showed me what I'd been doing wrong since I'd reached L.A.

I'd run myself ragged trying to find my people, but what I really needed to find was my own courage. Instead of trying so hard to be like everybody else, I needed to use my voice and tell stories that expressed who I really was. That way, other people might realize that *they* were like *me*.

ASIAN ACTORS
Casting Call

16mm short film that will go on the film festival circuit.

Pleae send headshot and Resume ASAP!

Deadline: September 14th!

*Teenage boy (15–18)
Mother (35–50)
Grandma & Grandpa (60–80)

Good cinematographers paint with light; great cinematographers paint with shadow. Trust what darkness can do.

If you cast an actor with long hair, be prepared for daily nightmares in continuity, making sure it looks identical from one shot to the next. (Same for bangs.)

Letting the audience see the world through a character's eyes—that is, putting the camera in a character's eyeline—is a subtle but powerful way of creating intimacy, of forging a bond.

I was grateful to learn all these lessons at USC. But the one that meant the most to me, both then and now, wasn't about filmmaking. Or anyway, it wasn't *just* about filmmaking. It was how to collaborate with creative people.

That was not an easy lesson to learn.

Before college, I could make my movies pretty much on my own. But a movie with any kind of scale is intensely, gorgeously, sometimes maddeningly collaborative. Before you can put a story on-screen for an audience to enjoy, you need to assemble a team. That means finding ways to describe the pictures in your head. You need to motivate people, to inspire them to jump out of an airplane with you, hoping that you'll make a parachute together as you fall. I've learned that this is a form of storytelling in its own right. And unless you want to be a dictator and make everybody miserable, there's no way to force it. Creative leadership, I came to see, is actually a form of creative partnership. Because in the end, you have to trust each member of the team to do their part to make a project real and save you from splattering on the ground.

My classmates and I grew closer during our years of working together this way. We helped one another, looked out for one another, bonded every week at our traditional Wednesday night dinner. (In those pre-smartphone days, we didn't have devices to distract us: We actually talked to each other.) Eight of us even moved into an old house that Everett had begun to remodel. For a while, it had no windows; we had only one bathroom. We called it the "Fight Club House."

As graduation drew nearer, we daydreamed about life after USC. How we'd go on helping one another, building the Hollywood careers that we'd wanted since we were kids. Most of us had no industry connections. Nobody was waiting to open a door for us or to show us the way. If we didn't look out for one another, who would? I began to see how the company I'd dreamed about since my Silicon Valley days could empower my friends to make the projects they wanted to make. I even got a head start. We called USC's Student Production Office "SPO," which rhymes with "go." My dorm became known as "Chu-SPO," a repository of resources that rivaled the university's. I filled binders with information about production services, phone numbers to call to obtain permits, names of restaurants that might donate food, a shit list of people you probably didn't want to work with. It was a hub for collaborating, a way to make each other better.

So it was awkward when, at a crucial stage of our education, USC put these twin desires—to build a Hollywood career, to help our classmates succeed—in direct conflict.

During senior year, USC gives directing students a chance to put together all that they've learned, to show the world what they can do. In course 480, they make a twelve-minute short film, shot on 16mm. Our handbook called it "'the big gig,' the proverbial feather in the cap, the goal to aim for." Excelling in 480 is no guarantee that you'll succeed in life, but it sure doesn't hurt. I mean, it worked for Robert Zemeckis.

The catch is that 480 isn't guaranteed. Out of dozens of students in the directing program, only *four* get chosen by the faculty selection committee. It's like USC's USC. But instead of competing against a bunch of anonymous strangers, as we did when we applied to the school, we'd be competing against our friends.

One night in junior year, all of us crowded into Norris Cinema Theatre to see what the 480 class ahead of us had made. Students, parents, professors: Everybody was dressed up, eager to see what the next generation of filmmakers had to offer. Was a new superstar director about to emerge? We younger students envied the opportunity to show our films with this sort of pomp and circumstance, on the biggest screen on campus. Which four of us would get chosen? Which idea would we pitch to the committee to give ourselves the best chance? I couldn't have been the only one who was silently wondering.

The lights dimmed. Everybody cheered. Each film was incredibly impressive and received a raucous ovation. The final film of the night was a romantic comedy about a young woman's search for love. It ended with a montage of her apartment door opening and closing, opening and closing, revealing different prospective boyfriends. Each of them did something awkward, weird, or disgusting.

The last time the door opened, nothing crazy happened. A regular-looking Asian guy just stood there. As I remember it, he was holding a flower. He smiled.

"Uhhh, *NO,*" she said, and slammed the door in his face.

Everybody laughed.

I looked around, genuinely confused. What was so funny? I didn't get the joke.

Then it clicked.

Unless I'd missed some hilarious detail that was apparent to everyone else, the joke—the whole joke—was that the guy was Asian. A single glance was all this woman needed to judge him unworthy of being a love interest. And people in the audience found it hilarious and laughed right along.

I couldn't believe what I'd seen and heard—that room-shaking laugh. *How can everyone be okay with this?*

I had, Lord knows, experienced a lot worse than that joke. But these people were my classmates, my teachers, my friends. That's really how they felt about Asian men? About *me*?

Today, I'd call bullshit on it, loudly and quickly. But at twenty-one, I wasn't capable of it. *Never complain.* As I left the theater, still reeling, silence seemed like the best response.

Then I realized what my 480 pitch would be.

No more adolescent spoofing of *Titanic*. No more wedding videos for hire. No more homework, even homework that meant as much to me as *Silent Beats*. It was time to take everything I'd learned and make something to show that the days of joking at the expense of people like me were over.

Since I am a competitive person—if you want to know the

BE THE GUY IN THE KITCHEN

I grew up watching my dad lead his gang of pirates in the restaurant's steamy kitchen—issuing orders, fine-tuning dishes, holding himself and everybody else to the most exacting standards—then step into the dining room a totally different man: suave, chatty, refined. To the public, he's the guy strolling around the tables, but I know that deep down he's really the guy in the back. And the guy in the back is my hero. If you ask him how he has kept up this routine for fifty years, he replies with his mantra: "Every day is opening day." I've taken that mantra to heart, because making movies isn't glamorous either, no matter what you see on the red carpet. That part is just my dining room. My kitchen is the long meetings with writers and producers, the weeks of rehearsals, the stressful days on set. It's banging our heads against the wall in the edit room and pacing the hallways during the sound mix. It's sleepless nights of doubting whether you've made something good. No matter how long you've been doing a job or how good people say you are, you need to care as if you've never done it before. You need to care as much as my dad does every time he puts on his chef's whites.

truth, an *intensely* competitive person—I decided it was time to show these fuckers who the guy at the door really was.

———

MY FILM —IF THE faculty committee gave me the chance to make it—would confront something I'd been ignoring most of my life: my cultural identity crisis. The confusions and tensions I felt while trying to live between two worlds. In 2001, this was fairly rare territory for a film to explore. A whole lot rarer than it should have been.

In the two decades since Wayne Wang's *Chan Is Missing* had been acclaimed as the first widely distributed Asian American film, the children of immigrants from China, Japan, India, the Philippines, and elsewhere across the Pacific had risen to new prominence in America, in terms of population, buying power, and cultural influence. A front-page story in *USA Today* around that time even described "The Asianization of America."

But what did Hollywood have to show for it—or to offer to someone like me? There'd been *The Joy Luck Club,* a widely admired film, but one that I was too young to fully appreciate or understand. The same went for Margaret Cho's *All-American Girl,* which lasted for less than a year on ABC. Mostly Hollywood went on serving up the usual stereotypes, the racialized nightmares: from Charlie Chan in the old days to *Sixteen Candles* in my time, along with the never-ending sexualization of Asian women. "The Hollywood representation of Asians in film has historically caricatured when it has sought to depict, damaged when it has aimed to entertain, and outraged when it has endeavored to inform," wrote Kenneth Li in *Eastern Standard Time,* a survey of Asian culture in America that was a huge help to me in understanding our predicament.

As I prepared my 480 pitch, I began to see that the lack of Asians in American media was a problem that compounded all our other problems. Why did strangers judge people who looked like me at a glance? In part because Hollywood had fed them a false understanding of who we were. Why did I feel apart from the crowd, unable to connect with other young Asian Americans who must have felt the same conflicts I did? In part because we didn't have an insight into one another's lives. We didn't know one another's stories because we didn't get to see them. And honestly maybe we didn't even know them ourselves.

My film would try to bring to light my experience—my shadow anxiety. It would tell the story of an Asian American kid struggling to negotiate his many worlds. He wanted to fit in at high school while also dealing with the pressures and expectations of his mother and his grandparents, who had emigrated from China. The crisis would arrive when he sees a couple of "cool" students bullying a quiet Asian girl. Would he stand idly by or intervene? Was it his place to get involved, or should he just ignore it, as so many of us were taught?

Since I was a mix of many influences, I wanted the film to be, too: It would include a singing Greek chorus, dance breaks, and a thirty-piece orchestra. A remix of many cultures to reflect a remix of a life.

I'd never seen that story on-screen, I told the 480 committee. But I had lived it.

When I saw my name on the list posted outside SPO—my classmates milling around, a queasy cloud of excitement, disappointment, and envy—I felt a surge of euphoria. *They were giving me my shot!* This was followed by a surge of fear. *Oh shit, how am I going to do this?*

A twelve-minute film. Big musical numbers. Very little time. Very little money.

More than ever before, I needed to put what I'd learned about collaboration to work.

THE DIRECTORS OF 480 films hired their production crews from the class below them. And younger students *wanted* to be recruited, because it gave them a much better chance of getting their own 480 someday. This feeling of desperate co-dependency was great preparation for working in Hollywood.

The problem was I didn't know the younger students. How could I identify the most talented up-and-comers, then convince them to work on my film and not somebody else's? Late one night, I figured out how to solve both riddles.

I went to the school's editing room around 2:00 a.m. No one was required to be there at that hour, but a handful of die-hard filmmakers were working late anyway, splicing film on their flatbeds.

"Hey, guys," I said, as I handed over the cookies and Red Bull I'd brought with me. "I want everybody in this room to work on my movie, because I want people who make things at two a.m."

Their faces lit up. *These were my people*. The ones who logged long hours trying to make something perfect, who so clearly loved what they did. Twenty years later, most of my classmates are out of the movie business, but almost everybody in that room that night is still working—some still with me.

No such shortcut existed for casting. Because Hollywood offered few roles to Asian actors, few thought they had a prayer of breaking in, so they had little incentive to try. We had to look everywhere. We contacted acting schools. We bought ads. We called casting agencies so often that they yelled at us. *Literally yelled at us.* For Joseph, the lead role, we ended up hiring a college student from San Diego who'd never acted before. But he had the right swagger. He understood what I went through because he was going through it, too.

I'd like to say that because the material was so familiar, production went beautifully. It didn't. Actors challenged me about why they were saying or doing things; I didn't have good answers. Neighbors got so angry when we filmed late at night that they called the cops. On top of all the other pressures, I was feeling a crazy sense of déjà vu. Nothing prepares you to watch strangers reenact scenes from your own childhood—especially when another participant in those scenes is watching them with you.

One of the big flash points in the movie is a multigenerational family dinner. (An Asian family working out its problems through food has now become a cliché, but again, in 2001, I hadn't seen it.) Everybody in the family would sip tea; Joseph would drink soda. Their argument about his Western ways would switch from Mandarin to English and back again. Joseph's grandfather would challenge him: *Why are you learning French at school instead of Chinese?*

That's the kind of question my dad used to fire at me. My dad, who was standing right next to me when we shot that scene. He had offered to help during the shoot, flying down to Los Angeles to serve as our de facto food designer. His dumplings looked good when the camera was rolling and proved to be irresistible when it stopped. The crew—a bunch of college students, remember—couldn't wait for me to call cut so they could devour the leftovers.

Did my dramatization of our family life jibe with Dad's memories? He didn't say.

The rules of 480 said I needed to screen my daily footage so my teachers and classmates could offer feedback. Some of their notes were technical, like when an actor's eyeline seemed too high compared with the shot before. But some cut deeper than technique. When the film's bullies made racist comments, a few of my classmates said it seemed cartoony, over-the-top.

"People don't say that kind of stuff so blatantly," they said.

I could only shake my head and think, *That just means they don't say those things to YOU.* Every taunt, every insult, was something I'd personally heard.

Outside of class, I received a different kind of feedback from the test audience I carried around in my head. *Who the hell are you,* I could imagine other Asians saying, *to put yourself forward as some kind of chronicler of the Asian American experience?* Did straddling my family's Chinese heritage and the "all-American" world of my non-Asian friends make me a sellout or even a "Twinkie"—yellow on the outside, white on the inside? Was I exactly what I was often accused of being? This was an exhausting cycle, a never-ending loop.

There's a reason I gave the movie the title *Gwai Lo.* When I was sixteen, I visited Hong Kong for the first time, because Larry had taken a job there. I felt a sense of belonging, an ease at being surrounded for the first time by a city full of people who looked like me—until somebody called me *gwai lo.* A local explained that it meant "foreign devil." So I didn't belong there, either.

Everybody seemed to doubt me. Sometimes even *I* doubted me. But I had to keep showing up every day, acting as if I had it all under control.

That was good preparation for Hollywood, too.

———

ON DECEMBER 14, 2001, my crew and I returned to the Norris Cinema Theatre. We sat together in the dark—our family members, teachers, and friends on every side.

Three other films came and went. I was impressed by all of them. Everybody was. At last, our turn arrived.

Here we go.

An old-timey TV appeared on-screen. Joseph's face popped up on the TV. He addressed the camera directly.

"So you want to know the worst part of it all?" he asked. Then came a montage of people saying stupid racist things to him. Like friends nicknaming him "Napalm" (which happened to me at my fraternity). Or kindergartners singing, "Chinese, Japanese, dirty knees, look at these!" (which happened when I volunteered at a grade school). Then Joseph appeared again.

"Yeah," he said. "Welcome to my world."

The TV disappeared. Now we were watching a montage of Joseph's early life.

"Ever since I can remember, I've had to deal with my 'orientality,'" he said in a voice-over. We saw more glimpses of people making fun of him. "All I wanted was to be accepted by somebody—*anybody*."

Then came the dinner scene: Joseph eating with his mom, his grandparents, his little sister. "Can I get a fork?" he asked.

They all freaked out at him. "A fork?! What about chopsticks?! *Ai ya!*" (My parents and grandparents used to say this all the time when they got frustrated or exasperated. I was proud to get it into the movie, especially when I found out how many other Asian American kids could relate.)

"If I wasn't a real Chinese, and if I wasn't a real American, then what the hell was I?" he asked, looking right at the camera.

Cut to the title of the movie: *Gwai Lo: The Little Foreigner*.

I could feel people enjoying it, which was a relief. In spite of the anger and dismay that supplied the initial spark, I still wanted to make something joyful. When three guys dressed like members of an all-American barbershop quartet began to sing, "You never know what your life may bring / No, you never know what song you'll sing," and the camera pulled back to reveal they were standing in Joseph's bedroom, it got a big laugh. (It might have gotten an even bigger laugh if there had been a full quartet, but I couldn't afford the fourth singer.)

As I look back now, plenty of moments in *Gwai Lo* feel very after-school special; some of them are downright cringey. If I had it to do over, there wouldn't be white guys singing to Joseph about his destiny—they'd be Asian. But I still sympathize with the young filmmaker who made it. He was trying, however clumsily, to wrestle with his cultural identity crisis.

The dramatized version of that crisis reached its climax when Joseph stepped up to the bullies. As soon as he did, they vanished. The audience could see that his primary struggle was within his own heart and mind. He needed to resolve that conflict before he could do anything else. The closing moments of the film showed the triumphant Joseph sitting down in the cafeteria. Instead of tossing his homemade dumplings in the bushes on the way to school, he dared to enjoy them—even if he did eat them with a fork. As the barbershop singers launched into the closing number, other kids took seats around him. He wasn't just Chinese, and he wasn't just American, but a strange combination of both. And that was okay.

I'd thought it would be a satisfying finale, and it was. When the credits rolled, people leapt to their feet. They crowded around to congratulate me. I tried not to drown in small talk.

I couldn't have imagined it going any better. But deep down, I wasn't excited. I was ashamed.

BY MAKING GWAI LO, I had, for the first time in my life, stepped off the path of assimilation. I'd revealed so much of myself—way, way more than in *Silent Beats*—by spending a whole movie calling maximal attention to my identity. I didn't like talking to my friends about these issues because it often just felt like victimizing myself. And we *definitely* didn't talk about them in my family. And now I'd put them on a big screen.

What had I done?

There's a grim irony in this: Joseph, my fictional alter ego who made such a bold, dramatic stand, turned out to be a lot braver than I was.

The circumstances that night added to my despair. In a few months, I'd have to start clawing my way toward that uncertain life in Hollywood. I'd need to convince people that I could direct the kind of big-screen spectacles that had attracted me to filmmaking in the first place. Yet for some reason I had made a 480 film—the calling card that was supposed to introduce me to the industry—that seemed likely to do the opposite, pigeonholing me as somebody who wanted to tell narrowly focused stories about his identity. Looking back on it now, I can see that *Gwai Lo* was a cry for people to see me as my authentic self. But at the time, I berated myself, thinking I'd made the dumbest decision of my life.

Why had I turned myself into the guy who did that Asian 480 instead of the guy who did that great 480?

By the time I got home that night, I had steered myself back to the familiar path: assimilate. Though USC expected 480 filmmakers to submit their films to as many festivals as possible, I didn't send it out. I didn't even make copies for the crew. I just kept delaying until everyone forgot to keep asking. As far as I was concerned, nobody would ever see *Gwai Lo* again. And pretty much nobody ever has.

At the time, it felt like the responsible choice, the one that offered me the best chance of realizing the dreams I'd nurtured in Silicon Valley: to make movies that would play on the big screen, to build a company of my own. The alternate scenario, where I would have embraced *Gwai Lo* and all that it said about me—that is, where I would have abandoned the old path of broad, mainstream success and cut a new one that was all my own, specific to my cultural identity—seemed risky, even foolish. It took me a lot of years and a lot of pain to realize that it was also the choice that would have led me to becoming a full human being.

SEEK THE REBELS

When Justin Lin made *Better Luck Tomorrow*, a movie about Asian Americans that went a long way toward blowing up the "model minority" myth—imagine Martin Scorsese's idea of a high school movie, with lots of guns and drugs—it sparked a famous shouting match at the Sundance Film Festival. I know because I was there. During a post-screening Q&A, a white critic stood up in the audience and harangued Justin and his cast for presenting an unflattering depiction of Asian Americans. In a flash, Roger Ebert was on his feet, yelling, waving his arms, defending Justin. "Asian American characters have the right to be whoever the hell they want to be!" he shouted. "They do not have to 'represent' their people." Ebert was right. I felt like I knew the kids in that movie and was excited to see them on-screen. I also admired the ferocity of Justin's vision. He made something unrepentant and was willing to max out his credit cards to do it. I saw that a new generation of Asian Americans—young artists with rebellious attitudes and immense talent—was about to remake the world. Over the years, I tried to keep up with what those rebels were saying and doing: seeking out their screenings, listening to their speeches, reading articles about all the feathers they were ruffling. It prepared me for the times when I'd face a lot of the same critics, giving me a quiet confidence that I wasn't alone. So seek the rebels. Learn from their battles. When your turn comes, you'll know how to fight.

"It's nothing to worry about," my agent told me. "But the rumor is Spielberg saw your short and is going to call you."

"Oh," I said. "*Steven* Spielberg?"

"Yeah."

I had stepped out of my friend Jerome's house to take the call, my Sony Ericsson T68i pressed to my ear. Above me, the streetlights started going all swirly. It's fair to say this is not how I expected my Friday night to unfold.

"There probably isn't anything to do till Monday, but just in case, keep your phone on this weekend. And don't think about it."

"Okay, sure. I definitely won't think about that *at all*."

I hung up. Then I freaked out.

By that night in early 2003, I had graduated from USC, though a little later than planned. *Silent Beats* had won the Princess Grace Award, which had given me the chance to stick around for an extra semester to make a new short called *When the Kids Are Away,* imagining what mothers do after their children leave for school. The success of *Silent Beats* (the attention at festivals, the prizes) had also caught the eye of some talent representatives who wanted to work with me: an agent, a lawyer, managers. (This was unusual—I was the only director in my class to put together a team before graduation. "Why you?" asked some of my classmates. It was a good question. I was proud of *Silent Beats* but asked it myself.) In late 2002 and early 2003, my new team arranged screenings of *When the Kids Are Away,* hoping it might lead to meetings with producers or studio executives. Anything to get Hollywood to notice me, to get me my shot.

A phone call from Steven Spielberg—assuming it wasn't a prank, and I was totally prepared for it to be a prank—went far beyond my wildest dream for the kind of attention that the short might draw.

I didn't sleep that night.

The next day, my agent called again. The prospective phone call with Spielberg was now off the table. He wanted to meet in person.

I didn't sleep much that night, either.

The next day, Sunday, I assembled my friends and roommates at my apartment for a celebration that doubled as a strategy session. A lot of my classmates had started down a trail marked for us by past generations of USC grads: You hustle to get an entry-level job as a producer's assistant or working in a mail room, then bust your ass to move forward. That map offered no guidance for someone in my situation. If I really got face time with Steven Spielberg, what should I do with it? What was my goal?

Jason—best friend, former roommate, costar of my Britney Spears video—was blunt: "Get a second meeting."

He was right. You can cover only so much ground in a single conversation. But if I could play it just right and start a *re-lationship,* then anything might be possible.

I spent the rest of the party/summit pondering ways to make that happen. At some point, Jason mentioned a project that he and his girlfriend, Danica, had been developing: a modern-day musical retelling of the Romeo and Juliet story called *Moxie.* I clocked it, then went back to freaking out.

The next morning, after a weekend that had lasted seven centuries, I drove onto the Universal lot. Mercifully, this wasn't one of the many times when the guard at the gate took one look at my face and my neon-green Volkswagen Bug and said, "Deliveries are around the side." On this day—March 3, 2003—he checked my ID and waved me through.

I thanked him and rolled up the window.

It was really happening. I was almost there.

I tried not to crash my car.

THE SPACESHIP LIFTED OFF; Elliott watched it fly away.

Turning from the screen, I saw that my brothers and sisters, sitting in the row next to me, were just as rapt as I was. They'd already seen *E.T.*—Howard had even brought his E.T. doll with him—but it was a new experience for me. Very new.

I was five, and I'd never been to the movies before. Never sat in the dark gaping up at a big screen, never felt the music and sound crash over me. On that summer afternoon in 1985, at the Old Mill mall in Mountain View, with my family all around me and a bag of Reese's Pieces on my lap, my life in movies began. Steven Spielberg's story about a boy's friendship with a lost alien set a standard that I'd judge every other film experience against, consciously or not, for the rest of my life.

Plenty of people love *E.T.*, of course, but in my family, it had a special significance. Watch it again sometime: You'll see that it's a remarkably nonverbal film. Elliott and E.T. need to find ways to express themselves without a full array of words—just like we did.

My grandparents spoke Mandarin. I didn't. To communicate with them, I had to rely on gestures and facial expressions. The same sometimes went for Mom and Dad: After decades in America, the right English word still might elude them. And even when we had the words we needed, we didn't always use them. Since we loved one another but didn't share our feelings, we were constantly trying to decode one another's signals.

Above all, there was Howard, who faced the biggest challenge in making himself understood. He needed the closest kind of attention, the most careful kind of listening. It's no wonder he loved his E.T. doll. He played with it so much its eyes fell off. Then he kept on playing with it.

My siblings and I watched that movie again and again on home video. We even adopted E.T. and Elliott's signature move. We'd touch the tips of our index fingers together, lock eyes with each other, and say, "I'll be right here."

It wasn't just *E.T.*, either. *Jurassic Park, Raiders of the Lost Ark, Close Encounters of the Third Kind:* All of Spielberg's movies left me feeling that I'd been taken outside myself, making me believe in a reality that was different from my everyday world, and bigger. On the morning I was set to meet him, the DreamWorks lobby rendered that feeling in three solid dimensions. The place looked like an Indiana Jones set, all adobe and wood.

It also featured a wishing well. I peered down into it, coming face-to-face with somebody's little joke: the shark from *Jaws* lunging up at me.

As if I weren't scared enough already.

IN EVERY MOVIE I made growing up—using every new device I got my hands on and every camera trick I learned—I wanted to do what Spielberg did, to spark people's imaginations in the way he kept sparking mine.

I figured every young filmmaker felt that way. Then I started film school.

Plenty of my professors—and classmates, for that matter—viewed Spielberg as unacceptably commercial. He was the director who had created the modern blockbuster, who triggered the avalanche of big-budget movies that aimed only to please, without the "integrity" of "serious films." I disagreed. To me, he had an unprecedented ability to bring masses of people into a story, to expand their view of the world. He restored a sense of awe about the wondrous parts of life. He gave you a message about the human experience that you didn't even know you were getting. Everything that others derided about his work was everything I loved and aspired to achieve in my own work.

Spielberg's production company is called Amblin Entertainment. (The name comes from the student film that helped him break into the business.) When people asked me about the kinds of movies I wanted to make after school, I would say, "Amblin-y."

My professors might not have given him the credit he deserved, but they couldn't ignore him: The man who had just directed *Schindler's List* and *Saving Private Ryan* was too important to the history of film. So USC offered a semester-long course devoted to his work. It was led by Drew Casper, who was as much a showman as a scholar. (When he taught *E.T.,* he rode into the lecture hall on a bicycle with a toy E.T. in the basket.) Beginning with Spielberg's student films, we surveyed his entire body of work, Dr. Casper pointing out how his craft had developed with blazing and totally intimidating speed. To me, the semester refuted forever the charge that he made only empty spectacles. *E.T.* left a roomful of film snobs weeping.

On the last day of class, as a grand finale for the semester, Spielberg himself showed up.

The chance to hear Dr. Casper interview him seems to have fried a circuit in my brain, because I have a vivid memory of how the two of them looked and no memory at all of what they said. At least not until the very end.

When Dr. Casper took questions from the crowd, Jason stood up. "What are you planning to do next?"

Spielberg said he was thinking of making a musical.

Jason practically levitated. He pointed at me, in the seat next to him, and said that the two of us wanted to bring back the American musical.

I don't know if Spielberg joined the rest of the room in laughing at us. I was too embarrassed to look. But if he did, he would have been in good company. Scorning movie musicals was the enlightened view in my college years. In my screenwriting course, I had tried to write a musical, only for the professor to tell me, in front of the whole class, that the musical was a dead art form. There hadn't been a hit live-action musical in decades. They were a waste of my time. "You should be writing a script that could get made," he told me.

But I couldn't help it. I loved musicals, from the classics like *Singin' in the Rain* and *Meet Me in St. Louis* to the animated triumphs of Disney's '90s renaissance. Above all, I loved Michael Jackson, whose videos made him the living embodiment of the modern musical. I wanted to see all this energy cohere in a new wave of big-screen musicals, and I was happy—and reassured—to hear that Spielberg did, too. Which is a big reason why, when the Princess Grace Award gave me the chance to make one more movie before leaving USC, I decided that *When the Kids Are Away* had to be a musical.

What do stay-at-home moms do when their children are at school? My short answer was: *They sing and dance.*

I wanted to do big ensemble numbers, with dozens of moms dancing up and down the street. The heart of the story would be shaped by my Michael Jackson obsession. The main character was inspired by his mother, Katherine; the production design evoked the time and place where he'd grown up: 1960s Gary, Indiana. One of the kids, Little Mikey, would have a sparkly glove and a toy monkey. I hoped the audience would leave with the idea that she had played a role in inspiring his work and that he had been chosen to carry the tradition of the musical forward.

Somehow, in early 2003, Spielberg had gotten a copy of my movie. (How, I'll never be sure. Four different people have claimed credit, which is about average for a Hollywood success story.) Apparently, unbelievably, he'd liked it enough to want to meet me.

And now here I was, crossing his lobby, heading for his door.

In spite of my pounding heart and sweaty palms, I noticed that the DreamWorks offices were a glimpse of heaven: people chatting, eating, talking about stories. When I'd come up with my Silicon Valley dream of leading a company, a place where creative people could work on stories all day long, this was pretty much what I'd imagined. But I couldn't savor the view, not when my brain was racing through the many things that might go wrong.

Spielberg might realize that I knew nothing about film. Or, in spite of how much I'd built up the meeting in my mind, it could be a quick handshake and goodbye. The scariest possibility of all was that it might go great. That my life would peak right then and there. What if my first great Hollywood adventure would also be my last?

Please, I prayed, *let this not be the end of the story.*

I reached the reception desk. I felt silly, but there was no other way to say it: "I'm here to see Steven Spielberg."

"WE'VE ACTUALLY MET," I said when we sat down in a small conference room near his office.

"Was I nice?" he asked.

"You were."

"Phew!" he replied.

(A couple of years earlier, I'd designed a fake security credential to sneak into the Oscars. I laminated a photoshopped image of a pass, then talked my way into the backstage press area, where I worked up the nerve to shake his hand, though not to give him a letter I'd written. It was very fulsome.)

To my surprise, rather than forcing me to try to make small talk and say how big a fan I was, Spielberg took all the pressure off and launched into how much he'd loved *When the Kids Are Away.* He said it was different from any student film he'd seen in a long time. How had I made something that did so many things so well, with such high production value? That had a big orchestra and dancers and period costumes? That was so joyful?

I learned it from watching you, I thought, but didn't say. Even though that was literally the truth.

The movie was as expansive as we could make it because I'd wanted it to deserve a big screen, the way his movies always did. The tone showed his influence, too. I'd wanted the movie to be a warm picture of family life, a celebration of mothers. (Again, never going to be the cynical guy.) That's why we'd shot it in Pasadena, in all that suburban sunshine. At one point my director of photography, Alice Brooks, and I had needed to persuade a cranky and late-arriving crane operator to help us get a moving crane shot of the neighborhood before we lost our golden light. In a word: "Amblin-y."

And the movie showcased little kids, another Spielberg signature. On set, I'd tried all the tricks that I'd seen him use in behind-the-scenes videos of *The Goonies* and *E.T.* to draw beautiful performances out of child actors. He had made it look so easy. *It was not easy.*

He said that after he watched those family scenes, he knew immediately that he needed to share my film with his wife, Kate Capshaw. Her reaction, according to him, was: "He gets us mothers."

"That's when I knew I had to meet you," he told me.

The more we talked about the movie, the more surreal the conversation became. Because the final explanation for how we'd made the film was by using tools that were just as new and unfamiliar to Spielberg as they were to me.

From the day my classmates and I arrived at film school,

our professors had drilled us on all the ways that shooting on film was superior to using a digital camera. Even I, a trueborn son of Silicon Valley, had to agree. But by the time I graduated, technology had leapt ahead. Sony and Panavision had developed a digital camera capable of filming in high definition at twenty-four frames per second, which is how most directors had shot most movies for decades. We prepped *When the Kids Are Away* at the same time George Lucas was giving that camera, the F900, its first test in a major Hollywood feature, *Star Wars: Episode 2—Attack of the Clones*. Lucas described it as "a giant experiment for everybody."

There was no earthly reason a couple of recent college grads should get their hands on technology that cutting-edge. But Alice and I wrote a letter to Bob Harvey, then senior vice president of sales at Panavision, that was nearly as effusive as the undelivered one I'd written to Spielberg. Miraculously, it worked. Once we learned the secrets of the F900, all sorts of new possibilities arose.

Since we didn't have to worry about burning through film (and our budget), we could shoot more and longer takes of dance sequences, which made us look more polished than we were. We could let the camera run during rehearsals, catching amazing moments from our child actors. Best of all, during postproduction, we could manipulate the color and frame until we found the right look. Doing this on film would've been financially ruinous, impossible.

This was all so new in 2002 that a filmmaking magazine interviewed me and Alice about what we did. It was so new that Steven Spielberg was curious to hear how it had gone.

It wasn't all shop talk, though. He wanted to know about my family, where I'd grown up, what I'd learned at USC—an institution that he said he was very proud to support. And we talked about what might come next.

"I've wanted to do a musical," he said.

"Oh, I know."

When we compared notes on our favorite musicals, he said his was *Oliver!,* then launched into a rendition of "Consider Yourself," the song that the Artful Dodger sings when welcoming quick-fingered young Oliver into his gang: "Consider yourself at home. / Consider yourself one of the family." I sat there as he sang the song to me, all the way to its final words: "Consider yourself—one of us!" The irony of him singing that song, of all songs, on the day of our first meeting didn't strike me until much later.

Eventually a couple of his senior executives joined us. They asked, in a casual way, what I was working on. The big moment had arrived.

I told them that some friends and I had been developing a new musical called *Moxie.*

"We'd love to hear about it when it's ready," they said.

"Oh, it's ready," I said. "We just finished it this week. We'd love to show it to you."

A couple of hours later, as soon as I got home, I recounted this conversation for Jason and Danica. Then I broke the bad news: There wasn't going to be a second meeting. After they'd consoled me for a while, I told them the truth: I was just kidding. (I was about to give them the greatest news of their whole lives. How could I resist messing around with them for a minute first?)

I'd gotten my second meeting with Spielberg. And this time, they were coming with me.

They screamed. I screamed. We all jumped up and down

and shouted into each other's faces. If this scene were directed by Spielberg (who likes to cut away from big moments to something comically mundane), we'd see the people in the apartment downstairs looking annoyed as the wineglasses on their table rattled back and forth.

They were so excited—so euphoric—that they didn't mind the ridiculous jam I'd put us in. Contrary to what I'd said, *Moxie* was nowhere near finished. It was barely even an idea. The three of us would spend the next week pulling all-nighters, racing to figure out how to pitch our movie. Or, come to think of it, how to pitch *any* movie. None of us knew.

Those few frantic days were like the condensed version of that whole phase of my life, after the call from Spielberg scrambled every expectation of what my beginning in Hollywood might be. I didn't know where I was going, but I was going there fast.

SOCIAL MEDIA DIDN'T EXIST in 2003—a lot of Hollywood execs didn't even use email—but gossip got around. Once people heard that Steven Spielberg had wanted to meet a twenty-three-year-old to talk about a student film, the whole town snapped to attention.

And here's the best part: The fact that I'd made a musical made them more eager to meet me, not less.

About twenty minutes after my screenwriting professor had told me that musicals were a dead art form, *Moulin Rouge* had reminded everybody of their enormous creative possibilities. Then, three weeks after the premiere of *When the Kids Are Away*, Rob Marshall's movie version of *Chicago* had opened huge. It racked up thirteen Oscar nominations, more than any other film that year. Just like that, musicals were the hottest genre in town. And here I was, a young filmmaker with a musical that even Steven Spielberg was curious about.

My team had taken a counterintuitive approach to getting me known. Instead of flooding the town with dozens of screener copies of *When the Kids Are Away,* they tightly limited access. We held invitation-only screenings—not too many of them—for producers and execs. That way, people would experience the movie the way a joyful musical should be experienced: in a crowded theater on a big screen.

Those screenings led to meetings. Dozens and dozens of meetings. Some were before my sit-down with Spielberg, some were after. In fact, visiting his office stands out as a crisp memory in an otherwise blurry season of forced smiles, conference rooms, and water bottles. As we crisscrossed the city, from Universal City to Santa Monica, from Burbank to Culver City, I started to wonder: *Is this what being a director is—just having meetings?*

I also took notes in my planner so I could keep all the new names and personalities straight—notes that today offer a frozen-in-amber record of my first encounters with Old Hollywood. One senior exec was "LAME," another "screamed at assistant." There were highlights ("kill to work with you") and little milestones ("front desk knows my name!"—that was after a meeting at William Morris, the agency that repped me at the time). There were also tantalizing roads that never went anywhere ("*SNL* musical?").

Perusing these artifacts of a very different time in my career and the industry, I find that my favorite entries record the beginnings of what would turn out to be decades-long relationships. Like the "Asian brotha . . . very put together"—that was Dan Lin, then an up-and-coming executive at Warner Bros. who is now the head of film at Netflix. Or the "ballerina" (we bonded over our shared dance backgrounds) who "got goosebumps" from what I said about *Moxie*. That was Donna Langley, who has become one of the most powerful people in Hollywood and is the head of Universal, the studio where I'm making *Wicked*.

Even though I was still on the steep part of my Hollywood learning curve and hadn't figured out how to decode what movie executives said—the mysterious terms included "turnaround," "rolling call," and "option"—one meeting felt different from all the others. It felt *real*.

Rachel Shane ("young and fun"), an exec at Red Wagon Productions, had come to the premiere of *When the Kids Are Away*. She loved it and asked to meet with me. Her company had the rights to remake *Bye Bye Birdie,* the 1960 musical about a pop star going into the army. At her invitation, I worked up an idea for what I would do with it.

It wouldn't be a period piece, I decided. It should be set here and now. In my version, Birdie would be a pop star whose fame is waning. His manager, Albert, would come up with a plan to reignite his career and get him street cred by manufacturing a fight that would land him in jail: a live, nationally televised broadcast and reality show in which he would use his last days of freedom to "do good" for his fans. Who would be America's luckiest teenager? It would deal with issues that actually mattered to young people in the twenty-first century: celebrity and the distorting power of fame.

When I pitched *Birdie* to Rachel, I was really pitching something much bigger than a single film. I'd worked out an entire creed for the modern movie musical. Its fundamental value was fearlessness. It seemed to me that a generation raised on MTV, hooked on *TRL,* and toting iPods around didn't need a clever conceit to justify why actors burst into song (as in *Chicago,* where the dances are all in the heads of the characters). Songs couldn't be merely extra forms of expression for the movie's characters. They needed to be tightly integrated into the story, otherwise a twenty-first-century audience would tune out. Dances need to be mind-boggling, *Matrix*-style, using technology to capture movement in a way it had never been seen on-screen before. It was past time for the entire genre to get an upgrade, a reboot, a remix. In short, I wanted to do for musicals what *Pulp Fiction* had done for the gangster movie.

To show what I had in mind for my modernized *Birdie,* I used my Silicon Valley know-how to manipulate images, so it looked like the actors I had in mind were already cast and even in costume: I had Seann William Scott as Birdie, Will Smith as Albert, Lindsay Lohan (who was about to blow up thanks to *Mean Girls*) as Kim MacAfee, and Will Ferrell as Harry MacAfee. But I'd barely started the spiel when Rachel stopped me.

She left her office and returned with Lucy Fisher, the co-head of Red Wagon and former head of Columbia Pictures. Rachel wanted her to hear it right away.

This time, I got to finish the pitch. But they told me to come back on a different day and do it again for Doug Wick, Lucy's partner. He'd just won the Oscar for Best Picture for producing *Gladiator.*

Soon after that, Rachel, Lucy, and Doug had me deliver the pitch yet again—this time for Amy Pascal, the highly respected head of Columbia Pictures.

By the time I got home from her office, I had a call from my agent. Columbia wanted me to direct *Bye Bye Birdie*.

How did it happen so fast—so ludicrously fast? Partly it was golden timing: Doug, Lucy, and I were selling a musical when the whole town was looking to buy. Partly it was the liberating power of ignorance. I had no fear about talking a big, bold game in Amy's office because, at twenty-three, I had no sense of how powerful she was. I didn't know that a studio head can end your career if you mess up. I didn't know enough to be scared.

The last factor might be the most important of all: Spielberg.

At my second meeting with him, he introduced me, Jason, and Danica to his lieutenants, a handful of people who were well on their way to running the town: Adam Goodman would become president of Paramount; Mike De Luca is now running Warner Bros. Once again, I had no idea whom I was talking to—or, in this case, singing to. Jason, Danica, and I, in our naivete, thought that when you pitch a new musical, you're supposed to perform it—to put on a literal song and dance. We brought a big chest with us full of wigs, hats, and stacks of images we'd printed at Kinko's—images we taped to walls around the room as the presentation went on.

It's a fair bet that we put on the weirdest pitch of those guys' careers. But it worked. On the way out, in the parking lot, we happened to bump into Steven and his wife. He didn't just congratulate us; he said we should teach a class on how to pitch. (I recorded this meeting in my planner too, which I'm now realizing reads like a teenage fanboy journal: "I ♥ him! Soo cool!! Met Kate Capshaw.")

The execs at Columbia moved fast because they wanted to

be able to say that they'd introduced me—that *Birdie* was my debut. Then I'd do *Moxie* for DreamWorks, with Spielberg producing. As insane as that sounds.

Very early on the morning of April 10, I ran to my local newsstand, at the corner of Pico and Robertson. That's how we got our news in ye olde Hollywood. My own face smiled up at me from the covers of *The Hollywood Reporter* (" 'Birdie' Redo Hatches in Chu's Hands") and *Variety* ("Tyro to Watch 'Birdie' "). I had to look up "tyro"—I was relieved to learn it meant "novice."

Both stories were light on details of my deal, which was fine, because I didn't want any further envy bombs to go off under my feet. Columbia was so determined to get me before Spielberg that it had offered incredibly generous terms, including a "pay-or-play" clause, which meant that I would collect my fee even if the movie didn't get made. Deals like that were rare back then and are all but nonexistent now. I haven't gotten one like it since.

If I hadn't been so young or in such a hurry, I might have noticed a crucial difference between Spielberg's early films and my student shorts (I mean, besides the obvious difference that his were giant blockbusters and mine were . . . student shorts). Again and again, they drew their power from how personal they were to him. *E.T.* was a reaction to his parents' divorce, when he wished he had an alien friend to keep him company. *Gwai Lo* had shown me that I could make something personal, too. But I had turned my back on that impulse. I'd stashed my identity far out of sight, and Hollywood had rewarded me for it with a shocking immediacy and beyond my craziest dreams.

But who had time to worry? I was too busy fielding celebratory calls from everybody I'd ever met in my entire life. On the night that the *Variety* and *Hollywood Reporter* stories ran, a few friends and I trekked over to Hollywood and Highland to watch my name scroll by on the news ticker. We took pictures, still not quite believing it was real.

I accepted everybody's congratulations, but something about them rang hollow to me. I knew deep down that I hadn't actually *done* anything yet. The sudden surge of acclaim was a projection—the industry's view of my potential, based on one short film that had shown some promise and exceptionally lucky timing. It was all happening too fast for me to process, let alone for me to control. Which meant that behind my smile, I was terrified. I thought, *I hope I'm the person they think I am*. Because in spite of everybody's apparent confidence in me, I knew that I had no real idea how to make a movie like *Birdie* or *Moxie*.

From the outside, it looked like I was flying. But I was really trying to figure out how to flap my wings.

"HEY, WHO ARE YOU?" said Tom Hanks.

Spielberg answered before I got the chance. "Oh, this is my buddy Jon."

It turns out that if you're a kid and you're sitting next to Steven Spielberg on a film set, people want to know what you're doing there. And they are very nice.

"So you're a new filmmaker," said Hanks. "What kind of films?"

A few months after the *Birdie* news broke, Steven had invited me to visit him on the set of *The Terminal*. The production had taken over a gigantic hangar—the size of four football fields—in Palmdale, north of Los Angeles. They'd built a full-sized airport terminal inside it with real clothes in the shops, real coffee at the Starbucks, and escalators that actually worked. I arrived that morning every bit as scared as I'd been the first time I'd met him. Maybe even more so. After all, I'd been to an office before, but I'd never been on a film set—a fluky side effect of missing the phase of your career where you work as a production assistant. I worried about which door to use, where to sit, what to touch.

When he'd welcomed me, Steven had tried to put me at ease. He'd pulled up a chair right next to his. I'd still felt an urge to scoot it back a little.

He'd invited me on this day, of all days, because he was shooting a musical number—and Hollywood now believed I was the hotshot young musical guy. Ultimately he wouldn't include the song in the movie, but nobody knew that as Catherine Zeta-Jones and a handful of dancers rehearsed on an escalator, and the production team made the thousand tiny adjustments needed to capture even the simplest moment on-screen.

Amid the bustle, Steven was relaxed, confident, chatty. I asked questions about what was going on; he answered them. He even asked a few of his own. When he saw me pop a piece of candy into my mouth—potential bad breath being yet another cause for concern—he asked for one. It was smushed and warm from my pocket, but he didn't seem to mind.

As we talked, members of his production team kept interrupting. Even I, the least experienced person in that hangar, could tell that something was wrong.

From what I could gather, the cameras were missing a crucial moment in Zeta-Jones's performance, and something—the blocking, the scenery, the laws of physics—was foiling their attempted solutions. They kept struggling, which meant the clock kept ticking, and the cost of the delay kept rising.

I began to feel uncomfortable, as if I were catching a glimpse of something I wasn't supposed to see. I began to feel an absurd sensation: worrying about Steven Spielberg and whether he might be in trouble.

He wasn't.

After a stricken assistant gave him one final bit of bad news, he excused himself from our conversation. He walked over to the escalator. He listened to his director of photography, Janusz Kamiński. Then he listened to the actors. Then he listened to other members of the production team. Then he acted. On the fly, he worked out a completely different way of filming the sequence, one that none of them had perceived but that everyone seemed to like.

Just like that, he was back in the chair next to me, and the whole enormous operation rolled on.

Damn, I thought. *That's what makes him Steven Spielberg.*

He hadn't gotten lost. He hadn't wasted any time or energy getting upset. He just grasped the problem and fixed it. Simple, efficient, elegant.

In doing so, he'd given me a precious gift. He had, once again, shown me the way.

Just as he'd made me fall in love with movies when I was five years old, just as he'd revealed all that they could do—move people, bring them together, harness a power much bigger than any of us—he'd now shown me the right way to make them. My teachers could lecture me, but they couldn't really make me understand what it was like to direct a movie. Neither could my peers. Only another director could do that. And in Spielberg, I had the best of all possible guides. He proved, in that instant, that you could make giant-scale movies with kindness, patience, joy.

Those hours at Steven's side made me feel that I belonged. I knew I wasn't among my peers on that set, but I knew for certain I was among my people. Film school had led me to think that in order to succeed in Hollywood, I would need to be disciplined and businesslike. But there was a lightness about Spielberg and his actors and crew. They acted like children, in the best possible way. They were deeply invested in a great game of make-believe in their gigantic, hangar-sized sandbox. During the lunch break, somebody delivered a dirt bike that Spielberg had ordered. He didn't know how to ride it, but Janusz did. We watched him zip around the set as Steven shook his head, smiling.

The great ones, I realized, *are still playing.*

He let me spend the whole day with him. Now that I've directed movies of my own, I belatedly realize how generous that was. After all those hours of watching him and talking with him, my fear and insecurity about my future melted away. I knew what I needed to do and I knew how to do it. The *Oliver!* lyrics he had sung to me in his office had come true: I felt like I really was one of the family.

I was still standing at his elbow when he called, "That's a wrap!"

The set, which had been so serene, burst into commotion. Actors bolted for wardrobe; the crew began packing equipment away. This rush for the exits always happens at the end of a long day, particularly when you're in Palmdale and know that you're going to spend hours in traffic before you get home. But before Spielberg disappeared, there was one last thing I needed to do.

"I have a gift for you," I told him.

I knew that he was a cigar aficionado, which I definitely wasn't. But a friend of mine knew all about them and agreed to pick out a great one. I pulled it out of my jacket pocket and presented it to him—in a Ziploc bag—to express my gratitude.

"Jon, thank you so much," he said, genuinely enthusiastic. "This is so nice, this is great."

He called over an assistant who had been carrying a suitcase around. At his signal, she opened it, revealing a humidor filled with the most beautiful cigars I'd ever seen. I watched him try to squeeze my cigar—still in its shabby plastic bag—into one of the available spaces, then try again, then try again. It was too small for the slot.

I was mortified. He was gracious. We shook hands.

"Come back any time," he said.

A huge gust of wind blew through the set, followed by a deep rumbling sound. Behind me, the hangar doors, seventy feet tall, began to part. Outside, on the tarmac, a helicopter waited, its rotors spinning. A red carpet led to its door.

With a few waves to his left and right, Spielberg said his goodbyes. He started walking down the carpet. In the months and years that followed, I would replay his exit over and over in my mind—always with regret. Was there something else I could have said or done in those moments to change what came after?

A couple of assistants trailed behind him. Before long, I'd

envy them, how they still got to talk with him, work with him, and watch him do what he did, after my own chance was gone.

I'd think back on how I might have looked to him, standing alone in the hangar doorway, backpack on my back, watching him climb aboard. Did he think about me after all the ideas we'd talked about fell apart? Did he even notice it happen?

If I'd managed to stay on the road that seemed, at that time, like my destiny—of my impossibly fast start, of *Birdie* and *Moxie,* of reinventing the musical—I would have talked about that set visit in every interview I gave. But when all my plans misfired, that day with Spielberg turned into a kind of orphan memory, detached from the rest of my life. It might as well have been a dream.

The helicopter lifted off; I watched it fly away.

"We live in a great time to do this movie," I had declared in my pitch for *Bye Bye Birdie*.

Pop music was in the right place: In the Napster era, audiences were hopscotching from one style to another as never before, which gave us all sorts of options for our score. In Hollywood, technology was in the right place, too: We had the tools to do gravity-defying dances that had never been seen on-screen or off. The dance world was more diverse and innovative than ever before. And the subject was timely. Millions of young Americans were signing up on Myspace and Friendster, making it the ideal moment for a story about the growing mania for attention, the destructive desire for fame.

Then there was the director. Never once did I feel like the smartest or most talented young filmmaker around, but after that fortifying day on set with Steven, I trusted that my love of musicals and my facility with the new wave of digital tools made me the right person for this movie. So I threw myself into prep, conceptualizing each musical number, refining the script, checking all the boxes that needed to get checked so filming could begin.

The job got very real very fast. The producers gave me an

office on the Sony lot, like an actual grown-up. For a young director, what's realer than chatting up Rob Marshall at the copy machine? To find our leads, I took meetings with what felt like half of young Hollywood and anybody with a hit record. It was another surreal round of conversations all across L.A. Britney Spears showed up looking stylish in a period polka-dot dress. Her face dropped when I said the movie wasn't going to be set in the '60s. Kirsten Dunst and I met at a café, where she protected me from encroaching paparazzi. I played tennis with Seann William Scott at his house in Malibu, trading ideas about Conrad Birdie as we volleyed. Everyone was curious about my journey since I was either the same age or younger than they were.

Our sharp, funny script got sharper and funnier when Tina Fey started working on it. Fresh off the success of *Mean Girls,* she had great ideas for how to give it a more satiric edge. Her revision seemed to me—to all of us—like the last piece we would need for filming to begin.

It won't surprise you, given all those years of tap classes and the press I was getting at the time (like a story in *Los Angeles* magazine saying I could be "the latest director out to revolutionize the movie musical"), that I spent a lot of time thinking about dances. More dances. Longer dances. Ever-more-elaborate dances. As my ideas grew, so did the budget. It's one thing to let an untested director, whose biggest project had cost $20,000, make a $25 million movie. It's a different and potentially far more calamitous thing when the budget projection passes $65 million and you haven't even started shooting yet.

We'd been prepping *Birdie* for a year and a half when Amy

Pascal called me into her office. I had a bad feeling—a trip-to-the-principal's-office feeling. So I braced myself to make my case again. I drew storyboards of some of the musical numbers and cut some video clips together to show where we were headed.

Once again, it seemed that my Silicon Valley know-how had saved my skin. "I was supposed to give you bad news," she told me, "but seeing that makes me want to see that movie."

She spent the weekend making up her mind. I spent the weekend quaking. It was like waiting for Spielberg's call, but in reverse. I had built my entire future around this movie. Now it was suddenly all in jeopardy.

A few days later, she summoned me again. Our conversation was a blur, but certain phrases stick with me. Phrases like "can't do it" and "too risky" and "pressure from Wall Street."

In other words: I was out.

It didn't feel real when I walked out of her office or when I sat down in mine. It still didn't feel real when I went home—another blur—and began to break the news to the people most directly affected by it. Collaborators. Mom. Dad. Larry. A few friends.

That night, I drove my girlfriend back to USC, where she was finishing film school. I parked in the loading dock area of the building where we used to rent our cameras. I couldn't bear to get out of the car. It was too embarrassing. As she walked off to class, I sat in the dark, looking at the people who had spent the past year and a half cheering my great big overnight Hollywood success. I thought about all the students who knew we were dating. They were about to hear of my epic failure, which made me embarrassed for her.

That's what made it feel real. *That's* when I started to sob.

For a long time I sat in my car and cried. I cried in a way I hadn't cried since the death of my grandmother.

Losing *Birdie* felt like having a baby taken away. Because I'd lost something deeper than a job. If I'd gotten the chance to do it, everything in my life up to that point would have told one coherent story. All the hard work, all the training, all the hustling, all the lucky breaks I caught, all the parties I missed, even all the goofing around with my friends—it all would have made sense.

Now nothing did.

THE NEXT DAY WASN'T more painful, but it was more humiliating. The news had leaked overnight, so there I was, splashed across the trades again. "This kid didn't stay in the picture," somebody snarked in *Variety*.

My phone rang and kept ringing. People calling with condolences. I did my best to sound brave. At some point I went to the supermarket: My dreams were dying, but I still had to eat. (Specifically, I needed Lucky Charms, which were my go-to comfort food when I needed to treat myself kindly. They still are.) My phone rang again while I was there—not with condolences this time, but with a job.

It was Jeff Robinov, one of the great Hollywood mavericks of recent times. He had broken into the industry a decade earlier as the agent who helped to establish the Hughes brothers and the Wachowskis. Lately he had risen to become president of production of Warner Bros., his renegade tendencies intact. In a town of chauffeured Bentleys, he rode a motorcycle to work.

"Jon, you know I've always been a fan," he said.

Actually, I didn't know. But it turned out he'd been keeping an eye on me since seeing *When the Kids Are Away*.

"Don't let this stop you," he said. "You're talented, and you will always have a home here at Warner Bros. Let's get a couple movies set up for you over here."

That was true to Jeff's character—and to the ways of Hollywood in those days. The place wasn't as freewheeling as in the heyday of New Hollywood, when studios let upstart directors like Francis Ford Coppola and Martin Scorsese and William Friedkin take wild creative swings. But you could still find execs like Jeff who were willing to trust their gut. Since the prevailing model of film distribution—wide theatrical release followed by TV broadcast and home video sales and rentals—didn't yield granular data about what exactly was working, why not roll the dice? Especially when the studios had enough cash to sustain the occasional loss (within reason, anyway). Hollywood had been gorging itself on DVD revenues. In 2004, that number flew past $15 billion and kept climbing, with no end in sight. Green-lighting movies was a gambler's art, and Jeff was a gambler.

He sat me down with Kevin McCormick, one of his execs, and said, "Find Jon a movie to make here."

So in quick succession I got attached to three Warner Bros. projects. None of them were perfect for me in the way that *Birdie* had been perfect, but I was excited about all of them. I thought any of them could get me back on my path.

But there's a strange fact of life about Hollywood that never changes, whether times are flush or lean. Between the movies that fail to get set up at a studio and the movies that make it all the way to their premieres, there's a wide limbo.

Month after month, for one reason or another, they just don't come together. There always seems to be a piece missing or a problem left to solve. They drift along in a kind of float space, with no up or down. One by one, that's where all three of my Warner Bros. projects ended up. They weren't bad; they just weren't extraordinary enough to get made.

Which meant that I was even more grateful than usual for Steven Spielberg. Other movies might fall apart or stall, but I still had him. And I still had *Moxie*.

Around DreamWorks, people knew Steven had "found" me, so the execs treated me well. He was enthusiastic about the project. And I was enthusiastic about him. Everyone was enthusiastic about everything. Except for the script.

A screenwriter turned in draft after draft of a screenplay that didn't really work. The more we tried to clarify the story, the more the movie slipped away from the vision that we had pitched with our chest full of props and wigs. Then an executive shuffle at DreamWorks cost us some of our champions. After a certain amount of struggling and switchbacks, there's no way to keep a troubled project on the path to production, no matter how great your producers are (in this case, Dan Jinks and Bruce Cohen, who had just won Oscars for *American Beauty*), no matter how much Steven Spielberg likes you.

We tried and we tried, then we had to stop trying. *Moxie,* like *Birdie,* was over.

There was no public humiliation this time, no tide of consoling calls, just a steady descent into grief. By then, my girlfriend had graduated from film school and started a new job.

"The guy at work says that he's seen this story before," she told me one day. "Most people who come out of film school this hot don't get a movie made."

She wasn't trying to be hurtful, but it stung. I shrugged it off. Well, I tried. Still there was no way to unhear what I'd heard. Especially since I knew "the guy at work" had burst onto the scene with a lot of hype, only to see it go nowhere.

Were they right? Had I missed my chance? Had everybody's belief in me—and my belief in myself—been a mistake?

It was a very lonely time. And not just because my girlfriend and I broke up soon after that conversation. I'd used some of the pay-or-play money from my *Birdie* deal to buy a condo in Mar Vista. At the time, it had been a source of pride—a 1,400-square-foot sign that I was well on my way. Now the place felt empty, stale.

Once again it would've helped to spend time with my old USC classmates, to get the kind of morale boost that we used to give one another back at school. But our fortunes had reversed. Now they were too busy at their jobs, making movies.

So, pretty much by myself, I had to make a decision: Should I view my failures—getting fired, being humiliated—as proof that the story I'd been telling about myself was wrong? That in spite of my blazing start, I'd gone as far as I would ever go toward the life I wanted to lead? God knows, nobody would've blamed me if I'd reached that conclusion. My dream of making big Hollywood movies and one day leading a creative company of my own really did seem like a childish fantasy at that point. Or should I find some way to pull myself out of this ditch, get back on the road, and keep moving?

In short: *Did I still believe in myself?*

The question was stark, but it wasn't simple. It turns out that if you want to change your life and reach a dream that seems to be receding beyond the horizon, then the question isn't something you answer only once. It's with you every morning. It's with you every night. The world is going to ask it and keep asking it. And every time it does, you have to give the same answer. And that answer has to be true—there's no lying.

So I answered yes. As I had before and would need to again. Though never in circumstances like these.

When nobody expected anything of me, I set expectations for myself. I created a regimen and posted it on my wall: a series of daily, monthly, and yearly goals. I woke at the same time every morning and made my bed. I walked my dog. I tried to learn a new word every day and to watch another film, taking careful notes on the shots that inspired me, so I would be ready when my chance came.

This routine, like all routines, was hard to sustain for very long. But the individual activities mattered less than the underlying purpose of all of it: preserving even a shred of my morale. I needed to frame my experience on my own terms, to put myself in charge of my own narrative. Sometimes I pulled myself out of my daily ordeal by pretending I'd already lived through it. Or I'd tell myself, *This'll make a great chapter in a book someday*. Good days would be exciting chapters; bad days would be harrowing chapters.

Every day, I willed myself to believe it.

I HAD ALL THE time in the world, and I had no time at all. The payout from *Birdie* gave me a way to cover my expenses, but it wouldn't last long. I vowed that no matter what happened, my parents weren't going to help me. Not financially, at least. In those painful days, I fell back on how they'd raised me.

STOCK YOUR
PANTRY

In our house, the pantry had everything. Actually,
it had more than everything. When you're the son of
restaurateurs, there's food, there are sauces, there's
equipment—it all piles up. When I try to make something creative, especially when I start a new project,
it's not always easy to come up with an idea out of the
blue. I have kids, I have chores, I'm thinking about a
lot of other things. So over the years, I've made my
own pantry—my place to store all my ideas. Years ago,
I liked to cut images out of magazines and organize
them in a file cabinet. I'd also record music videos
and commercials off MTV and catalog them in a Word
doc. These days I keep folders on my computer with
lists of things I'd love to see in a movie: characters,
locations, even color combinations. Any time I have
an inspiration or a dream, or see something that
triggers my brain, I put it in these folders. That way,
when I read a script and need to come up with a
point of view, I can jump-start my creative process
by digging through my folders. If we got good ideas
the way characters do in cartoons—as a lightbulb over
our heads—none of this would be necessary. But in
my experience, creativity isn't a light with an on/off
switch. It's a fire that needs constant feeding.

How many times had Mom said, "Don't feel sorry for yourself"? Or Dad said, "Don't say there's nothing you can do"? *Never complain.* Their training made the difference between feeling depressed and plunging into full-on depression. They had drilled it into us from the time we could walk: *You might encounter people who are smarter or better connected or more talented than you, but never let anyone be more hardworking than you.*

In my case, that meant pitching. Lots and lots of pitching. Or, as I explained it to my parents, lots and lots of trying to convince people to give me a job.

Sometimes my agent or managers would hear of a project that needed a director; other times, I'd work up an idea of my own. Each pitch required a couple of weeks of preparation. I'd write a presentation, work out a visual component (usually by creating graphics on my Mac), and rehearse the pitch until I knew it inside out. I never memorized, because I didn't have that kind of brain. I was more of a visual/spatial guy. So I'd bring a cheat sheet—a sort of outline—but instead of key words, I'd draw little symbols that would remind me of what I wanted to say. Then all I'd have to remember were the shapes and their order. Weird, but it works.

When the big day arrived, I'd show up in a studio conference room or a producer's office, fake my way through some pleasantries, then make my case. I'd hit the five or six crucial story beats: Once upon a time *this,* then one day *something happened that changed everything,* which led to *this,* which caused *this,* which created *that.* No two pitches were alike, but they were all some version of why I was the greatest of all possible candidates to direct this, the greatest of all possible movies.

Because I'd established myself with a movie involving children, I got invited to pitch on a lot of family stuff—like *Poker*

Kid, about twenty-four-year-old Phil Hellmuth winning the World Series of Poker. But I didn't hesitate to pitch on far-flung material, like *Psycho Funk Chimp,* a comedy about the hunt for a precious toy. Being my parents' son, I didn't wait for opportunities to come to me—I tried to create my own, even if it meant repeating myself. I worked up a pitch for *When the Kids Are Away: The Feature Film.* In this version of the story, four women who had been elite spies in the '70s would reunite when an old nemesis abducts their kids, seeking revenge.

I felt like a player who'd been drafted into the NBA and just needed two minutes on the court to show what I could do. A few times I thought a coach was putting me in. Studios would give me a little money to develop an idea. Since I never stopped pitching, I suddenly found myself with a lot of work to do. In fact, I worked all the time. But I wasn't *making* anything, for the first time since I was eleven years old.

It turns out that sometimes, when you're really down, it's not the insults that sting the most, it's the praise. Because even as my career floundered, USC kept inviting me back as an honored alum, a success story, a model to the students. This was humiliating, but I had the same interest in sustaining the illusion that the school did, even though my visits would invariably lead to somebody asking me, "So how's it going with *Birdie?*"

That hurt. A lot. But not as much as my trips back home.

My parents had reveled in my overnight Hollywood success. They loved it when my name popped up in the Mandarin-language press, because it meant they didn't need to explain it to their friends. Nothing delighted them more than hearing "Wow, your son did this or that." But once *Birdie* went away, my name stopped appearing in their newspapers—or any newspapers. So when I got attached to some movie, I had to tell them myself.

"So when does it come out?"

"Well, it doesn't necessarily *ever* come out."

"So what are you doing?"

I tried to explain development to them: the intricate dance of writing, the studio gatekeepers, the casting challenges, the budgeting.

"How is that directing?"

I stopped telling them what I was doing, or failing to do. In the absence of any updates, it would have been totally reasonable for them to say, *Maybe this isn't working out for you, son. Maybe you should try something else.* If they had said that to me even one time, it would have destroyed me. My fragile confidence wouldn't have survived it. I really might have given up on directing and gone to work for some tech company.

But they never said that to me. Not one time did they give me a reason to doubt myself. Their support kept me going through the darkest days of my young creative life.

BACK AND FORTH ACROSS L.A., I had to go on pitching. Some meetings went well, but like Jay Gatsby, the hero of my favorite novel, I found that the green light remained just out of reach. (I also pitched a version of *The Great Gatsby*. Baz Luhrmann's version squashed mine.)

Almost none of the projects that I was invited to pitch on ultimately reached the screen. Pretty clearly, I wasn't getting access to anybody's most promising material. As months of failure stretched into years, I needed a fresh basis for hope.

I found it—or maybe created it—in Steve Jobs.

My hometown hero had reached unimaginable heights. The introduction of the iPod had made him a cultural force, not just a tech-world leader. People were excited about carrying a thousand songs to work or school, but to me, the real significance was that everybody suddenly had a 5GB hard drive in their pocket. Life was digitizing: music today, other things—maybe *everything*—tomorrow.

I kept talking up Apple to my friends. When I'd gotten my *Birdie* payout, I'd invested a chunk of it in Apple stock.

In those years when all I did was pitch movies and try to prop up my crumbling self-confidence, Steve was never far from my mind, because he was the greatest pitchman I'd ever seen. I'd already watched every Macworld presentation he made, even skipping school to watch them in person. But now I studied them.

Most speakers—in tech, in Hollywood, wherever—were satisfied to read boring prepared remarks. Or, worse, they seemed like they were acting. Steve talked to the audience the way you'd talk to a friend. He'd describe a problem, one that he knew you'd been having, too. Then he'd walk you through solutions that hadn't worked, then turn, with unassailable logic, to the solution that worked best: a new Apple device that, more often than not, you urgently wanted to buy. It made sense—perfect "no duh" sense. That was his magic.

I adopted that approach for just about every pitch I made in those years. I still use it.

The Steve pitch that meant the most to me wasn't for a laptop or an operating system; it was for a worldview. In 2005, he gave Stanford's commencement address. He had survived a cancer scare a year earlier, so wanted to share some bittersweet truths about life. He did it by telling three simple stories. (Structure was a huge part of what made his pitches so effective: You always knew where you were.) One of those stories recounted how he got fired from Apple, and all his dreams seemed to be smashed, but later he realized it was the best thing that could have happened to him.

"You can only connect [the dots] looking backwards," he said. "So you have to trust that the dots will somehow connect in your future . . . Because believing that the dots will connect down the road will give you the confidence to follow your heart, even when it leads you off the well-worn path, and that will make all the difference."

I needed that affirmation so badly. I seized on his insight as a kind of mantra. If he could find a way back to the path he'd originally been on, and use failure in the service of greater success, maybe I could, too.

The more I watched the speech—and I watched it a lot—the more I got an idea fixed in my brain: In spite of my lowly station and his preeminent one, and the fact that we worked in different fields, our paths were going to cross. It sounds desperate, like the kind of hero worship that countless Macolytes felt for him. Except that in my case, this far-flung notion started becoming more plausible—and quickly.

At Macworld a few months after his Stanford speech, Steve unveiled a new iPod with a video screen. *The New York Times* said Apple was helping to create "a revolution in the way cultural content is distributed." Steve also announced that the iTunes Music Store would begin to sell TV shows. A crucial threshold had been crossed: Video on demand had arrived.

"I've got a feeling we're not in Kansas anymore," Steve said from the stage.

A year later—after Apple had sold forty-five million episodes of TV shows and Pixar had been acquired by Disney, making Steve the company's largest shareholder—he announced that the iTunes Store would sell full-length feature films, too. Thanks to a leap in the iPod's screen resolution (to 640 x 480 pixels), Apple could now offer what he called "movies in your pocket."

Having grown up where I grew up, I celebrated it as a major breakthrough. Silicon Valley was dragging Hollywood into the twenty-first century. Movies, like music, were going digital. There was no stopping progress. And progress was on the way. Though not for my career.

The harder I worked, the less I had to show for it. Around this time, I was invited to pitch yet another retelling of *Romeo and Juliet* (yeah, Hollywood is littered with them). This time, Shakespeare's star-crossed lovers, the iconic embodiments of youth and passion and poetry, would be dogs. I pulled all-nighters for days, rehearsing my pitch, even hand-drawing storyboards. On the morning of the meeting, facing a table of studio executives, I made it halfway through my spiel when a voice in my head piped up: *This is crazy. What the hell am I talking about?*

I didn't book that one, either.

At last, I managed to get a project on track. I was hired to direct *The Prom,* a kind of John Hughes movie for today: satiric, but with heart. Amy Andelson, my assistant at the time (and future creative collaborator), and I set up a workspace at the production company's offices. We attached Shia LaBeouf to play the lead. We scouted locations in New Orleans and made plans to fly back in a couple of weeks to finally, *finally,* start filming.

That's when I got a secret phone call at our office. My agent had heard bad news. The financing on the movie had fallen through. In spite of the progress we appeared to be making, the entire operation would have to shut down.

I hung up and shared the news with Amy. She looked as stunned as I felt. We glanced around the office, where work seemed to be humming right along. The executives were probably quietly strategizing about how to cut everything off. We realized there was no point in dragging this out. Immediately, as in a scene from an office comedy, we started grabbing our stuff and hauling it to our cars—one small pile at a time, to avoid detection.

The producers called me in. Unaware of the tip I'd received, they said there'd been a setback, but everything was going to be fine. I nodded along. The first chance I got, I was out of there.

Didn't anybody ever make a movie in this town?

After nearly four years of trying, I hadn't made one. And I was beginning to think I never would. Because my time had run out. The *Birdie* money was gone.

Since I had promised not to ask my parents for money, I had only one way to pay the bills. I sold my Apple stock.

I hated to do it. Beyond the sentimental reasons, the timing couldn't have been worse. A few months after I parted with every share I owned, Steve Jobs would unveil the iPhone, aka "the God phone." Within a year, the stock price would more than double. Later, it would split, then split again, as Apple became the most valuable company ever traded.

And in the end, I still had to ask my parents for money.

———

HOLLYWOOD HAS INFINITE WAYS to keep people from quitting, to prevent them from moving on with their lives. It's so ingenious, it's almost diabolical.

Just six more months and this movie will be in production, I'd tell myself as another project began to flounder. *Just three more people need to say yes.*

By 2007, these table scraps were no longer enough to keep me from starving. I could persuade myself to keep working—or even get out of bed in the morning—only if I avoided any jolts of reality. Like a friend casually asking, "So what are you working on?"

I began to pull away from other people and spend more time alone, which of course made all my problems worse.

I was getting desperate now.

At a loss for what else I could do, I fired my managers. It was a painful conversation, since they'd been with me since film school. But something—*something*—had to change.

I found new managers, Allen Fischer and Brian Dobbins, and they brought me a fresh batch of projects. Some seemed very promising, some less so. Way down near the bottom of the list was *Step Up 2.* The original movie had been a surprise hit. It had made enough money for Summit Entertainment and Disney that they'd decided to make a sequel. But since it had also turned its leading man, Channing Tatum, into a big star with a significantly higher fee, the budget math worked only if the sequel was a direct-to-DVD release.

Allen and Brian told me not to direct it. They didn't need to worry. Though I hadn't seen Spielberg since the demise of *Moxie,* I clung to a piece of advice he'd given me: I should be extraordinarily careful about choosing my first project—to hold out until I found one that meant a lot to me, that would allow me to do my best work, that would define me for the town. Some of the projects I'd tried to line up in those many long, bleak years would have brought me awfully close to contradicting his advice. But a direct-to-DVD sequel, pretty much the lowest form of directing gig, would blow right past it. There was no way I could take that job and keep telling myself the story I'd been telling, about how I was still making a quick rise through Hollywood, in spite of a couple of delays.

I'm not that person, I told myself. *I can't be that person.*

Since I plainly wasn't going to take the job, I figured there was no harm in telling my parents about it. So the next time I called home, I mentioned it.

"Since when did you become a snob?" replied my mother.

Talk about a jolt of reality. I never saw that response coming. I didn't know what to say.

"You're a storyteller, right?" she continued. "Well, if you're a storyteller, you should be able to do it in any form. Even a direct-to-DVD movie."

I'd called them from the loft of my condo, which meant that as I listened to her, I was looking at the Ikea Billy bookcase where I archived the dozens of black three-ring binders from my pitch meetings. A giant shelf of nothing.

During the years I'd spent making those pitches, I'd sustained myself with a story about who I was and the trajectory I was on. Mom was asking me to see that the story wasn't true. She wanted me to acknowledge what that wall of binders had been trying to tell me. I wasn't making a meteoric rise. I wasn't destined for any special prodigious success. My story might have helped me in the early days of my ordeal, but now it was holding me back. It was an anchor, not a beacon. If I wanted a chance to build the kind of life I'd dreamed about—or any other kind of creative life, for that matter—then I needed to let go of that story. I had to write myself a new one.

I wasn't sure if that was possible. Could I decide, just like that, to reach out and pop the bubble of my self-image? The question might sound abstract now, but it didn't feel that way at the time. Because the clock was ticking. My managers were waiting for an answer. Did I want to put myself up for *Step Up 2* or didn't I?

Or, to put the question another way: Whose advice was I going to follow—Steven Spielberg's . . . or my mom's?

To Allen and Brian's consternation, I agreed to go for the movie. I was determined to be a storyteller again, no matter where or how I got to do it.

As ever, I had a lot to give, and I gave it all. I worked up a pitch for the film's producers, Adam Shankman and Jennifer Gibgot, that called for more dance—*lots* more dance—than the original. And this time, the movie should incorporate street dance styles. They liked my ideas but said there was no way to afford them on a direct-to-DVD budget. So they went back to Disney: Maybe *Step Up 2* deserved a theatrical release after all?

The decision fell to Oren Aviv, Disney's president of production. Facing him across his desk, I threw everything I had at him. All my Silicon Valley know-how had gone into creating a video preview of the dances I had in mind, all my Steve Jobs hero worship informed the way I framed the speech.

I'd done enough pitches to know what would happen next: the "we'll get back to you" smile, the surreptitious checking up on me with people around town. But that wasn't Oren's style. Not when he happened to have an open weekend on his release calendar.

Less than twenty minutes after I sat down with him, he said, "If you can have it in theaters by February, let's go."

It was already May. To be ready that quickly, we'd have to write a script, get it approved, find a cast, scout locations, build sets, and be ready to start filming in less than twelve weeks. That didn't seem possible. But what choice did I have? Or, more to the point, what did I have to lose? And what would my parents say?

I shook his hand. "Let's go."

EVERYTHING WAS HAPPENING OUT of order. Everything was upside down.

After years of trying to get a green light for movies that had complete screenplays, now I had a green light for a movie without one. With casting, budgeting, and location scouting underway, I spent long hours with the writer, trying to hammer out a story that made some kind of sense. In fact, we needed someone so fast that we hired the business affairs executive at the studio to write the script. Oren needed to sign off—a step I didn't take for granted, after seeing so many projects stall or die at moments like that over the years. He needed our draft on a Saturday afternoon so he could read it over the weekend and release a tranche of money the following Monday so we could begin prep.

This is going to sound fake, but it actually happened: On Friday night, with the finish line in sight, our hard drive crashed. Everything we'd done was gone. I began doing anything that anyone had ever done to salvage a busted hard drive, including bringing it to a twenty-four-hour hard drive recovery service—like an emergency room for computers. Nothing worked.

Technology had saved my ass so many times. Was it really going to ruin me now?

I remember thinking, *We have no choice. This is what I've waited my whole life to do.* So we stayed up all night, reconstructing what we could remember. We stayed up the next night too, subsisting on Red Bull and terror. We sent Oren the screenplay on Sunday, hoping we could survive the delay.

Ten weeks later, I was in Baltimore, shooting a movie at last.

Most twenty-seven-year-old directors have served as somebody's apprentice, learning their way around a movie set before they attempt to run one. I still hadn't done that, so pretty much all my lessons arrived in a bunch. The biggest one was: When you're making a movie, *nothing goes according to plan.*

From our first day on set, problems piled up, the kinds of problems that would have challenged even a more experienced director. The weather. Our locations. A lead actor tearing an ACL *on the first take.* Every time, the crew looked to me—the new guy, the rookie, the kid—for answers.

They wanted to see what I was made of. *Who was I?*

I wanted to see, too.

The answer probably surprised them. It definitely surprised me. When I finally got on my own film set, I became a different person: bolder, more decisive, more willing to walk into a fire. Not because I was brave but because I was scared as shit, and acting decisively was the only way I knew how to get through it. Being forced to solve problems rapidly and constantly—not simple math problems, but creative puzzles without easy solutions—forges your character. You must be present. Long-term plans are necessary, but once you step on set, all that matters is what you shoot that day, at that hour, in that moment. I knew that I had no choice. So I vowed that I wasn't going to quit until I got what we needed.

That feeling carried through every minute of shooting. It even spilled into my life away from set, where I found new confidence, so different from the doubt and dismay of how I'd felt during the long years after *Birdie* fell apart.

We finished our crazy sprint just in time. In spite of all the challenges we'd faced in Baltimore, we even enjoyed ourselves doing it. On Valentine's Day 2008, five seemingly endless years after *Birdie* had been announced, my first movie had its world premiere.

This was definitely not how I had expected my first opening night to unfold. It didn't mark the arrival of a Hollywood wunderkind. The trades weren't going to say that I reinvented the movie musical. Steven Spielberg wasn't going to give me a hug at the afterparty. But none of that mattered to me now. I was so proud to finally be walking a red carpet that I cut out a piece of it. (I still have it.) By not giving up on myself, by insisting that I could write a new story about my life, I'd pulled myself out of the ditch. I'd put myself back on the road. I'd get another chance to work my way toward the kind of life I'd dreamed about.

Or anyway, I would if people liked the movie.

Some cast members and I met for dinner to celebrate what we'd achieved—or what we *hoped* we'd achieved. It was opening night, so none of us could be sure.

Then we headed to the Grove, the multiplex in Hollywood. We timed our arrival so we could sneak into the back of the theater and watch the audience for the last few minutes, to see if we'd held their interest—a time-honored ritual for many filmmakers in L.A. We pulled open the doors. We ducked inside.

People were literally dancing in the aisles.

We stared, not believing what we saw. Then we joined them.

There's a cynical view of Hollywood that says the only kind of success that really matters here is financial success. When it comes to choosing which movies will get made, or judging how well they've done, the ultimate consideration is whether they could make, or already have made, a bunch of money.

That's a deeply unromantic way of thinking about what makes Hollywood tick. It's also basically true.

You can find plenty of people around Hollywood who have good taste and lofty ideals, who really do care about aesthetic innovation, building a better world, and what the critics think. But Hollywood, as an institution, lives for the scores that are posted every Monday morning in the form of the weekend box office grosses. (The situation might seem different lately, when there's so much talk about subscribers, engagement, or vaporous projections of future users. These metrics are all roundabout ways of arriving at the same destination: dollars.)

This truth about life in Hollywood was revealed to me on the opening weekend of *Step Up 2*. The critical response was mixed, but the box office totals exceeded expectations. Which meant that even though I was the same guy who had, after a fast start, struggled for five years to get his emails returned, Hollywood looked at our grosses and found 22.1 million reasons to think I knew what I was doing.

For the first time since film school, I could ponder which movies I'd like to direct and not have it feel like just an exercise in warding off despair. A list of potential projects I made around this time shows what a transitional moment I was in. It includes some projects that look backward to earlier in my career—such as, if you can believe it, *Bye Bye Birdie*. The project had broken my heart, but I couldn't let it go. Now that I was back on the path that runs toward Hollywood success, I thought I might get another chance at it, just a little later than originally planned.

But the list also includes some projects that look forward to later in my career. Like *Wicked*.

I'd seen the show years earlier, in San Francisco, during its pre-Broadway tryout run. The musical, an adaptation of Gregory Maguire's novel about the witches of Oz, captivated me from the start. I loved how cleverly Stephen Schwartz's songs and Winnie Holzman's script turned *The Wizard of Oz* inside out. Even though the creative team was still making changes to the show, it already felt like a hit to me. The audience went wild for "Popular," Glinda's mantra, sung (hilariously by Kristin Chenoweth) as she tried to give Elphaba a makeover, and "Defying Gravity," Elphaba's song of defiance, sung (gloriously by Idina Menzel) as she turned away from Glinda in pursuit of what she thought was right.

I loved both of those songs, but the one that meant the most to me was "The Wizard and I," Elphaba's dream of reaching the Emerald City. Though her schoolmates mock her for her green skin, she feels sure that the all-powerful Wizard will welcome her—even celebrate her. When I saw the show for the first time, I was riding high: *Birdie* and *Moxie* were both on track. So I identified with Elphaba's hopefulness about the future. Later, when all my plans fell apart, a different aspect of the song began to resonate for me: Elphaba's uncertainty. She wants to prove herself but doesn't know if she's ready. Which is how I felt, too: believing in myself and doubting myself all at the same time.

That song helped me get through some very dark days. The entire show did. I knew that somebody was going to turn it into a movie, and I wanted it to be me. But I also knew that a young director with only one professional credit wasn't likely to get a shot at *Wicked*. So I didn't even try.

I was weighing more realistic options when Oren Aviv called, wondering if I had ideas for where to take the *Step Up* franchise. After we hung up, I described the call to the people sitting around me. Somebody joked, "What do they want to do—*Step Up 3D*?"

Everybody laughed. I didn't.

"That would be really fun."

My lifelong love of dancers is a big part of why I've gravitated to musicals. Twelve years of tap lessons helped me understand the trade-off they make: They push the limits of what a human being can do, achieving all sorts of astonishing effects, but they beat up their bodies in the process. Fred Astaire, Ginger Rogers, Bob Fosse, and Michael Jackson (especially him) had all been superstars, but their successors had been trivialized, shoved to the background. A 3D movie, with dancers flying off the screen, would be an amazing way to put them front and center again.

That movie—*any* movie made on a reasonable timeline—

was going to take years (two and a half of them, by the time we finished it). The prospect of that timetable made me deeply anxious. As I looked back on the unhappy years when I couldn't get a movie going, I discovered something about myself: I need my fix. When I couldn't make anything, I couldn't get the fix I depended on, that feeling of deep satisfaction that comes only from being immersed in creating something that I'm about to share. The rest of the world goes away. There's a drive to do whatever it takes, to stay up all night, to ignore the cost—financial or otherwise—to blow past the gatekeepers, to just keep going and going until some new expression is out where the world can see it.

There's a wise old saying: *You are what you do every day.* If I was a storyteller, then I needed to be telling stories—*making things*—and sharing them with people every chance I could get, not just at the end of two and a half years. And if the things I made involved a camera and a screen, so much the better.

Luckily, in 2008, I had a way to do that. Everybody did.

When you read the words "tech" and "Hollywood" in the same sentence these days, it tends to be because the former has wreaked havoc on the latter. The relationship between the two spheres didn't need to be so destructive. It could have been healthier, more productive, and more empowering, for both the people who do the creating and producing and the companies that do the financing and distribution. For a little while, in certain ways, it really was.

Take it from me. It may seem like I got my groove back in 2008 because of *Step Up 2,* when all those dollars got the attention of the industry. But when I reflect on it now, what really got me back on track—what gave me a new spark, what helped to shape everything that came after, including my view of myself—was the internet.

THE STORYTELLING TOOLS I grew up using in Silicon Valley—the digital cameras, the editing software—all pushed creativity in the same direction: They gave more creators more chances to share their visions with an audience. During the early years of the new millennium, that democratizing wave swept the world, empowering a whole new generation of creators. If you had the moviemaking urge that I'd had as a kid, you suddenly had lots of ways to satisfy it.

The final bottleneck was distribution. What do you do with your small-scale cinematic gem when you've finished it? Burning it to a big stack of DVDs, one disc at a time, was not an inspiring choice. A scalable solution finally arrived when video compression made files smaller and broadband internet expanded farther, allowing torrents of data to flow. Dozens of video-sharing websites popped up to serve the legions of newly empowered creators, but one site outpaced all the rest.

YouTube was, like me, born and raised in Silicon Valley. In fact, it embodied a lot of the place's stereotypes. The company was founded by young programmers who worked above a pizza parlor and sometimes put the bills on their credit cards. In the true spirit of Silicon Valley, they chased exponential growth, and they got it.

When I started paying attention to YouTube, a few months after it launched, I loved catching glimpses of what people were making all over the world. But above all I felt the shock of the familiar: people who looked like me, talked like me, even told jokes that I got—jokes that a lot of my real-world friends didn't.

Asian Americans were some of YouTube's first and most enthusiastic users. One study showed that Asian Americans streamed more than double the online video as the average user. In the mid- to late aughts, you could spend days watching the work of Asian creators like Ryan Higa or Wong Fu Productions. Some videos made fun of Asian family dinners. Others, from crews like Jabbawockeez and Kaba Modern, showed an unsuspecting world that Asians can dance. So many videos about boba!

Without a central organizing force, one video at a time, Asian Americans began shifting the way they were perceived by American society—and by one another. Watching those videos, reading the comments, gave me something I'd never had before: proof that other people could relate to my in-between identity. YouTube soothed my still-unresolved cultural identity crisis, the feeling that I didn't fit in with other Asians—or other Americans—that had dogged me since I was a kid. I began to understand that many, many other young Asian Americans were proud of their family heritage *and* eager to immerse in mainstream American culture. They—*we*—didn't pit one side of themselves against the other but yearned to reconcile the two.

I wanted to be part of what I was seeing. So in 2006, I posted the only videos I had on hand: my class projects from USC. The response was . . . underwhelming. The videos sat there in the site's depths, all but completely ignored. It was the world's usual response to my work in the dark days before *Step Up 2*. But a few months later, when I was driving across town to some misbegotten pitch meeting, my phone went crazy, buzzing in a way it had never buzzed before.

A torrent of messages. Hundreds—then thousands. I thought I'd been hacked.

I looked for someplace with an internet connection where I could change my passwords. Hustling into the first place I saw, the Beverly Hills Public Library, I noticed that all the messages had something to do with YouTube.

I opened a browser and clicked my way to the homepage. There, in a featured spot, was *Silent Beats*.

I thought it might be a personalized view, feeding my own content back to me, so I clicked refresh.

Silent Beats was still there.

How could this be?

Unbeknownst to me, YouTube had hired curators to dig through the daily avalanche of newly posted material to find videos worth showcasing. They were nicknamed "coolhunters." (Steve Jobs was partly responsible for the move. "Your videos are shit," he had told one of the site's founders.) Once a curator put *Silent Beats* where the site's millions and millions of users could see it, they ate it up. As I refreshed the page, the video's view counter spun like the dials on a slot machine. Every few seconds, somebody left a comment or a "like" (which explains why my phone had freaked out—I'd set an alert for whenever I got a new one).

I had found a new audience, at a time when I was desperate to have one. And I knew that on YouTube I shared the company of countless young Asian Americans who could relate to my experiences. That combination made my next move obvious—almost inevitable. It was time for me to share *Gwai Lo*.

Except that I still couldn't do it. I was still too self-conscious.

Still too determined to break into Hollywood as a mainstream filmmaker, not an Asian storyteller. Still unwilling to look closely at my cultural identity, my past, my self.

WHEN I FELT THE urge to keep making things in the early days of preparing *Step Up 3D,* YouTube was the obvious place to do it. Adam Sevani, the young actor who had played Moose in *Step Up 2,* felt the same impulse I did, though we came at it with different motivations.

For me, it was the desire to keep working with dancers, particularly some whom I'd discovered on YouTube. For Adam, it was a crush on Miley Cyrus.

After rocketing to fame on the Disney Channel as the singing superstar Hannah Montana, she'd started posting a series of video blogs with her best friend and backup dancer, Mandy Jiroux. *The Miley and Mandy Show* looked like something my friends and I might have cooked up in high school—a lot of goofy faces and silly voices in somebody's bedroom—except that, thanks to YouTube (and to the chagrin of the Disney corporation), millions of people were watching.

Adam and I decided, for our respective reasons, to challenge Miley and Mandy to "the biggest online dance battle in YouTube history." (The joke was that there hadn't really been dance battles on YouTube before.) We invited dancers from around Los Angeles to come to a dance studio and join us in the challenge by sharing their best moves. We named ourselves the Adam/Chu Dance Crew, ACDC for short. (Yes, the band eventually objected.)

We didn't coordinate with Miley's team before calling her out via (what else) a YouTube video. We weren't even sure if she would notice. But a few days later, after our challenge had gotten tens of thousands of views, she and Mandy posted a response: a squad of her dancers performing a tightly choreographed routine to "4 Minutes," Madonna's song featuring Justin Timberlake and Timbaland. It also included a real slap in the face to me and Adam, two guys from the *Step Up* franchise: an appearance from the stars of the original movie, Channing Tatum and Jenna Dewan.

A million people watched Miley and Mandy's video in its first twenty-four hours. Then it was picked up by Ellen DeGeneres for her TV show. Then by *Access Hollywood*.

Adam and I had to come back hard.

While we prepared our response, our audience surged. Thirty-two thousand subscribers might not be a Miley-and-Mandy number, but it was more than Bad Boy Records at the time. We threw everything we had at the next video: dozens more dancers, including some of the new Asian stars of YouTube, plus the lead actors of *Step Up 2,* plus a constellation of names that had never before appeared in the same sentence, let alone a dance battle video—Adam Sandler, Chris Brown, Amanda Bynes, Lindsay Lohan, and Diana Ross.

The battle went back and forth all summer, occasionally spilling out into the real world, like when Ellen invited ACDC to perform at her fiftieth birthday party. All of it built toward the grand finale: a live showdown on national TV, when Miley hosted the Teen Choice Awards.

The M&M crew scored higher on the giant "applause meter" (which we didn't realize was going to be a predesigned graphic), but we didn't care. We'd already gotten our win.

Those dance battle videos required many, many hours of the kind of lowly work that a lot of Hollywood directors would consider beneath them. I did pretty much all the filming and editing. But to me, at that stage of my life, it was *better* than Hollywood. The constant scrappiness, the DIY spirit, the chance to work with friends like *Step Up 2* castmates Christopher Scott and Harry Shum Jr., the attempt to use new tools in new ways: It felt like Silicon Valley to me. Like I'd come home.

NO SOONER HAD I finished *Step Up 3D* (once again, mixed reviews; once again, box office success—$159 million worldwide) than I got a much clearer look at the internet's enormous potential to create, destroy, and everything in between. A full immersion, in fact.

"Have you heard of Justin Bieber?"

Adam Goodman was on the phone. He was the president of production at Paramount, though I'd known him since he'd been a studio exec at DreamWorks, in my bygone tyro days.

"I think so," I told him. "The internet guy."

That was one way of describing Justin, who was, at sixteen years old, a worldwide celebrity with an album atop the *Billboard* chart. What set him apart from other pop stars—what made him "the internet guy"—was that he'd been discovered on YouTube. Just a regular kid from a small Canadian town who now inspired Beatlemania screams every time he left his house.

Paramount had acquired the rights to make a 3D film of his upcoming show at Madison Square Garden. But the concert was less than a month away and it still didn't have a director. Adam knew that I'd just come off a 3D movie, and he remembered me from my over-the-top *Moxie* pitch. He wondered if I'd be interested. I said I'd get back to him.

I hung up thinking a concert movie might be fun but not

taking the idea much more seriously than that. Then I went to YouTube.

I'd been impressed by Justin's videos when he'd blown up the year before. But this time, I scrolled all the way back to the earliest comments on his videos and saw how he started. First his mom had left one, then his neighbors, then total strangers. Those fans had connected with one another, and pretty soon a community had formed. Their enthusiasm had launched Justin with so much velocity that within two years he could sell out the world's most famous arena in twenty-two minutes.

Those comments made me feel like I'd been on the ride the entire time. It was a fairy tale: a kid chasing a dream—the kind of story I like best. Only this time it had a Silicon Valley twist because of the outsized role that the internet had played in creating one of the biggest stars in the world. I started to imagine ways to tell Justin's story using the comments and his songs.

It all sounded great, Adam told me when I called him back, but the decision wasn't entirely up to him. I'd need the approval of Justin's manager, the one who had discovered him on YouTube and set the entire crazy story in motion.

"He's a lot," Adam said.

I assured him I could handle it, then called the number he'd given me.

"I don't think you're the right filmmaker for this," said Justin's manager, Scooter Braun.

A challenge. I relish a challenge.

I explained why I *was* the right filmmaker for this. It seemed to me that Justin represented a new generation, young people pursuing their dreams in a connected world—a world that I was part of and knew well. So the movie shouldn't be a concert film; it should be a full-fledged musical documentary, told by someone who really understands the internet. Justin's story could be a new generation's *Rocky*. (The reference wasn't accidental. I'd read online that it was his favorite movie.)

A tiny pause, then: "Okay. Let's go."

The next day, I arrived at the Arena at Gwinnett Center, just outside Atlanta. Scooter was waiting for me.

"Come with me. You have your camera?"

I did. Once again, I'd gotten my hands on the perfect tool at the perfect moment. The Canon EOS 5D Mark II was the size of any old point-and-shoot still camera but was capable of capturing video in full HD at twenty-four frames per second. Nothing like this had existed for filmmakers before. It could just about match the performance of the camera we'd begged Panavision to use when shooting *When the Kids Are Away,* but it was small enough to toss in my carry-on bag and a tiny fraction of the price.

Scooter led me through the arena and out the other side. Above us loomed a parking garage. All six levels were lined with girls—girls and their moms, hundreds of them. They were staring down at us, hoping for a glimpse of Justin. All of them were singing "One Less Lonely Girl," one of his more popular songs.

"Shoot that," Scooter said. "That's what this is all about."

We walked to the tour bus. It was time to meet Justin. Inside, he was goofing around like a regular sixteen-year-old. In other words: pretty much every kid in the world except for him.

"Hey, Justin, this is Jon," Scooter said. "He's going to make your movie."

Justin turned my way. Immediately, in a single glance, I understood why millions of people were obsessed with him. When he looked at you, you felt like the center of the world.

"*What* movie?"

Oh shit, I thought. *This is gonna be crazy.*

I embedded with the tour for the next few weeks, shadowing Justin as he performed in places like Nashville, Indianapolis, and Columbus, then swung north to Toronto for the closest he would come to a hometown gig, then pivoted south for the big finale in New York City. While a reality TV crew captured the action backstage, I used the tiny dimensions of my 5D, and the fact that it needed so little light, to capture his more private moments on the bus without his shields going up: doing homework with his tutor, playing video games alone in the middle of the night.

I loved spending time with Justin and the crew, but life on an arena tour—all buses and backstage hallways—is unnerving. Alienating. Surreal. You're in a bubble. You lose track of which town you're in, what time it is, or where you're supposed to sleep, if you get to sleep. Watching Justin in those very weird circumstances helped me understand the paradoxes of living an extremely online life.

I'd always felt pretty savvy about the internet, thanks to my Silicon Valley head start. But Justin was way savvier than me. He was a child of it, so it came so naturally to him. He was an incredibly quick study, so would find things that he wanted to learn on YouTube, like speed Rubik's Cube or yo-yo tricks, and practice until he mastered them.

At a time when it wasn't physically safe for Justin to walk down a city street, his phone gave him a connection to the world. He could look at his fans, and they could (and did) look back. The number and intensity of those connections gave him power. After coming offstage one night, he tweeted to his four and a half million followers: "This TOUR is

INCREDIBLE!! Only problem is this guy keeps following me show to show. @jonmchu why r u following me dude?" My follower count began to skyrocket by hundreds a second. It was like when YouTube promoted *Silent Beats,* only this time it wasn't because a Google-owned company with a globally viewed homepage had selected me. It was just a single sixteen-year-old.

Those connections also provided Justin with a kind of insulation. When he had a direct line to millions of people willing to follow him anywhere, what could a record label or anybody else do to control him, or even guide him? Especially since he wasn't putting on a show for them—he was offering his authentic self. And there was a clear difference between the two. When we tried to interview him on camera, he gave answers that were formal and unrevealing. But when he talked into his laptop camera, recording a video for fans, he was relaxed, comfortable, truthful—the real Justin.

Now and then I'd find him alone, without anybody else—online or off. He'd be writing lyrics, slotting them carefully into a different folder for each stop on his tour. Those moments told me that he wasn't just a pop star; he was a real musician. They gave me reason to hope that he was going to be okay, even amid the enormous pressures and constant scrutiny of his massively connected life.

Justin may have been an extreme case, but it seemed to me that he embodied a generation-wide change in the way young people related to technology. That was the point of the movie, which we titled *Justin Bieber: Never Say Never.* The scale might be different, but the intensity and scrutiny are the same: Today, in the era of TikTok, Snapchat, and Instagram, every kid is that kid.

EATING SHIT

This happens all the time. I do it every
that every leader does, but somehow we
about it. I'll be on set, trying to make the day, when
I'll get a complaint from a producer, a condescending
"suggestion" from the studio, or a dirty look from
somebody who doesn't like one of my choices. Each
time, the hairs on the back of my neck stick up, and I
have to decide: Am I going to stop what I'm doing and
push back? The way I see it, a big part of my job is
resisting that urge. Leaders need to prioritize the
goals of the project, not the needs of their egos. It's
not weak to let things like that go—it's strong to
promise yourself that no one and nothing is going to
keep you from making your movie. If that means
eating shit from time to time, so be it. Just try not to
taste it. And know that everybody else is doing it, too.

IT WASN'T JUST ASIAN AMERICANS and it wasn't just
YouTube: The whole world seemed to be going online. The
more people turned to the internet for their entertainment,
the less they needed to pay for movies and TV shows, particularly in the highly profitable formats that Hollywood depended on. When the Great Recession cut into people's
spending and streaming video became more widely available,
both DVD sales and cable TV subscriptions began to decline,
taking precious dollars with them.

ere Silicon Valley and Hollywood—my old home and
y new one—becoming better friends or turning into ene-
mies? Maybe both? The closer you looked at the relationship,
the more confusing it got.

Take Netflix. The Los Gatos–based company was a survi-
vor of the '90s dot-com boom-and-bust, mailing out DVDs in
its famous red envelopes. It had generated revenue for Hollywood through those DVD rentals and a free add-on streaming
option. But in 2010, it shifted its strategy, introducing a
streaming-only subscription. It even started to call itself "primarily a streaming video company." The stock price tripled in
a year.

It was definitely a mortal threat to Hollywood . . . unless it
was no big deal? Nobody could be sure. Jeff Bewkes, the chief
executive of Time Warner, offered the snappiest version of the
no-big-deal position: "It's a little bit like, is the Albanian army
going to take over the world? I don't think so."

Hollywood's struggle to find new revenue streams without
further choking the old ones led to a lot of experimentation,
which gave me just the opening I needed to do more experi-
menting of my own. After the Miley-and-Mandy dance battle, I'd started to percolate another idea—a more ambitious
attempt to tell stories through dance. *If dancers are like real-world
superheroes,* I remember thinking, *then why not create a superhero
series about them?* I dreamed up *The Legion of Extraordinary Dancers,* a sprawling good vs. evil story—like a comic book on-
screen. This time, I didn't think YouTube was the right
platform. I would need longer run times than the site's viewers
tended to like. I also needed money for production costs,
which YouTube didn't provide. (It would do so, in some cases,
a couple of years later.)

I found exactly what I needed in Hulu. The streaming service, a joint effort from the corporate owners of ABC, NBC, and Fox, had begun serving up network programming a couple of years earlier. In that pivotal year, 2010, it began to supplement those shows with original online-only content: a low-cost way to draw more viewers to the site, to create more inventory for ads, and, above all, to prevent any more eyeballs from straying to YouTube and Netflix.

My idea for a comic-book series about dance—ten-minute episodes in which dancers showcased the unbelievable things they could do with their bodies—was just what Hulu wanted. Working with friends and colleagues, and backed by Paramount Digital Entertainment, I threw myself into the project. I dreamed up an elaborate mythology with my collaborators, then wrote all the episodes and directed the first few.

Hulu gave us a lot of freedom and we used every bit of it. I even hung a pirate flag in our production office, a tribute to the one that Steve Jobs had flown above the Macintosh building in the early days of Apple. ("It's better to be a pirate than join the navy," he'd explained.) It felt to me like maybe my adolescent dream of leading a company of fellow creators— my version of Pixar—might be starting to come true.

We called ourselves "dance adventurers," because we were constantly trying things, the crazier the better: a robot love story in the style of a noir comic book, ballerina assassins ambushing a villain in a grocery store. The mix of approaches from one episode to the next (comedy, relationship drama, split-screen storytelling, plots running backward) may have seemed scattershot, but it was highly strategic. Plenty of signature moments in my later movies exist only because of the laboratory for filming dance provided by *The LXD*. My creative partners—Alice Brooks, the director of photography, and Christopher Scott, the choreographer—did more than stock a toolbox with techniques, styles, and moves in our Hulu days. We developed a shorthand. We began to fuse ourselves into a team.

My collaborators and I started promoting *The LXD* while we were still in production, mainly by posting trailers to the YouTube channel that we'd used for the Miley-and-Mandy dance battle. Although we were months away from our official premiere, our online series started opening some offline doors. The producers of *So You Think You Can Dance,* one of the most popular shows on TV, saw the trailer, loved it, and asked us to come on the show. We also got invited to perform a TED Talk. Dance has "never had a better friend than technology," I said in my introduction. (Afterward, Bill Gates asked us for a photo. While we were setting up the shot, he did the robot: one of the strangest of that year's collisions of technology and self-expression.)

An even bigger invitation came from Adam Shankman, who had produced *Step Up 2* and was about to direct the Oscars. After seeing the *LXD* trailer, he asked us to perform on the show to a medley of nominees for Best Score.

Adam's invitation would bring this phase of my life, and its many fusions of creativity and technology, to a crescendo. I'm not talking about what happened on Oscar night. I'm thinking of that afternoon—of the encounter that made performing for eighty million people feel like an anticlimax.

THE CEREMONY THAT YEAR, like every year, was a celebration of Hollywood traditions: the tuxes and gowns, the tributes to screen legends. But in 2010, even the Oscars reflected the promising alliance of digital technology and storytelling. *Up,* the latest computer-animated movie from Pixar, was nominated for five Oscars, including Best Picture—the first animated film in that category since *Beauty and the Beast* in 1991.

Forty-five minutes before the broadcast began, I was soaking up the vibe, enjoying how it felt to be at the summit of moviemaking with a real pass (not a fake one that I'd designed for myself), when everything froze. All the people. All the sounds. My thumping heart.

Steve Jobs had walked in.

It was really him. Not on a Macworld stage, not on a magazine cover, but right here in front of me—headed into a VIP area. Thanks to *The LXD,* I was a VIP, too. Nothing stood between me and my hero except my fear.

From across the room, trying to work up the courage to talk with him, I could see that he looked gaunt. The previous year, his cancer had returned. He'd taken a medical leave from Apple so he could receive a liver transplant. In person, he looked frailer than he had just five weeks earlier, when he'd unveiled the iPad. "We've always tried to be at the intersection of technology and the liberal arts, to be able to get the best of both," he'd said that day. It was a mission statement for me, and maybe for everybody, in the rapidly changing world of 2010.

Somebody handed me a glass of champagne. I downed it and kept staring. All those years of revering the guy, and now *he was right there*. He was talking to Bob Iger, the CEO of Disney—a conversation that no mere mortal had a right to interrupt. So yes, I was scared. He had a reputation for being brusque with people, even cruel. I thought it was almost always in the service of his vision, pushing himself and everybody around him to realize some picture in his head. Still, I wasn't going to risk incurring his wrath. He meant too much to me.

Some of these thoughts must have come out of my mouth as I was thinking them, because Harry Shum—friend, actor, *LXD* choreographer—laughed a little.

"I did, like, six iPod commercials. *I'll* talk to him."

Harry marched off, just like that. I initiated some choreography of my own. I turned away from Steve, then started backing up. So if he looked at me, it would seem like I was talking to somebody else and not being a creeper.

Harry, hand on my arm, spun me around.

"I want you to meet my friend Jon. He loves you."

We are shaking hands now. Even gaunt from illness, this face is still the one that has stared back at me from posters in almost every bedroom I've ever had.

I feel self-conscious about being red, stupidly red, from the champagne. Also about my hair being a stupid mohawk. *Jesus.*

"I'm from Los Altos," I say.

"Oh, my hometown! How's it going, neighbor?"

"Something something Chef Chu's," I say.

"Chef Chu's! I used to go there when I was younger." So a family legend is confirmed.

I brace myself to say what I've wanted to say since I was fifteen years old: "I'm so thankful for the tools you created. I'm a director now, and they allowed me to find my voice. I'm not sure what I'd be doing without them."

"That's so great to hear," he says, smiling. "The hometown boy is here!"

I get the sense that he's about to wrap things up. I can't let that happen. He still doesn't understand what he means to me.

What else can I say? It hits me just in time.

"Also your commercial really moves me. I memorized it. I say it to myself all the time."

"Which one?"

"The 'Think different' one."

"How does it go?"

"Here's to the crazy ones," I begin. "The misfits. The rebels."

I recite a few more lines, then stop. I don't want to waste the man's time. But he leans in. He turns an ear toward me so he can hear me more clearly. He stares at the floor. Waits.

I get the message. I keep going.

I try not to skip a word or stutter. I don't notice when somebody to my left snaps a picture.

When I reach the line "Because they change things," Steve turns and looks up. He starts saying it with me.

In sync, face-to-face, we recite it together, all the way to the big finish.

"Because the people who are crazy enough to think they can change the world are the ones who do," we say.

Steve smiles. He shakes my hand.

"Jon, that means so much to me. Thank you for sharing that."

I'm about to effuse some more, but Bob Iger saves me.

"Steve! You met one of our directors, Jon."

"No, no—he's my *neighbor*," Steve says.

"He did the movie *Step Up 2*. Have you heard of it?"

Steve begins to say that he hasn't, but just then his wife, Laurene Powell Jobs, turns to join us.

"Oh, our daughters love those movies!"

And Laurene is smiling, and Bob is smiling, and Steve is

smiling, and *I* am smiling (and still very red). And I know that this conversation has reached its dreamy conclusion. I tell Steve it was great to meet him and head back down to planet Earth.

I'm a few feet away when it hits me: *I didn't get a picture.* How had I finally met my hero, my idol—I, who use cameras for a living—and failed to get a picture?

I am stewing. Harry is amused. The show starts in ten minutes. How can I bother Steve Jobs again so quickly? Especially by asking for a photo, which I know he doesn't like. I don't want to spoil what feels like the greatest moment of my life.

I'm about to let it go when I get a strange conviction— a feeling that I'll never forgive myself if I let this opportunity pass. Eighteen months later, I will be deeply, painfully grateful for that impulse. I will be on a movie set in New Orleans, in the midst of what I remember as a difficult day, when an assistant will take me aside and break the news about Steve. And even though time is money on film sets, I will excuse myself from the actors, find a bathroom, lock the door, and weep.

I grab Harry and walk back across the room.

"Steve," I say, "I know you don't like this, but could we take a picture? It would mean so much."

"Of course, Jon," he says. "We're neighbors."

Harry takes my iPhone, points it at us, and looks at the screen. What does he see?

Two sons of Silicon Valley. A young man and his hero. One of them fulfilling a boyhood dream, one with just eighteen months to live. Two people who, walking different paths and working at much different scales, had combined creativity and technology to get from Los Altos all the way to Los Angeles. Even farther than that—all the way to the *Oscars,* to the very heart of Hollywood.

Together. Smiling.

Click.

The creative experiments of *The LXD* succeeded—and success took a toll.

The internet, I was learning, makes insatiable demands. You need to feed the beast. Once you've built an audience, you need to invest time and effort in keeping it. Once you've lined up sponsors, you need to contend with their expectations, which might involve the pressure to make more, even if you don't want to. The boundlessness of the internet can make you crazy if you let it.

The offers and sponsorship deals began to open a new path for me: to become what we'd now call an "influencer." For example: A soda company wanted us to make videos for its new marketing campaign, suggesting that everybody should dance to celebrate its bubbly new taste. But did promoting a soda brand clash with the kind of healthy lifestyle that dancers value? I hadn't expected that I would need to navigate those kinds of complexities when we started out. And I didn't want to muddy what had begun as a creative endeavor among friends.

I knew it was time to slow the pace of *The LXD*. But I treasured the work that we'd made and the lessons I'd learned.

I saw enough of the influencer economy to sympathize with young people who try to navigate its demands today: the constant gnawing need to do more, to work longer hours, to fixate on the shows you're not making, the people you're not reaching—all while trying to survive your "real" life. And I was grateful for the leadership experience I'd gained for the creative company that I planned to run someday.

But that day would need to wait, because I had movies to direct. Lots of movies.

Though I'd made three studio films, I was still traumatized by how much of my twenties I'd spent in development hell. So now that I was on the right path and finally getting movies made, I wanted to make more as quick as I could. This was no time to get distracted, not by shiny side projects, not by the demands of a personal life, not by anything.

Lucky for me, in Hollywood, momentum is real. The place operates according to a simple flowchart. If your movie earns money, you get to follow the arrow that points to making another movie. (If it doesn't, you get to read about other people making movies in the trades.) At thirty-one, I wanted to position myself for a long career, to eventually make the big, inclusive spectacles I'd always dreamed of making. The smart move, it seemed to me, would be to diversify the kind of movies I'd been directing, to show more of what I could do.

Like making a gigantic action movie.

Since the Justin Bieber documentary had grossed $99 million at the box office (the highest domestic gross of all time for a concert movie—a record that would stand for a decade), Paramount offered me a couple of other projects. One of them was a *G.I. Joe* movie. Huge battles, elaborate stunts, pyrotechnics: It would definitely complicate any effort to pigeonhole me. Also, I'd loved playing with G.I. Joes as a kid and couldn't resist the idea of doing so again, only with a $125 million budget. That was bigger than all my previous budgets combined.

The movie, *G.I. Joe: Retaliation,* was a sequel. If you're keeping count—which I wasn't, because I was grateful to be making anything—that means I directed three sequels in my first four films. I thought they gave a Hollywood newcomer like me an advantage. People in the industry could compare my approach with the previous director's and see what made me distinctive. In the case of *G.I. Joe,* I hoped that my experience filming movement in the *Step Up* movies and *The LXD,* when we shifted not just what's within the frame but the frame itself, would set me apart. After all, from a technical perspective, a fight sequence and a dance sequence aren't so different (though don't tell my stunt coordinators). Both work best when they're essential to the story, showing another step in the emotional journey of the characters. Both rely on action, not dialogue, saying what a paragraph never could. And if you do them right, nobody can look away.

In preproduction, we decided to push those possibilities as far as we could. We dreamed up a nine-minute-long, dialogue-free action sequence, in which ninjas would fight on the sheer face of a mountain. I imagined sword fights, zip lines, giant swings, an avalanche. Getting it right would require specialized input from the stunt directors and their crew, plus best-in-class visual effects from Industrial Light & Magic. But it would also take playing with 3¾-inch-tall G.I. Joes.

We arranged the couches and chairs in our production office to stand in for mountains, then used string and tape to represent the zip lines. We sat on the floor, the way a lot of us did when we were kids, and staged battles with the action figures (never say "dolls"—Hasbro doesn't like it). That's how we decided where the camera would go, which parts we would shoot in front of a blue screen, which on the side of an actual mountain. Anybody who walked past the office could tell you that we also decided how it should sound. All of us vocalized *boom* and *bang* and *swish* as we played—sorry, *planned*—with our action figures.

But the best thing about the project was getting a chance to direct a genuine, bona fide, face-on-a-billboard movie star: Dwayne "the Rock" Johnson.

"You look like my cousin," he said on our first day on set. (His father was Black, and his mother, Samoan.)

I wasn't sure how to respond to that. Then he threw his giant arm around my comparatively tiny shoulders, leaned in, flashed his billion-dollar smile, and said, "Isn't it crazy that someone that looks like you and someone that looks like me are here, getting to do this big-ass movie?"

I'd never thought about how I looked to the cast and crew. I was too busy trying to do the job. But I loved that he gave me that perspective of what we were embarking on.

He treated me like family the whole time we worked together, which meant a lot on that gigantic set, where it was easy to feel overwhelmed by the enormity of it all. (We shot part of the movie in a NASA facility so big that it had its own microclimates.) His kindness meant even more when my *actual* family was around. My parents visited the set one day; Howard came with them. He knows everything about movies—more than I do, more than almost anybody does—and he knows *even more* about professional wrestling. So meeting Dwayne, who'd of course been a WWF champ before becoming a movie star, was like two dreams come true. The Rock talked with him, laughed with him, and even yelled his tagline—*"Can you smell what the Rock is cooking?"*—for him so loudly that an assistant director had to tell him to keep it down. Howard will never forget it. And neither will I.

G.I. Joe: Retaliation received what I'd begun to think of as the standard response to my movies. Critics didn't love it, but the audience did, so it made a bunch of money all over the world. Which meant that I got to make another one. I immediately started to develop the third installment in the franchise, even though it would take a while before we could start production. The Hollywood flowchart had already pointed me toward a different movie that I'd decided to make first. Well, sort of decided.

One afternoon, Justin invited me over to Scooter's house. They told me there was going to be a second documentary, and Justin wanted me to direct it, and they weren't letting me leave until I said yes.

Even now I'm not sure if they were kidding. But I didn't need any arm-twisting. I jumped at having another chance to be at the center of the pop culture universe, especially since it gave me a chance to show more of what I could do. This time, Justin also wanted me to be the creative director of his tour. I'd never even directed a high school play, and now the world's biggest pop star was giving me a chance to direct what felt like it ought to be the world's biggest concert.

After years of making things to be seen on screens, it was unbelievably liberating to play in three dimensions. I wanted the show to be an immersive experience for Justin's fans, like going on a Disneyland ride with twenty thousand other people: shifting sets, elements that flew over their heads, pyro. In fact, I took a lot of inspiration from *Captain EO,* the Michael

Jackson short film that had been a highlight of our Disney trips when I was a kid. *Captain EO* was advertised as being in 3D, but it was even more immersive than that, because the effects stretched into the auditorium: smoke, wind, lasers. The experience was fresh in my mind, because when *Step Up 2* had turned out to be a big hit, and Disney chairman Dick Cook had asked me if there was anything he could do for me, I'd requested a screening of *Captain EO* for me and the dancers. Since the movie had left the parks a decade earlier, we had to trek out to a secret Imagineering warehouse full of retired attractions. The dust didn't matter: The place was magical, and so was *Captain EO*.

As Justin's tour rolled from city to city and continent to continent, I guided the documentary through postproduction. But as we neared the finish line, it became clear that a piece was missing. We needed to have a conversation with Justin about his life. The impossible pressures that I'd seen building on him a couple of years earlier, the strange mix of power and vulnerability that came from being a pop star who was also the internet's main character, had begun to affect him. He wasn't a kid doing homework on the bus anymore. He'd had his first run-in with the law, an argument with a photographer that nearly turned into a fistfight, and enough embarrassing headlines to suggest that bigger problems might lie ahead.

"Are you conscious that you are the perfect candidate to become a train wreck?" I asked him, camera rolling.

He laughed me off. I pointed out that he lived in a bubble.

"No one can tell you no," I said. "So now what?"

He assured me that he had a good head on his shoulders. He said it wasn't going to happen to him.

I'd grown to care about Justin by this point, so I wanted to believe him. I wanted him to have a happy, healthy life and get to make his music. I still want that for him.

WHEN THE FILM WAS nearly done, we held a screening for members of Scooter's staff. I planned to watch them watch the movie, then adjust the moments that hadn't connected.

Fifteen or twenty people crowded into my office. But I ended up watching only one.

She sat in the front, on the floor. Once the movie started, she laughed everywhere I hoped people would laugh and cried everywhere I hoped people would cry.

Either she's a big fan of Justin's, I figured, *or she really gets me.*

Afterward I asked about her. *Who is she? What's her deal?* Scooter's assistant, a friend of hers, talked with her, then filled me in.

Her name was Kristin. She wasn't currently seeing anybody. And here was her number.

I had to fly to China the next day to make arrangements for the movie's release. But I didn't want to let the moment pass, so I decided to ask her to dinner while I was still overseas. I'd heard that she was a graphic designer, so instead of typing an email, I wrote an elaborate letter on the stationery of my hotel. I added illustrations all over the page, then took a picture of it. I aimed for "funny and quirky," but when I saw it on my phone, it looked like a crazy stalker letter.

This is bad, I thought. *They're going to put this on the office refrigerator.*

I decided to hedge my bet by turning what I'd written into

a plain old email. It still seemed risky. But it was almost time to get back on the plane, so I said a silent *screw it* and hit send. (I don't recommend this strategy.)

I spent the next thirteen hours thinking that it was the stupidest thing I'd ever done. My email was almost definitely being forwarded to everyone at Scooter's company.

When I landed early the next morning and turned off airplane mode on my phone, her reply was waiting for me. She said it was a nice message to wake up to. And yes, she would go out to dinner with me.

But our dinner didn't happen, not the way we'd planned. Justin was supposed to come to my house to watch a cut of the movie, but he showed up three hours late. (He was a nineteen-year-old superstar—it happens.)

I was embarrassed. Kristin was understanding. Dinner turned into late-night drinks.

We went to the Polo Lounge, my favorite old-school Hollywood haunt and just about the only classy place open that late. We ordered the famous soufflé as soon as we sat down, since it takes a while to arrive. Would we find enough to talk about until then? I'm not much of a drinker but ordered a Grey Goose and tonic, hoping to calm myself down. But now was my face going to turn red?

I tried to stop worrying and listen.

She'd grown up in Arizona, then had gone to NYU to study design. After working with Pencils of Promise, a nonprofit run by Scooter's brother, she'd moved to L.A. to work with Scooter himself. Now she was handling some of his highest-profile design projects, like album covers for Justin, Ariana Grande, and the Wanted.

I told her some of my story too, but I wasn't sure if we

were connecting. Then, somehow, we landed on the topic of fonts. Her eyes lit up. We proceeded to talk about typefaces for half an hour: what we liked, what we hated, how we used them.

She told me her favorite font was Akzidenz. Thank God it wasn't something like Zapfino! I knew right then we'd be all right.

I wanted to see her again and didn't want to wait, which got me into trouble. The next night, I was ten minutes into a long-scheduled meeting with Alice Brooks when I said I was sorry, but I had to leave early. For a date.

Alice was a little bit exasperated and more than a little surprised. We'd been friends and collaborators since our USC days, so she knew how I felt: that no relationship was going to interfere with my work, not after the struggle to get to that point in my career. She shook her head and watched me go.

"She better be your wife," Alice said.

A YEAR LATER, KRISTIN wasn't my wife, but we were together—in London.

Because *G.I. Joe* had shown that I could be trusted with a major franchise, Lionsgate hired me to direct *Now You See Me 2*. The movie would tell the story of a team of magician-heroes who need to steal an all-powerful computer chip and save the world. And it would film in England.

I hadn't consulted Kristin before taking the job, just told her I'd be doing it. She was thrown by my abrupt announcement that I was about to spend nearly a year on the other side of the planet. I can appreciate why. By that point, I'd already introduced her to my parents, at the opening night of *Justin Bieber's*

Believe. (When she started to feel awkward holding my hand through one red carpet interview after another, she retreated to someplace less conspicuous. But my mom told her to go stand by me, so no girls thought I was single.) Kristin had even spent Christmas with us in Los Altos, braving the mayhem of Chu family dinners: the onslaught of dishes, everybody talking at once, me being paraded around the restaurant by my mom.

I cared so much about Kristin, but it just had never occurred to me to let a girlfriend have a say in whether I took a project. Work came first for me, and as far as I was concerned, it would go on coming first for as long as the Hollywood flow-chart allowed. Besides, experience had taught me that movies and girlfriends don't mix. Whenever I'd gone into production while dating somebody, the relationship always wrapped before the movie did.

But this time, I wanted the relationship to last. Thankfully, so did Kristin. She stayed in London for weeks at a time. We grew closer, in spite of my hesitation. She was different from anybody I'd dated—from anybody I'd *known*. She was kind, so unbelievably kind, but she pushed back when she thought I deserved it. And she exuded a sense of calm I'd never experienced before, one that I was definitely not experiencing during those months in London. Because face-to-face with a cast full of stars and legends, I was scared out of my mind.

On my first day working with Morgan Freeman, who played the (apparent) villain of the movie, we finished the first take, then I said, "Let's do it again."

Morgan said, "Why?"

He knew what he wanted to do with the scene. He felt that he'd already done it. If I wanted the scene done a different way, I needed to give him a damn convincing reason.

I respected that, even though it put me in a jam. I tried to spell out my thinking.

"Well, it's gonna be the same," he said.

I suggested some adjustments, which might make it play differently.

He paused, thinking. Then said: "Okay, let's do it again."

We did it again.

"Was that any different?"

It wasn't. I didn't know what to do. Before shooting started, I had dug out my old USC textbooks, to brush up on the dos and don'ts of directing actors. None of them offered tips for how to overcome the resistance of a screen legend who has so much gravitas that he's literally the go-to actor for playing God.

But there was something I didn't realize: The entire time that he was challenging me, he was smiling at the crew, as if to say, *I'm fucking with this guy.*

Hazing, I'd later learn, was part of Morgan's love language. It was the playful vibe he wanted to set at the beginning of the shoot. Behind it, though, was a test—a real one. Actors know that for all their fame and their talent, the filmmaking process leaves them largely powerless. No matter what they do in front of the camera, a director can change their entire performance in the edit—and, if the director has bad taste, ruin it. Morgan wanted to see if I knew what I was doing.

I understood how he felt, particularly since I was so young. Actors tend to expect that new directors will show up with a lot of ego, making demands that might or might not serve the movie's best interests. When they see that's not how I operate, it usually disarms them.

It disarmed Morgan, which was a relief. But that still left

every other star in this all-star cast. Once again, my dance background helped me: I felt like I was dancing with each actor separately and with all of them together. Each one had a different reason for being there, a different goal, a different method. As director, it was my job to connect their individual wants and the scene's needs. So we needed to move in sync, hopefully without mashing anybody's toes.

I was lucky that their ringleader, on-screen and off, was Mark Ruffalo. On the first day when all the actors were in the room, he gave me a hug and said, "We're down with you, Jon. Tell us what to do." Which is not to say that he always made it easy for me and his scene-mates. The man never gave the same performance twice. Every take was different, but somehow they all felt truthful. His style was so in-the-moment that he would even react to something a crew member in his line of sight happened to do. I finally had to tell everybody to hold still while the cameras were rolling.

Jesse Eisenberg was a writer himself, so we'd have smart, focused conversations about what a scene was trying to achieve. He could execute like a pro, even in scenes with the freewheeling Mark, where the collision of their very different methods was fun to watch. Daniel Radcliffe was like Jesse. At the table read, he already knew his lines. The other actors were playfully furious with him for making them look bad. But then Dave Franco made them look bad, too: In a movie that required a lot of precise card tricks, he was the best card thrower by far. Woody Harrelson was fast and funny and liked to riff his way through his scenes, hitting his marks, weaving in and out of the script like a pro. Lizzy Caplan had a category all to herself: totally hilarious, ridiculously fearless. The cast was a bit of a boys' club, but she more than held her own. She was usually the one who would push a joke as far as it could go, leaving people on the floor laughing. That constituted a major victory, since the actors spent a lot of their time trying to make each other break character. Some days, I felt like a chaperone on the best field trip ever.

Above all there was Michael Caine, who brought something unique and precious to the shoot: the fact that he was Michael Caine. Wherever he went, the rest of the cast would follow—myself included—listening to him tell legendary stories about *Alfie, Dirty Rotten Scoundrels,* and countless other movies he'd made in his incredible life. He also taught me a lesson about power, on-screen and off. In one scene, he was supposed to confront another character. I wanted him to show his authority by getting in the guy's face, but he wouldn't do it.

"Jon, people with power don't get into other people's faces," he told me. "They don't have to. They make other people come to them. The less I do, the more powerful I am."

I held on to that insight and used it a few years later when making *Crazy Rich Asians*. It's the reason Eleanor, Michelle Yeoh's character, barely acknowledges her son's new girlfriend the first time they meet. She establishes their power dynamic while barely saying a word.

By the time we wrapped production, I'd shed a lot of my fear about directing big stars. I was proud of what we'd achieved. Which made it all the more mysterious: Why didn't I get more creative enjoyment out of the experience? It should have felt amazing, like a career milestone—a *life* milestone. And somehow it didn't.

So what was missing?

Part of the answer was obvious: Kristin was missing. When she was back in L.A., we'd talk on the phone for hours, wishing we were together. But loneliness couldn't be the only explanation for my feeling of unease. For directors, loneliness is a constant—a given. During the flurry of meetings I'd had after graduating from USC, Rob Reiner had tried to warn me. "You're neither cast nor crew. You're not going to be bonding with any of them," he said. "Any decision you make, somebody's going to whisper what an asshole or an idiot you are. It is what it is. Be okay with it."

No, this had to be something else, something deeper. The movie was everything I could have asked for and should have left me feeling fulfilled, and it didn't.

Wasn't this the path I'd chosen? I was a storyteller, telling stories. And wasn't I making my way along the path of Hollywood success, picking up speed with every project? I already had another *G.I. Joe* movie lined up. After that, there'd be *Now You See Me 3*. That's what I'd been working so hard for.

Wasn't it?

A YEAR LATER, BACK in Los Angeles.

Because I wanted a home, and not just a place to live, I started eyeing a house across the street from my apartment in West Hollywood that was being renovated. Because Kristin and I were starting to talk about a future together, we climbed the fence of the house late one night, to daydream about what our life there could be. Nobody warned us the place had a very loud alarm, so we had to scramble back to the sidewalk, amid blaring horns, then run like hell, dodging the law enforcement

UNCOMFORTABLE
CONVERSATIONS

Being a creative leader involves a lot of dreaming
and "yes, and"—ing, but it can also mean managing a
team that isn't reaching its full potential. No matter
how hard you try to foster a healthy environment, one
where everybody feels empowered and makes a contribution, it might not survive a problem with the
group's approach to work or a team member having
an attitude flare-up. Much as I dislike confronta-
tions, my years in Hollywood have taught me that
situations like those need to be addressed *right away*.
I'd even say that your success is directly related to the
number of uncomfortable conversations you're willing to have and how quickly you're willing to have
them. Speaking honestly and directly—even bluntly—
with an underperforming team or one of its wayward
members can be essential to keeping a project on
track. That doesn't mean you should be cruel. In fact,
it means the opposite: Be empathetic. So have the
hard conversation. Embrace it. It's a sign of progress.
And in my experience, it's never as scary as you
think it'll be.

that was rushing to the scene, laughing the entire time. Now I
had to buy that house.

Spending time with Kristin—sharing late-night milk-
shakes at Swingers or sitting in bed, drawing on our iPads,

comparing designs—made me stop feeling lonely. But my unease lingered. My friend Liat gave me a clue around this time, though she didn't realize she was doing it.

"You have the best job," she told me. "You're, like, '-ish.' You've made a lot of movies, so you're successful-*ish*. And people kind of know you, so you're famous-*ish,* but not so famous that you can't go out. And you make movies, but they don't change the world or anything, so you're great-*ish*. You're just below the radar, and you get to have a good life, and you don't have to deal with pressure."

"That's terrible!" I shot back, much to her surprise. "I don't want to be '-ish.' That's a huge insult! Why would anybody want a life to be '-ish'? I don't want to be '-ish'!"

It bothered me—but not enough for me to do anything about it. I promised myself that I would deal with it later, when I had the time. At the moment, I was much too busy to deal with personal stuff, which seemed to me like the best kind of busy to be. After the terrible stretch when I couldn't get anything made, I was about to finish my seventh movie in seven years.

The success of *G.I. Joe: Retaliation* had earned me the trust of the folks at Hasbro, the toy manufacturer that also controlled the rights to *Jem and the Holograms*. I'd grown up watching the animated series with my sisters. For three seasons in the late '80s, Jerrica Benton, a young woman who ran a record label, used a powerful computer bequeathed by her father to create holograms that allowed her and her sisters to transform into a rock band. We loved it: The show was about empowerment, split identities, and cool technology, and the songs were pretty great, in a tongue-in-cheek way. I thought the show could come back as a live-action movie, set in the present day.

The theme of having an alter ego seemed more relevant than ever in the social media era. In my version, Jerrica/Jem would be famous thanks to a YouTube clip and would struggle to balance her real everyday life with her publicly created one. It was, in no small part, a fictionalized, outsized version of Justin's story.

By now, I'd had plenty of experience with passionate fan bases, from Justin's "Beliebers" to the guys covered in G.I. Joe tattoos. None of it prepared me for the Jem fans. My approach to the material, wanting to tell a basically grounded story about a young woman struggling with her identity, wasn't what a lot of them seemed to want. At least not from me. I got hate mail, racist abuse, even death threats.

In spite of the vitriol, I loved the actual experience of making the movie. The cast was stellar, the music was fun, and the story was about something that mattered to me. Still, as we neared the end of the project, I began to see that the doubters might be right. My attempt to make a more earnest *Jem,* one that a new audience of kids might respond to the way my sisters and I had, was missing the boldness and outlandish fun that had meant so much to the original fans. I had miscalculated, attempting to take the brand in a direction it didn't naturally go. But by then it was too late to make a change.

The reviews were mostly scathing. That had never bothered me much, because I mainly cared about the audience liking my movies—in particular, liking them enough to show up in healthy numbers. On both of those metrics—audience response and box office—*Jem* failed completely. In fact, it failed *historically. The Hollywood Reporter* declared that it had "the worst opening ever for a major studio release playing in at least 2,000 theaters."

All I wanted to do was die or, if I couldn't manage that, at least hide out for a couple of months. But in a truly sadistic coincidence, *Jem* opened on the same weekend that I was scheduled to deliver a keynote address at the Film Independent Forum. I had promised to stand onstage for thirty minutes and tell a theater full of up-and-coming filmmakers the secrets of my recent success.

The night before the speech, I drafted an email canceling my appearance. As I was about to hit send, I froze. At one of the lowest moments of my life, I felt a surge of defiance. I was a storyteller, wasn't I? Well, I certainly had a story to tell. It might not be a tale of triumph, but I could still give an honest account of my experience. The audience might relate to it, maybe even benefit from it. I was going to stand for something, even if it hurt.

On the morning after our catastrophic opening night, my feet walked me across a stage at the Directors Guild of America. I clutched the lectern and tried not to puke.

"So, this is a bit awkward," I said to nervous laughter. "Only because I'm supposed to be here this morning talking about how great it is to be in the movie business. (*weakly sarcastic*) It's so awesome! (*back to queasy resolve*) But currently— I don't know if you've looked at box office numbers—this morning specifically, it hasn't been the greatest. So you might get some real shit today."

I recounted my career for them. How I'd failed with *Birdie,* then succeeded with *Step Up 2,* then blah blah blah. It was true enough, if all you had to judge it against was my IMDb page. But as I delivered the speech, I began to see, with painful clarity, that the person whose movies were itemized on that IMDb page was not really me.

If I'd wanted my listeners to know the real me, I would have told them about *Silent Beats*. I would've described how I'd gotten my flash of inspiration in the middle of the night while I was helping my mom recover from cancer. Where did that kid go, and that pure burning desire to get a story onto a screen? I would've told them about *Gwai Lo,* too—how I'd found the courage to make myself vulnerable, to expose my life, my family, and my cultural identity crisis to the world. Why, after making something so personal, had I buried it—and kept it buried for fifteen years?

One answer was obvious: success. Steven Spielberg bestowing his blessing on *When the Kids Are Away* had sent me zooming down the path of conventional Hollywood achievement, toward making hits like other people's hits. When *Birdie* and *Moxie* failed, and my career went into that ditch, I could have altered my course. I might have ventured off to make a searingly honest independent film that would have shown the world who I really was. Instead I clung to my self-image as Hollywood's rising star, battering away at the studios, pitch after miserable pitch, until I found a way back to the path I'd been on. Thanks to *Step Up 2,* Hollywood gave me a chance to make things before I'd figured out what I wanted to say.

As long as the hits kept coming, I didn't see any reason for changing course. I was too busy traveling down the road that others had marked out for me, never questioning where I was going—or, more important, why. Now, at last, failure had burst the bubble that my successes had built for me. In trying to be the embodiment of what others expected of me, I'd lost my way. I'd lost my *self*.

My unease during *Now You See Me 2,* I now realized, had been my first inkling that there was something broken, something empty, about the way I'd been making movies. That living for commercial success, the rush I'd get from a hit, could never completely fulfill me. That thinking of sequels as a great way to get known around town was just a clever way to hide. The second or third installment of a series might reveal my taste or my style, but nothing that was really personal to me. I hadn't revealed that in my work since I'd left college. That's why, as I stood onstage that morning talking about my seven movies, I felt that my career hadn't even begun.

Delivering that speech was mortifying, but it served a purpose. It forced me to say out loud, with a bunch of people listening, that I was still a filmmaker. I had to take accountability. Even on that terrible morning, I wasn't about to quit the business, although there was a moment or two when I thought about it. So what had to change? I couldn't just swap out one set of projects for another set of projects and think that I'd fixed anything. My decisions about work had to be the symptoms of a deeper, more personal cause.

I didn't know what that was. But I knew that in order to find it, I would need to go back. Not just to where I'd come from, to my early work or even my childhood. I would need to go further than that.

My parents had done so much to make me who I was. Their teachings and their example had shaped me and my siblings at every step of our lives. But what had made them who *they* were? They'd never wanted to share, and I'd never tried very hard to find out. Silicon Valley, like Hollywood, has powerful tools for redirecting your gaze. Who wants to bother peering into the past when there's always a new new thing peeking over the horizon?

I'd always called myself a storyteller. Since the night I

stayed up editing my first home movie, I'd been learning my craft: how to reveal character, how to trace a narrative, how to bring hidden motivations to light. Yet I'd never turned that lens on my family's history. If I was ever going to do it, it had to be now—even though merely thinking about it made me so self-conscious that my skin itched.

I needed to resist the incentives that Hollywood had dangled in front of me and the impulses that Silicon Valley had bred in me and *stop moving*. And turn around. And look at myself and my family and the stories I'd been telling myself. And keep looking until I began to understand.

I might have been giving a speech about movies that morning, but my career wasn't on my mind. I needed to look back because it was the only hope I had of figuring out who I really was, of closing the gap between the life I'd been leading and the one that I wanted to lead—one that I hoped would have Kristin at its center.

That's what I was thinking about as I gave that speech, looking out into the audience, seeing her sitting there, sobbing.

The camera would be at a low angle, near the ground, so you could almost feel the sand. The bodies of beachgoers would fill the foreground of the frame. Then the camera would rise, revealing many more of them, stretching deep into the background.

A title card would say "Half Moon Bay—1969."

That's how it makes sense to me to begin telling the story of my family's past.

I haven't shared much of that past with you in this book, for the simple reason that they never shared much of it with me. When my brothers and sisters and I were little, they didn't volunteer much about our history. In fairness to them, we always had so much going on, it's not as if we pushed them particularly hard for details. But when I got older, and felt lost in my life and my work, I started asking about where they'd come from. And I didn't stop.

As I assembled their story—from anecdotes, offhand comments, even old pictures—I began to see it in filmic terms. Which isn't a surprise. After all, those are the storytelling tools I've learned to use best: how to gather pictures, words, and sounds and, with imagination and sensitivity, form a coherent narrative. Using my director's brain gives me the best chance of seeing the people in my family as living, breathing individuals with their own vulnerabilities, insecurities, and unfulfilled dreams.

Yet in spite of all my experience going through this process for the projects I'd developed, I didn't know what I would find when I turned the lens on my family. Or how I would feel when I found it. Or what it would be like to share it—which I'm doing for the first time here.

If I ever film this story, and not just imagine how it might be filmed, I'd shoot my establishing shot of Half Moon Bay with a superlong lens. That's the kind that creates a helpful illusion. It seems to bring faraway things close to you.

And faraway people.

The camera would push in slowly, keeping the Pacific on the left side of the frame. The beach, which lies just south of San Francisco, would be on the right. We'd glide past people playing volleyball, slightly obscured by smoke from the barbecues in the foreground. Music from various vintage radios would fade up through the walla, which is what we call the murmur of background noise on set: Elvis, the Temptations, Dean Martin. Eventually one song will drown out the rest: "Bad Moon Rising."

The crowd would be, for the most part, a sea of white faces. In the middle of this field of California blond, one group looks different: They're Chinese.

As the camera pans to their beach blanket, we discover that it's a handful of friends, including a pair of young women. They're nineteen or so, wearing modest bikinis. Now we're close enough to hear their voices—but they're speaking . . . Russian?

Cut to an extreme close-up of a Russian language text-book. It's in the hands of one of the girls. She has amazing long hair, falling nearly to her ankles. The black strands mostly conceal her eyes and make a sharp contrast to the white sand. Her name is Ruth. She's my mom.

From off camera, sand comes flying toward the book. Everybody laughs. Ruth's friends are teasing her for bringing homework to the beach. She closes the book—not before marking her place—to look around. In close-up, she has an innocence, almost hiding from us, but is still inquisitive about every detail around her.

Cut to her point of view: Happy beachgoers on every side. In handheld medium shots, she observes these strange people and their rituals. She has been in America for only two years. She hasn't yet mastered English, which she didn't speak at all when she arrived. I'd been a kid when I'd first heard that part of my mom's story. At the time, watching her breezy command of every room she entered, I'd figured that adjusting to a new country and a foreign language must have been like every other challenge she faced: a matter of willpower, quickly dispatched. After the disappointment of *Jem,* when I felt the need to revisit my past—when I started asking my parents new questions and asking them old questions for new reasons—I realized it couldn't have been quick or easy. Not even for her.

Ruth looks down, reopens the book. She says a few more Russian words, maybe practices her numbers—"*Tri . . . chetyre . . . pyat . . .*"—before "Bad Moon Rising" gets a lot louder, drowning her out. The camera whip pans away from her. Far across the beach, a group of gangly young men are cutting across the sand. They're all wearing suits. They're also Chinese.

Close-up on their bare feet. Tilt up to their hands, holding socks and shoes. Tilt higher to their faces. Most of them look uncomfortable to be slipping and sliding through the sand. One doesn't. When a soccer ball bounces into the frame, he deflects it and, without breaking stride, flick-kicks it back. He's got some easy swagger, Lawrence does. He's my dad.

We cut to his point of view, letting us see the beach the way he sees it. Like Ruth, he's studying the customs of these foreign people. What's browning on those grills? How is it being served? Over the shoulder of one of those cooks, movement attracts his eye. We rack focus—that is, we show him shifting his focus to look at something far away—as a gust of wind catches the longest, darkest, most beautiful hair he has ever seen.

From above, in a bird's-eye shot, we see the boys change course. They are heading toward the girls.

Back at eye level, in medium over-the-shoulder shots, we watch everybody say hello. The boys hadn't made a random visit to the beach, it turns out. Lawrence knows Margie, Ruth's friend. In fact, he flirts with her a bit. (That's how my mom remembers it, anyway. My dad claims otherwise. It's one of many places where their recollections don't add up to a single tidy narrative. They remember events differently, or they don't remember at all, or they *do* remember but won't tell me. It's another reason, as I have pieced their story together here for the first time, it comes to me most naturally in cinematic terms.)

If we go with the odds and say that it's likelier than not that Lawrence—young, handsome, streetwise—might flirt a little with a pretty girl at the beach, then it's also likely that his friends would enjoy watching the exchange. But now Margie is making an introduction.

"Lawrence, this is my friend Ruth. Ruth, this is Lawrence."

"Hi there."

"Hello."

The boys take a seat, though it's not easy to get comfortable on that blanket, not when they're so overdressed. (They've come from a lunch party, they explain.) Ruth can tell that they're older than her, but she's used to that. Most of the Chinese boys her own age are from Hong Kong, which means they mainly speak Cantonese. Her fellow Mandarin speakers tend to be grad students who came from Taiwan. Lawrence looks to be about that age, though he doesn't carry himself like any grad student she's known.

By the time the boys join them, Ruth and her friends have been at the beach for a while. Margie leans close to her: "Let's get away from these old dudes." Ruth laughs and nods.

Lawrence and his friends are still folding their jackets when Ruth, Margie, and their group pick up their stuff and go. As they zigzag through the beach blankets, the ambient sounds get louder: the crashing waves, the laughing kids, "Bad Moon Rising."

By the time I was born, my parents rarely showed intimacy toward each other. But I don't see how they could get married, raise five children, and stay together for all these years without some sort of spark on the day they met.

Ruth, trailing the group, glances back across the crowd. She didn't mean for it to happen, but she locks eyes with Lawrence, who has been watching her leave. Embarrassed, she turns away, but it's too late. They both know what happened.

———

A FEW DAYS LATER, it's blazing hot in San Francisco. A wide establishing shot shows the sun beating down on the city, even as it dips toward the Pacific. But somehow the sound doesn't match the image: Why do we hear thunder if there's a clear blue sky?

Cut to an extreme close-up of a tiny flower. (I'd ask the production designer for something bright—specifically tropical.) A fat raindrop falls on one of its leaves. Then another. Cut to the surface of a lake, where the drops begin to fall more quickly. For some reason, we hear people cheering. What is going on?

In a new interior establishing shot, we see the entrance to the restaurant where the raindrops—fake ones—have been falling from the ceiling. A wooden sign flanked by tiki torches says "Tonga Room." Even though we're outside the restaurant, we're still inside a hotel: the beautiful old Fairmont, at the top of Nob Hill. I'd ask the composer for Muzak that feels ostentatiously classy.

Lawrence steps into view: sharply dressed, new shoes. He walks most of the way across the frame, stops, and walks back. He's not the type to pace around, but here he is, pacing around. He looks off-screen. He sees something that brings his shoulders down. From his POV, we watch the door to the women's room open. Out steps Ruth.

She throws him a smile, a shy one. He throws one back, less shy.

Now here she comes.

Cut to them standing face-to-face. It's a profile two-shot,

so they share the frame, which lets us see what's most important about this moment in the story: how each of them is responding to the other.

"You're going to love this place," he tells her in Mandarin.

He guides her toward the door, pulls it open. Close-up on his hand touching the small of her back. That's new. Now her shoulders relax.

Inside, the rain is still falling: a nightly special effect to delight the customers. People are talking and laughing. The place is *alive*. A Steadicam pursues Ruth and Lawrence as they walk past an artificial pond in the middle of the room. Lawrence looks off-screen and grins.

Cut to a table of young people, mostly men: It's Lawrence's brother and their friends. When they see him coming, they let out a cheer. They were already loud—the table is strewn with empty bottles—but the party's really starting now.

They slide over to make room.

Lawrence turns toward Ruth, but before he can say anything, the lights go out. The whole restaurant cheers. Cut to an extreme close-up of Ruth's face, up-lit by a candle on the table. She's puzzled but intrigued. What's about to happen?

The lights flare, more colorful now. From the back of the pond, a bandstand floats into view. Cut to a close-up of each musician as they begin to play: guitar, ukulele, drums. They launch into an island version of "Let the Sunshine In."

A 135mm handheld, to give a sense of intimate proximity: Lawrence leans toward Ruth, but she can't hear what he's trying to say—the band is too loud. He gives up, takes her hand, and eases her to her feet. With his eyes, he says, *Trust me*. Then he leads her to the dance floor.

In a series of floating Steadicam shots, we see that he's a smooth dancer. She's a little stiff—she doesn't know the steps—but she's trying. The other dancers like what Lawrence is doing, so they give him room, which means they give her room. She's miles out of her element now, getting a kind of attention she's never gotten before. Not that she minds.

Finally, she thinks, *a Chinese boy who knows how to dance.*

As the chorus kicks in and the camera whirls around them, creating lots of motion blur, I'd ask the editor to start cutting faster. Amid Lawrence's moves we catch glimpses of him in his younger days, dancing in Hong Kong or racing down a sidewalk with his friends; from Ruth, we cut to her singing with her little brothers and sisters in Taiwan, performing at a ballet recital, or walking somewhere alone, long hair swinging.

As the song reaches its big finish, everybody claps for this young Chinese couple that just held the dance floor. Back to that 135mm handheld shot. Lawrence leans in and says something that makes Ruth laugh. The subtitle reads "Let's eat."

They thread their way to the table, accepting congratulations. As the next song begins, a young man draws near. *Would Ruth like to dance?*

I haven't decided how I'd film what happens next, because I haven't decided whose story I believe: my mother's, that Lawrence shooed the guy away; or my father's, that she was free to dance with anybody if she wanted to—she just didn't want to.

Either way, the guy leaves.

The music shifts: It's gentler now. The camera cuts around the room, from table to table, from booth to booth. In one shot—so quick you'd almost miss it—I might show a married couple with five little kids. It would be a bit of foreshadowing. Every year, on their anniversary, my parents would bring us to the Tonga Room. They'd offer a rare glimpse into their past by telling us how they'd had their first date here: how they'd danced, how they'd talked. This tradition, like so many traditions, had a paradoxical effect. The more times we heard this story, the more inevitable it began to seem. It got harder and harder to imagine how life could have turned out any differently for my parents. I would need to live through the collapse of my own so-called destiny, when I lost *Bye Bye Birdie,* to grasp that nothing in this life is foreordained. I'd need to have enough relationships of my own, happy and otherwise, to see that if two people come together and stay together, the reason is never as simple as fate. Especially when people have as much stacked against them ever meeting as my parents did.

By the time the camera returns to Ruth and Lawrence, dinner is over. Their friends are stuffed; most of them are drunk. Someone tells the waiter to bring the best dessert on the menu anyway. Lawrence doesn't notice. He's too absorbed in a story that Ruth is telling. As she speaks, the camera cuts back and forth to the kitchen, where the chefs prepare their specialty: a half pineapple filled with coconut, sliced peaches, and cherries. We see how dexterous they are, how delicious this whole night has become.

Her mother and father were born in Shanghai, she is telling him, but they met in Taiwan. That's where their families had fled during the terrifying exodus of the late 1940s, when Mao's forces overran the country. At first, Taiwan wasn't much safer. Ruth's mother had hidden under a hut when resentful locals attacked the new arrivals. But they found safety in Tainan, where Ruth's father worked for a Western company. Ruth grew up there, teaching Sunday school from the time she was twelve. They built a comfortable life, but when the United States changed its immigration laws in 1965, they left home, hoping to start again.

"So here I am," the subtitle says.

As she finishes her story, the chef puts the last touch on the dessert: setting its brandy sauce aflame. Now it's Lawrence's turn. His story isn't nearly as smooth or as straightforward as Ruth's. The camera cuts from his face to the dessert on its perilous journey to their table, one waiter's hand to the next.

He was born in Chongqing shortly after Japan's massive campaign of air raids against the city: thousands killed, whole neighborhoods destroyed. His family moved to Shanghai, but tragedy followed. When he was five, his mother went to the hospital for some routine ailment, but a doctor's error or negligence or stupidity killed her. Lawrence's grieving father sent him back to Chongqing to be raised by his aunt and uncle, but within a year, he needed to flee again. Mao's forces stormed the city. Family connections got him a seat on a military plane, one of the last flights to safety. Since he's telling this story at dinner, he probably omits the next part: The flight was so dangerous and so precipitous that everybody on board vomited.

In Taipei, he reunited with his father, who had a new wife now. From the outside, they appeared to be a real family, but to Lawrence it would always feel like a broken one. He might not mention that part at dinner, either.

His story is cut short by dessert. As soon as it touches the table, everybody grabs a spoon and makes a joyful lunge for a share. More laughing, more jokes.

Lawrence isn't like the other boys, Ruth is noticing. He's worldlier than they are; he's savvier. For his part, Lawrence is relieved that she doesn't seem to care about college credentials, because unlike most of the young men at the table, he doesn't have any. I'm not even sure he graduated middle school. He moved to Hong Kong at sixteen and started working shortly after that. Today, more than sixty years later, he hasn't stopped.

Lawrence's hand darts out of the frame. It comes back holding the check. His friends complain, but he insists that he's going to pick up the tab. At twenty-six, he has already decided on the kind of life he wants to lead: prosperous, successful, magnanimous. So what if he can't afford it yet? Ruth takes notice.

Everyone staggers to their feet and heads for the door. A couple of Lawrence's friends croon along with the band's rendition of "Can't Help Falling in Love," arms slung over each other's shoulders. Lawrence holds Ruth back.

Cut to that 135mm lens again. This time, we are far away, peering between bar patrons, almost voyeur-like, in a two-shot of them facing each other. Just them, alone, with the band out of focus in the background. We aren't supposed to be seeing this moment.

He thinks, *I've never met anyone like this before*. He leans down and kisses her on the cheek.

It's not a big deal for him, but for her, it's a first.

Oh no, she thinks. *No other boys will want me now.*

She looks at him. He looks at her. A peal of thunder. Blackout.

———

A TITLE CARD READS "A few weeks later." The camera glides down a suburban street: single-story houses, warm colors, lots of trees. Amblin-y.

Los Gatos, just south of San Francisco, is nothing like what Ruth had expected of America. Movies had primed her for skyscrapers, teeming crowds, roaring traffic—Manhattan, basically. Instead she got cozy bungalows and cherry trees: the late-'60s version of the California dream.

As the camera pushes in on one of the houses, we hear people talking to each other—and *over* each other—in Mandarin.

Interior: living room. A middle-aged man has his feet propped up, a football game on TV and a drink in his hand. (Even now, whenever I smell cognac, I think of my *gong gong*—my grandfather.) He is oblivious to the commotion all around him: a toddler crawling on the floor, a slightly older girl scratching away at her homework, a teenage boy tinkering with a model airplane.

Cut to the kitchen: a close-up that drops us right into the middle of the action. Two women, a mother and her daughter, bustle back and forth among a half dozen Chinese dishes. As the older woman—my grandmother Bu Bu—puts the finishing touches on the oxtail soup, a spicy beef dish, and maybe sea bass, the younger woman, my aunt Lois, shuttles them to the table. They are just about done.

"*Chi fan le,*" says Bu Bu, loud enough for everybody to hear it. At least that's what she used to say all the time when I was a kid, to let everybody know when our family dinner was about to begin.

That's when the door swings open and Ruth steps in, trailed

by Lawrence. She looks nervous. He doesn't, but that's only because he's better at hiding it.

Ruth introduces him to everybody. The response is underwhelming. Bennett, Ruth's father, acknowledges Lawrence but goes right back to his game. Lusan and Benji, the bookworm and the model-airplane builder, just stare. Only the toddler wobbles over, says hello, and looks down at Lawrence's shiny shoes, waving at her reflection. Ruth picks her up and carries her to the couch kicking and screaming. Lawrence gives a self-conscious laugh and sneaks a look at his shoes. It could be that he doesn't want anything to happen to them because he's taking them back to the store in the morning.

Maggie, my grandmother, steps forward to welcome Lawrence to their home. Then, in a no-nonsense voice, she tells everybody to sit down. As she directs traffic, the camera follows the quick glance that Lawrence throws at Maggie's feet. They're impossibly tiny. She always wore shoes that were much too small for her, a painful legacy of growing up in a society where many women—including her own mother—had their feet bound.

The sight rattles him. He shakes it off. In a two-shot, he turns to smile at Ruth. She smiles back. They all sit down.

Smash cut to an overhead shot of the table. The meal is mostly over and the plates are mostly empty. Bennett, Maggie, and their children are listening to their guest.

"I was full of America," Lawrence says. He is describing how it felt to step off a steamship in San Francisco in 1963, taking his first look at his new land. The previous year, his father had designed the Taiwan pavilion for the World's Fair in Seattle, then settled in San Francisco. That gave Lawrence his opportunity to start a new life. Three days after he moved into his family's apartment, he got a job at Trader Vic's, then one of the hottest restaurants in the city. "Right from the start," he tells Ruth's family, "I was always working, always hustling, but also learning."

"And your father?" Maggie asks.

Lawrence takes this cue to launch into another long story—the only kind he tells, then or now—about his father's exploits as a restaurant owner. First there was a doughnut shop in San Mateo, then a Chinese restaurant in Menlo Park called Mandarin House.

The camera is at eye level now, not moving a lot, letting us enjoy Lawrence in full charm mode. Ruth has a tight little smile. She can tell that he wants to impress her family, but she also knows that her parents don't love flashiness. Her father, in particular, is staying awfully quiet.

Trying to steer the conversation onto safer ground, she tells everyone that Lawrence has an idea for a business of his own. He takes the hint and begins to sketch his grand vision—literally. He starts drawing on a napkin, the way he still does when he's planning a new dish. He says the time is ripe for Chinese food to win over the American public. Instead of a single sit-down restaurant like his father's, he wants to create a chain of Chinese fast-food restaurants in every town in America. "Like a savings and loan," he says. (This is more than a decade before Panda Express started building franchises.)

"So," Bennett says, breaking his long silence, "you know how to cook?"

Lawrence repeats that he worked at Trader Vic's, where he

made a close study of its operations. And he has worked at his father's restaurants, learning the ins and outs of—

Bennett turns to Ruth. "But he knows how to cook?"

"I have instincts," says Lawrence. "I know how to sell."

From off camera, a little voice—Ruth's brother, Benji—pipes up with a question. "So what did you think of *this* meal?"

Ruth shoots a sharp look Benji's way, but it's too late. The kid has already rolled his hand grenade down the table.

The room falls silent. All eyes turn to Lawrence, including the baby's.

The camera pushes in on him. He smiles. Then he begins. He goes dish by dish, explaining what he liked, how the sauces worked, what the different combinations mean. He digs even deeper into his past—how Taiwanese food is so good because all the fleeing mainlanders brought their cooks, who spent their off-hours trying to impress each other.

It sounds, to be fair, like bullshit. Bennett's expression makes clear that he thinks so. But it's also undeniably a good story.

Now all eyes turn to Maggie, whose response matters most. You need to look closely to see it—so we'll shoot it up close—but she flashes a little smile. Lawrence's big speech was good enough to satisfy her.

The tension breaks. The kids go back to eating and chattering. Ruth and Lawrence relax. As he scans the faces around the table, he turns at last toward Bennett, who is staring at him. Lawrence freezes. It's a heavy moment.

From Lawrence's POV, we see Bennett's face in close-up. It's impossible to read his expression. Then the camera moves down to the table. The bottle of cognac is in front of Bennett. He slides it toward Lawrence.

They raise their glasses for a toast. They drink.

Lawrence scans the table again, smiling. Only this time, he has a quizzical expression. There's something unusual, something distinctive, about Ruth and her siblings—and even more so their father. Later, he'll ask Ruth about it. She'll share a story that had been passed down to her, as it had been passed down to her father.

According to family lore, Bennett's grandfather Murray was the son of a Chinese woman and a prominent American businessman. Their arrangement, whatever it was, has been lost to time. But it seems that the American made some allowances for the child—my great-great-grandfather—without formally acknowledging his parentage. When I heard this story during my childhood, it seemed like ancient history, something that mattered only to the elders. In particular, Bennett, my *gong gong,* sure did love to talk about Scotland, reputed to be his American ancestor's family homeland. But as an adult, when I started asking more questions about our past, trying harder to understand why we faced the world the way we did, this strand of family history stopped seeming like a small thing. It began to seem like a big thing, maybe even the main thing.

Because in Shanghai, and later in Taiwan, my mother and her relatives were persecuted for the way they looked: their height, their fair skin, their unusual eyes. People stared, asked embarrassing questions, and were sometimes openly hostile. The family could have accepted this abuse, or gotten angry with the people who othered them, but it seems that they chose a third path: obstinacy. They found the strength to insist that the quality that others despised or found shameful was actually precious—not a curse, but a gift. Ruth's grandfather—who was named Murray, like his father—fully embraced his Western inheritance. He became a Presbyterian minister. He adopted British habits that confounded his neighbors, like eating three-minute eggs for breakfast. Ruth remembers his little egg cup, his careful timer, his tiny spoon.

Then came the family's move to America, the tornado that turned everything upside down. Here, persecution didn't come from being white, it came from being *Chinese*. As they struggled to get their bearings, every social cue from the dominant culture led them further down the path they were already traveling, toward embracing Western ways. In Asia, that impulse had put them at odds with the mainstream; in America, it did the opposite. It made them prime candidates for being melted down in the melting pot.

This history makes it a little easier to understand why my siblings and I were raised the way we were, so unlike our Asian friends: with our etiquette classes and matching Polo outfits and tennis lessons. In light of that training, is it any wonder that I shelved *Gwai Lo* after a single screening and buried the impulse I'd had to make it in the first place? Or that I spent a decade in Hollywood without ever once putting my family or our heritage on-screen? For somebody determined to blend in at all costs, it was easy to brush aside the little reminders of our family history that popped up from time to time. Like the interviewers who would look at my facial features and tell me I must be Filipino, no matter how much I insisted I'm Chinese. Or the "Directed by" credit on all my movies, which includes my middle initial. The "M" stands for "Murray."

Sitting at dinner with Ruth's family, Lawrence is unaware of this past—and of this future. The present is giving him all that he needs. In a close-up, we see him taking in the scene, basking in it. He's a handsome guy, and he has gone on plenty of dates, but he has avoided a serious relationship. He had been waiting for someone with a tight, loving family, like the one he lost when his mother died. It has taken him twenty years and a trip halfway around the world, but he's beginning to feel that he has found it.

Under the table, he grabs Ruth's hand. She bats it away. A moment later, she changes her mind and grabs his. They hold on.

THE CAMERA TRACKS LOW behind a sports car—another luxury that Lawrence can't afford. From our vantage point, above and behind the car, we watch it roll through the little towns of what is not yet called Silicon Valley: Palo Alto, Mountain View, San Mateo. Circling, circling.

At a busy intersection, the car stops. From inside the car, we faintly hear Elvis beginning to sing "Blue Suede Shoes" on the radio.

"There," says Ruth.

"Where?" says Lawrence.

Cut to inside the car. From the back seat, we see Ruth, in the driver's seat, reach across Lawrence, in the passenger seat, to point at something on his side of the road.

"There," she says.

When Lawrence turns to look out the window, the camera

shows us what he sees: a strip mall at the corner of El Camino Real and San Antonio Road. It's a little island in the midst of a vast parking lot. A beauty parlor, a laundromat, an accountant's office. None of it seems very tantalizing, except for the empty storefront with a FOR LEASE sign in the window.

Lawrence rummages in a pile of street maps and scrap paper at his feet and picks up a napkin. He presses it against the window and makes a quick pencil sketch of the building, including the sign. Then he draws a big, emphatic circle around the empty storefront.

He turns to Ruth, grinning.

"There," he says.

As the light changes and the car plunges ahead, "Blue Suede Shoes" gets louder. Much louder. The rest of this scene is a montage, the mad scramble of a twenty-six-year-old Chinese immigrant, who doesn't speak much English, and his nineteen-year-old girlfriend, who doesn't speak much more, to open a restaurant.

We cut to an auction: Lawrence is bidding on used kitchen equipment, paddle in the air, a tense expression on his face. Then we cut to a narrow kitchen, where he and a few guys are trying to wrestle the equipment into place. It doesn't look like it's going well, but the camera doesn't linger—there's no time.

Cut to the front area of the restaurant, where customers will place their orders. It's a couple of weeks later, and Ruth and her siblings are busy painting the walls. As the oldest, she's calling the shots. Lawrence emerges from the kitchen holding a morsel in chopsticks, the other hand cupped beneath it to catch the sauce. He feeds it to Ruth, then waits for her response.

"Mmmmmm," she says unconvincingly.

Lawrence frowns and goes back to the kitchen.

Elvis keeps singing.

Cut to Mandarin House, Lawrence's father's restaurant: elegant, quiet. At a desk in the back office, Lawrence sits before an open book and a sheet of paper. The book is a dog-eared collection of his father's recipes. The sheet is a numbered list of the twelve dishes that will constitute his menu. Twelve isn't many—it's a lot fewer than Mandarin House's offerings—but Lawrence figures that the only way to replicate the success of his prototype coast-to-coast is to keep it simple and quick, like a lunch counter.

A shadow falls across the desk. Lawrence looks up.

In a reverse angle, we see his father towering over him: his father the artist, the gifted designer, who ran a restaurant but was happier singing Peking operas. (My dad says the creative streak skipped a generation and landed on me.) He holds something up for Lawrence to see: a beautifully intricate sketch of a logo for the new restaurant.

Cut back to a close-up of Lawrence's face, beaming.

Cut to the sunny exterior of the restaurant. Beneath the full-sized version of the Chef Chu's sign that Lawrence's father had sketched, a banner says "GRAND OPENING." Ruth, her parents, Lawrence's parents, and a handful of customers are standing on the sidewalk, waiting. Ruth would like to keep them occupied, but she has run out of things to say, and the door remains closed.

We cut to the kitchen: Lawrence is on his back on the floor, frantically trying to get the steam table to turn on. This is not a leap of imagination—the thing really did malfunction on opening day.

The prospect of Chef Chu's not being there, of my parents' plan failing, is too painful for me to imagine—like Bedford Falls turning into Pottersville and never turning back. No matter where my life has taken me, the restaurant has always lingered in my mind as a safe harbor, a psychological anchor. *How could it not be there?* For my parents, in those scary early days, that possibility was very real. Overwhelmingly real.

Lawrence has a phone pressed to his ear, talking to a guy who might be able to tell him how to fix the table. (He doesn't have the money to hire somebody to do it for him.) As a last resort, he opens the circuit breaker box. He flips a switch, then looks back to the steam table. The cook nods—it's finally working.

Cut back to the sidewalk and the waiting crowd. Disheveled and sweaty, Lawrence pushes open the door. He smiles.

The Elvis song ends. Blackout.

OVER BLACK, A TITLE: "Six months later."

When a door opens, the light from outside shows us that we're in a living room, totally dark because it's very late. Lawrence stumbles in, exhausted from the workday. He shuffles toward the couch and pitches forward onto it facedown. Ruth, entering a step behind him, flips a switch. A ceiling light stutters on.

"Your shoes," she says.

He grunts and tries to kick them off, but he gives up: He's too tired.

She flips through that day's mail. In an extreme close-up on her hands, we can see that she's now wearing an engagement ring, modest but sparkling. One letter makes her stop flipping.

"Anything?" he mumbles into a cushion.

She hesitates, weighing whether to tell him about the letter that's clearly a tax bill. She drops the stack on a table.

"No," she says, crossing toward him. She perches on the edge of the couch.

Extreme close-up: He turns to look at her. "Why aren't they coming?"

"Who?"

"Customers. Students. Anyone. Even when they come, they don't come back."

"You should ask them."

"How? I need to be in the kitchen."

She sighs. He's right.

"Okay," she says. "I'll do it."

He laughs. "You'll be in school."

"No, I won't. Not anymore."

He laughs some more, then realizes she's not making a joke.

"I quit," she explains.

This wakes him all the way up. "You can't do that."

"I can. I did."

Lawrence flings himself upright, staring at her. "But your parents—"

"Understand."

"But customers—"

"Will start coming."

"But we—"

"Will make this work."

He looks at her, dazed. She looks back, poised.

Fate didn't bind my parents together. Neither did Cupid nor kismet nor any other implacable cosmic force. They were united by sacrifice and shared risk. By a belief in each other and in a common dream. By a determination not to let the other person down. By the recognition that each of them had what the other needed.

He stands up, staring. Then he starts walking toward the door: quick, purposeful steps.

"Where are you going?" she says as he pulls open the door.

"Back to work."

THE MUSIC CHANGES. No more peppy Elvis tunes now. The excitement of scrambling to open the restaurant gives way to the daily grind of trying to save the restaurant. Long hours, thin margins, fear. The song should be something melancholy, bittersweet: "Que Sera, Sera," maybe. I used to hear my mom humming it to herself around the house.

As a kid, I didn't understand why my father worked so much. We'd go on family trips—why wasn't he with us? I'd take a bow after some tap recital I'd done with Jennifer—why wasn't he there? Knowing more about these anxious weeks and months in 1970 helps me to understand. He decided that without his maximal effort, the restaurant had no chance. And even then, nothing was guaranteed. The restaurant wasn't just a business to him. It was tied up with his wish for a loving family life. He developed the habit, never broken, of doing whatever he needed to do to help it survive. But first he needed to find out what that was.

Cut to a series of close-ups: the faces of customers. We

don't hear any questions, only their answers. They look directly into the lens.

One says, "Well, it'd be nice to sit down, you know?"

Reverse to Ruth, smiling and nodding.

Now we see the restaurant expand to include a seating section, in what had been part of the beauty salon next door. Just like that, Lawrence's original vision—the chain of restaurants all across the country, Chinese lunch counters from sea to shining sea—was gone. He realized that making even one restaurant work would be perilous enough. But to hear him tell it, the change didn't feel like a compromise. Because for the first time, he had something to lose.

As a customer says, in voice-over, that she'd like to have a place to bring the kids and not worry when they make a mess, we see Ruth training her sister to be a hostess: how to guide customers to a table, how to present a menu.

Now we cut to another face in close-up: a Stanford student.

"Well, the selection."

Reverse to Lawrence and Ruth standing side by side, talking to the kid.

"What about the selection?" says Lawrence.

"Here, have more rice," says Ruth, adding a scoop to the kid's order.

"Hey, thanks," says the kid. "I wish we had more choices. My roommate and I would be here all the time."

Swish pan over to the roommate, just off screen, eating from a take-out container. "Totally," he says, mouth full of lo mein.

As a different customer talks, in voice-over, about the dishes she likes at other Chinese restaurants, we see Lawrence remaking his menu. Half the items on the original list have been crossed out, and a bunch of new ones are scribbled in. The new lineup is, by some measures, less authentic than what his father is offering at Mandarin House, but authenticity isn't on his mind right now. Survival is.

In close-up, we see a customer take a bite of one of the new dishes. He wrinkles his nose. The camera rises until we see Ruth's face. She is standing next to the customer, watching. As she turns toward the kitchen, the camera follows her gaze. It alights on Lawrence, who has been watching her to see if it worked.

He shakes his head. In a close-up, we see him cross out a line on a recipe and scribble in something else.

What else can he do?

Cut to a wide establishing shot of Lawrence taking a cooking class. The teacher demonstrates a Western technique, like how to use a grinder to make hamburgers. Lawrence listens along with his fellow students, then begins to try it.

Cut to a close-up of his hands operating the machine. For some reason, hamburger doesn't come out—the filling for dumplings does. The camera pulls back to reveal that Lawrence is in the restaurant's kitchen, teaching his chefs how to adapt what he'd learned to make their own recipes.

I feel such kinship with him in that moment. Trying to adapt Western techniques to Asian materials is exactly what I struggled to do at USC when I made *Gwai Lo*.

I wish I'd heard that story sooner.

Now we see reactions to the new dishes, a quick string of them: some smiling, some uncertain, an occasional glimpse of kids laughing and throwing rice around.

At one point, an Asian woman gives the camera a chilly smile. "It's not for us," she says.

At another point—or, if it's true to life, at several points—
a white face looks into the camera and says something horrible
and racist. I don't need to jog my parents' memories to find out
about those. I grew up hearing customers say them. Anyway,
what matters is my parents' reaction, or lack of reaction.
Under so much pressure, burdened by so much doubt, how
can you stop to unpack a cruel remark about your food, your
looks, or where you "belong"?

You can't. They couldn't. They just kept going. *Never complain.*

Cut to a shot of Lawrence at a desk, pencil in hand, scribbling. He's tweaking a recipe again, still looking for a way to
meet his customers where they are. As he looks up, thinking
about what to try next, he notices an envelope.

A tax bill. Second notice.

The camera stays on his face as he opens it, sees the number,
winces. There's no way he can pay this. He puts the letter
down, leans back in his chair, looks at the ceiling, sighs.

The ceiling fan spins, faster and faster.

Lawrence's chest moves up and down. The moisture on his
skin from the steam in the kitchen makes him almost glisten.
He's tired. Takes a deep breath, maybe the deepest he's ever
taken. A tear forms.

He knows what he needs to do to keep the restaurant alive.
And he hates that he needs to do it.

His hands go over his face, blocking the fan. He
screams—but right when he does, cut to:

Silence.

Ruth's parents' kitchen once again. Not a big family dinner
this time, just Ruth and Lawrence sitting across from her
mother and father, Bennett looking sterner than ever. Law-

rence appears to be in the midst of another long story—tables of facts and figures are spread before him—when Bennett closes his eyes and raises his hand: *Stop.*

Lawrence stops.

Bennett holds his pose for a few seconds, thinking. Then he reaches into his pocket. He pulls out a checkbook.

As Bennett begins to draft the check, Ruth's mother leans across the table. "As long as money is coming in, don't change the color of the door," she tells them.

They smile at her. They turn to each other and smile some more. Only when they break eye contact and look away do they let their true emotions show: Neither of them looks confident that this is going to work. The siblings in the other room laugh mischievously at the couple. Ruth shoots them a deadly stare.

NINE MONTHS AFTER OPENING DAY, three months after the menu change, we're with Lawrence in the kitchen. There's no music now.

The cooks and the kitchen staff have gotten better at their jobs. Through practice and willpower they've tightened their routines, figuring out how to integrate Western techniques and Chinese ingredients. Still, on this night, it's a struggle. For some reason, the orders are piling up faster than they can plate the dishes.

Lawrence wipes the sweat off his forehead and steps out of the kitchen, his chef's whites partly unbuttoned. Ruth walks over, looking just as harried.

"What's going on?" he asks.

"I don't know."

They stare at something they've never seen before: a line that stretches from the hostess stand all the way out the door. We'd bring up the walla.

Ruth approaches a customer. "We're happy you're here," she says. "What brings you tonight?"

"Oh, you know," she says, tugging a folded-up paper out of her bag.

"May I?" Ruth says.

"Sure." As Ruth brings the paper to Lawrence, the customer adds, "I thought we'd be early enough to beat the rush. We'll know for next time."

Ruth unfolds the paper. It's a restaurant review. Cut to a close-up of her and Lawrence, their heads close together, as they skim the paragraphs, mumbling key phrases as they read.

It's a rave.

They look at each other, stunned. Without saying a word, they walk to the door, push it open, and step outside.

The line stretches around the corner of the building. Most of the people are holding the review.

Lawrence and Ruth look at each other again. This time, they laugh. The same thought has flashed across both their minds: *We made it.*

But there's no time to celebrate.

From Lawrence's POV, we watch Ruth walk down the line of customers, smiling, her newfound charisma on full blast. She chats them up as if she's been doing it all her life, thanking them for waiting, asking what they need.

Overhead shot of the front door as it swings open. A couple walks outside, happy and full after their dinner. As Lawrence takes a rapid step back to let them pass, he catches a glimpse of his reflection in the glass panel on the door: He looks a mess. In a quick series of inserts, we see him pull himself together. He tugs the bottom of his chef's whites to straighten them out, then buttons his top button. He runs his fingers through his hair. He rolls his shoulders back.

The next customer in line is reaching for the door handle to go inside, but Lawrence gets there first.

He pulls it open. He smiles.

"Welcome," he says. "I'm Chef Chu."

NEW MUSIC COMES IN now: a remixed version of "Que Sera, Sera." An upbeat tempo.

The camera cuts to a wider establishing shot. It's on the sidewalk that runs along San Antonio Road, far enough away to take in the entire strip mall. We see Lawrence holding the door open for the customers he's just greeted, who thank him and step inside.

Time lapse.

The line begins to move forward at an exaggeratedly quick pace. The sun begins to sink.

In ones and twos and little groups, customers enter for their dinner and, eventually, leave.

The restaurant's sign clicks off. The cooks and waitstaff go home.

Lawrence and Ruth are the last to emerge. He locks the door behind him.

They embrace. Even sped up, it lasts for a while.

They walk off-screen arm in arm.

Now time moves faster still, in a series of jumps that skip

ahead by weeks or months or more. The building keeps changing. The neighboring businesses keep closing, and the restaurant keeps expanding.

Lawrence and Ruth are in the foreground of the shot,
standing with their backs to the camera, watching the transformation. After one time jump, Ruth is holding a baby: my
brother Larry.

After another jump, Larry has become a toddler, standing
next to Dad, grabbing his hand. Ruth holds baby Chrissy.

Then Larry and Chrissy are both toddlers, and my mom is
holding a third baby. My parents aren't looking at the restaurant now. They're facing each other, staring down at the infant
Howard, wondering how they can provide for this special
child.

Time skips again. My mom's hair is shorter now. My dad is
wearing a suit—a good one—finally able to afford the life he
always wanted to lead. The restaurant's success has created
new possibilities: endorsement deals, investments, a cookbook. He and Ruth turn off-screen and wave at someone passing by. They've become community leaders.

Another time skip: Now Lawrence is holding baby Jennifer. Ruth continues to hold Howard. I needed to become a
father myself to appreciate what my parents must have faced in
these years. How each child, arriving so soon after the last,
must have brought new challenges. How Mom and Dad must
have depended on their own siblings, someplace just out of
view, to help them get by.

The older kids stand to either side of Mom and Dad, looking at a building whose transformation is, at last, complete.
From its tenuous origins, the restaurant has expanded to fill
every inch of the strip mall, which my father now owns. My

parents are looking at proof, in three sturdy dimensions, that their hard work and sacrifices have brought them some version of the American dream. They'll never again be forced to flee. Their children will never want. And if material goods and financial success can't protect their children—if, for example, old prejudices slow their path toward realizing their own American dreams—a well-practiced mantra will come to their aid: *Never complain.*

In the foreground, the family tableau shifts one final time. Now Ruth is holding another baby, her fifth. He's safe and happy in the world that they've been preparing for him, a protective bubble so seamless he won't even know it's there.

THE TIME LAPSE ENDS. The family fades out of view. We are looking at the restaurant on a sunny afternoon.

Overlaid title: "1990."

Cut to the sidewalk in front of the restaurant. The camera trails a boy who's lugging a backpack toward the entrance. As he pulls the door open, the camera switches to his POV, so we see what he sees.

Inside, the restaurant is transformed. It feels much bigger now that so many walls have been torn down. To the left, a staircase leads to the upstairs dining room.

The camera stops at the window that looks into the kitchen. In the distance, Chef Chu is busy preparing a dish. A cook who had been leaning over a cutting board suddenly straightens up, popping into the foreground of the shot. He waves at the camera.

"*Lao ban!*" he calls over his shoulder to Lawrence. "Your son is here."

Lawrence looks at the camera. His face lights up. He nods in the direction of the dining room, as if to say, *I'll be right out.*

In a medium shot, the boy—still seen from behind—keeps walking. He waves at the hostess.

"Hi, Jon!" she replies.

With a heave, I toss my backpack onto the banquette near the bar. I slide behind a table.

"Ready for a lava flow?" the bartender calls.

Before I can answer, my dad has arrived, looking sharp in his chef's whites.

"I'll take care of it," he says, pulling out a chair. He slides a bowl of freshly made potstickers in front of me. "How was school?"

As I tell the story of my day, the camera stays on his face. Twenty years have passed since the restaurant opened, but Lawrence has barely aged: still handsome, still energetic.

He nods as he listens to my story, then stops nodding. Behind him, at the bar, a customer has asked the bartender about an item on the menu. Lawrence knows just what to do.

"Be right back," he tells me.

He introduces himself to the customer, then launches into an explanation of the dish. He has come a long way since that dinner at his future in-laws' house. He speaks with authority now: a little history, a lot of description, a bridge between the culture he was born into and the one that he has spent twenty years mastering, one customer at a time.

The light shifts. The front door has swung open. My mom, looking much more elegant than in her younger days, swoops in. Dad interrupts his lecture for a quick hello; Mom says a quick hello back. I've watched this greeting a million times. Sometimes when they saw each other, it was barely even a greeting. But the sheer staggering number of times they've said it gives it weight. Amid successes and failures, amid countless changes, good and bad. A lifetime together, measured in quick hellos.

Mom is walking toward me. "You need a haircut," she says. "Is that all you ordered? You need to eat more."

Before I can answer, she's on the move again. A young couple is waiting for the hostess to seat them; Ruth decides they have waited long enough. She greets them and leads them to where she thinks they should sit. (She doesn't introduce herself, but she carries herself with so much confidence they do whatever she tells them.) Once she walks into the dining room, I lose sight of her. A low divider wall blocks my view. But I can hear her chatting with whichever friends or regulars happen to be there. She's talking about her day, maybe her round of golf, or Christina's ballet.

Clunk.

Insert: a lava flow that the bartender has set on my table, fizzing and swirling. I say thanks and grab my chopsticks, ready to dig in. I dip the first dumpling in the garlic soy sauce, then pop it into my mouth.

Cut to an extreme close-up of my face. My expression—eyes closed, a smile—registers that the food tastes delicious. But that's *all* it registers.

At ten, I couldn't appreciate the history behind what I was eating or the sacrifices on my parents' part to make it possible for me to eat it. I was too focused on other things: blending in with my friends, being like the people on TV, becoming an all-American boy. I would stay focused on those things for years. For decades.

Only in looking back could I see that my family's history

wasn't a story that played out a long time ago on the other side of the ocean. And it wasn't something that ended when my parents opened their restaurant and started their family. It was still unfolding, and I was part of it. Though I neglected our heritage and even tried to run from it, I grew up steeped in it. The taste of those dumplings: ginger, soy, sesame. The sight of Bu Bu's tiny feet; the feel of her hands on mine, making wontons. The sound of my grandfather's voice as he sang his Peking operas.

These things weren't on my TV growing up. They weren't in the movies that studios hired me to direct. But they were part of me. I'd turned thirty-five without knowing who I was, because I'd ignored the sleeping dragon in me. It was a mistake to ever think I could. It's why I open *Crazy Rich Asians* with the quote attributed to Napoleon: "Let China sleep, for when she wakes she will shake the world." That didn't come from Kevin Kwan's book and wasn't in the movie for Rachel—it was there for me. The sense that something was rising in me that had been dormant all these years. And it was about to take over my whole being. But before that . . .

I open my eyes. I look off-screen: first one way, then the other. *Where did Dad go?* He's no longer chatting up the customer by the bar.

I turn around on the banquette. Behind me, the divider wall is inset with a pane of glass. Through it, I can see the dining room. *There he is.*

As I lean close to get a better view, we cut to my POV. The camera sees what I see—what I won't understand for a long time to come: my mom and dad, together in the world they'd built for us.

Cut to the reverse: Now the camera is in the dining room, aimed at my face. The camera slowly racks focus until the glass panel itself is the sharpest thing in the frame. There's an etching on it, a design that my parents picked out for this place shortly after I was born: two grown-up fish swimming with five little ones.

A few months after the premiere of *Jem*—that nightmare weekend—my agent and managers were well on their way to getting my next set of projects green-lit. These movies were, for the most part, like the movies I'd made before. More sequels (and sequels of sequels). More extensions of brands. After the time I'd spent reflecting on who I was and where I'd come from, gaining a new understanding of the threads of family and tradition that had done so much to shape me, that wasn't going to work anymore.

"Clear the decks," I told them. "I need to start fresh."

I'd changed. I was different. I needed to make something that reflected who I was.

"Okay," they said. "What is it?"

It was a good question. I didn't know the answer.

"Well, what's your dream project?"

I didn't know that, either. Five years of failing to get a movie made, followed by eight years of taking jobs that kept me moving along the flowchart of conventional success, had pretty much driven the notion of "dream project" out of my head. But I'd reached a point where I could think that way again. *Jem* notwithstanding, my movies had made plenty of money for the studios. I no longer felt grateful to executives merely for hiring me; I no longer felt lucky just to be there.

So it was time to find something that scared me. Something that only I could make. Something that inspired me, and might mean as much to people, as *Silent Beats* had. Whatever it might be, it was likely to be small and personal. So the only thing I could tell my team with any confidence—and it's a hard thing to say in Hollywood—was: "We're probably not going to make any money for a while."

From the start of my career, my relatives had peppered me with ideas for what I should do next. Their ideas tended to be months or years behind what was happening in Hollywood. As part of my new approach to life and work, I decided to pay a little more attention to what they had to say. That's when my sister Chrissy told me to check out *Crazy Rich Asians,* Kevin Kwan's bestselling novel from a few years back. Then my mom told me to read it, too.

I called my agent to ask him about it.

He said, "How did you know?"

The producers had sent him the screenplay that morning.

I read the novel first. It told the story of Rachel Chu, an Asian American professor of economics, going to Singapore to meet the family of her boyfriend, Nick Young. Some of it was foreign to me—I'd never been to Singapore. But in other ways, the book satirized a world I knew inside out. It depicted a collision between old money (represented by Nick's extremely wealthy family) and new money. I'd watched that conflict play out in Silicon Valley in the '90s, when dot-com tycoons started flinging their millions around, generally to the horror of Asians who had been there for a long time. Kevin captured how gaudy it could be and how hilarious. But he also found glimmers of elegance amid the excess. I remembered how stylish my aunties looked in their posh outfits from Taiwan, how charming my uncles could be when they got drunk and sang Elvis songs at Christmas parties.

I saw how much fun it could be to drop an audience into this delicious *Wizard of Oz* world, amid characters who, as Kevin put it, "made Upper East Side girls look like Mennonites." A movie version of this story would need to be vibrant, outsized: like a Disney animated musical without songs or animation. Which was closer to my natural style of filmmaking than anything I'd gotten to do in Hollywood up to this point.

Something else came flying off the page—something even more exciting at that moment in my life: *Rachel is me*. I remembered how it felt to be in her situation, a young Asian American visiting Asia for the first time: the mix of delight and alienation, of pleasant and unpleasant surprises. Rachel loves Singapore, then gets accosted by people who want to sabotage her relationship with Nick; I loved Hong Kong, then got called "foreign devil."

I thought this story was just what I wanted. I also thought, *They're not going to get this made without me*. Only a handful of Asian American directors were making big studio movies in 2016, and none of them was likely to be drawn to a splashy romantic comedy the way I was. For my pitch to the film's producers, Nina Jacobson and Brad Simpson, I didn't just share Instagram images of the over-the-top opulence I wanted to put on-screen, the kind that get tagged #RichAsians. I also talked about how I planned to marshal the studio resources we'd need, the practical tactics that you don't learn in film school but do learn from experience, if you survive long enough to get experience.

For the first time in all the pitches I'd done in Hollywood, I included my family. Photos of Mom and Dad and my brothers and sisters. Stories about the restaurant. The personal details I'd never been ready to share before. As it happened, this story was even closer to my family than I realized.

After the producers hired me, I got to know Kevin and learned how he'd written the book. He surprised me by saying he was good friends with my cousin Vivian. He'd loved listening to her stories about our extended family. In fact, some of them provided raw material for the novel—like the fact that Rachel is from Cupertino, because that's where Vivian grew up. At one point in the book, somebody defends Rachel by saying, "One of her cousins is even a famous film director." In other words: me.

It was unbelievable. Was I somehow destined to make this movie? I didn't know, but learning about the connection between my family and Kevin's novel brought me a sense of calm. It made me surrender to the process. To trust that everything was happening for a reason.

HISTORY MATTERS IN HOLLYWOOD, and history wasn't on our side. When the studios decide if or how they're going to green-light a movie, they consider how comparable titles have fared. But the last major release with a Westernized Asian cast was *The Joy Luck Club,* more than two decades earlier. So for our pitch meetings with executives, the producers and I pointed to other kinds of history: my track record, the ongoing popularity of Kevin's novel and its sequels, and, backing up the rest, the recent demographic history of the United

States. Asians were the fastest-growing segment of the population: a cohort of eighteen million people who hadn't seen themselves on a big screen in a generation.

We pitched the movie to executives all over town, making a familiar circuit around the famous old studios. When it was over, we felt best about the offer from Warner Bros., the studio that was practically synonymous with Hollywood. (It released *The Jazz Singer,* the first talking picture, in 1927.) But at the last moment, the ancient routine of dealmaking was upended. The Albanian army arrived.

You'll recall that back in 2010, when Netflix had declared itself "primarily a streaming video company," plenty of media executives dismissed the notion that it could ever pose a threat. One of them even likened it to the lowly Albanian army. Later events showed that the analogy didn't hold up. Albania doesn't have a secret superweapon.

At Netflix's headquarters in Los Gatos, a flywheel had started to spin. Hundreds of engineers had begun collecting personal data from viewers—something the studios couldn't do—and feeding it into a proprietary algorithm. It let the company tailor each viewer's homepage to be maximally appealing. It also helped to identify the kinds of content that would entertain existing subscribers and attract new ones. Instead of the studios' old green-light process, with its guesses based on history and executives' scattershot taste, here were predictions backed by math.

All of a sudden, the Albanians couldn't lose. Netflix began to produce its own TV programming and immediately had buzzy hits like *House of Cards* and *Orange Is the New Black*. The new content brought in new users, which yielded new data, and the flywheel spun faster. By 2015, Netflix was the best-performing company in the S&P 500, its stock price more than doubling that year.

The company's next move was so familiar to me I felt like I was back in high school, watching the dot-com boom all over again. It used its astronomical valuation and cheap debt to expand in every direction: a pure expression of Silicon Valley's grow-at-any-cost logic. In early 2016, it was one of the top buyers at Sundance, which barely dented the $6 billion it had vowed to spend on content that year. There was plenty left over for other appetizing projects that might come along. Like ours.

Netflix offered more money for *Crazy Rich Asians* than Warner Bros. did. Way, way more money. And it didn't stop there. It guaranteed us two sequels, so we wouldn't have to worry about critics or viewership, we could just make our art. It also promised to deliver more visibility to our movie, all around the world, than we could ever hope to get from a conventional studio marketing campaign.

According to long-standing Hollywood custom, Netflix's offer would lead Warner Bros. to make a higher counteroffer. On a Friday afternoon, all of us—producers, lawyers, Kevin, and I—gathered on a conference call to find out what it was. In one of the strangest moments of my career, we learned that the studio had *lowered* its bid. I still don't know why it turned the screw on us that way, but it was brutal. Especially since Warner Bros. said we had only fifteen minutes to decide. Then the offer was dead.

So which would it be, the streamer or the studio?

It seemed to me that the producers and lawyers were leaning toward Netflix, but they deferred to me and Kevin. And Kevin deferred to me.

Apart from the insult of Warner Bros. cutting its offer, Netflix spoke a language that just made sense to me. Empowering creators, building networks, replacing old systems with newer, more efficient ones: That's what technology is *for*. With *Crazy Rich Asians,* Netflix was promising to do for the visibility of Asian storytellers what YouTube had done a decade earlier, only at an exponentially vaster scale. Earlier that year, all at once, it had expanded its service to 130 countries. It was accessible in a half a billion households—and climbing. Choosing Netflix would put us on the side of the future, making our movie part of what its CEO called "the internet TV revolution."

My recent trauma with *Jem* made a streaming release sound even better. Since Netflix shared viewer data only sparingly and had preapproved two sequels, there was virtually no chance that our movie could be judged a failure. We could declare victory for ourselves and for Asian American storytelling no matter what happened.

It's Netflix—let's go.

There were so many reasons to say it. Yet I was having a hard time saying it.

One reason was John Cho.

A few months earlier, the graphic designer William Yu had started an online campaign to highlight the lack of Asian American representation in Hollywood. In particular, he wanted to show how Asian actors didn't get a shot at the biggest roles in the biggest movies, *even when the characters were Asian*. And even though studies showed that movies with diverse casts overperformed at the box office. He made his point by editing John Cho's face into posters for some recent hits. There he was in Matt Damon's astronaut helmet in *The Mar-*

tian, in James Bond's tuxedo in *Spectre,* in a cute embrace with Emilia Clarke in *Me Before You.*

I loved to see it. Hollywood really had been shortchanging Asian actors—and writers and stories and audiences—forever. (I got another taste of it myself around this time. In my first face-to-face meeting with the now-disgraced Harvey Weinstein, he asked me how *Star Trek Beyond* was going. I didn't direct that movie—Justin Lin did.) But I also realized: *Wait, I'm Hollywood.* If the movie business needed to change, then people like me needed to change it.

On that all-important conference call, somebody proposed that we accept Netflix's offer, then use a portion of the windfall to support organizations fighting for greater Asian visibility. But that didn't make sense to me. The purpose of those causes was to get a seat at *this* table, to be where we were at this moment. Hollywood was the party we hadn't been invited to yet. The moviegoing experience had a cachet—a glamour, a sense of aspiration, a validating power—that no streaming service could match. Our movie might be seen by more people on Netflix, but if we chose Warner Bros., the studio's legacy and stature might give it more impact.

Wasn't that what we were after? Wasn't that the point of #StarringJohnCho?

It bothered me that Netflix asked for no commitment from the people who watched its movies. I mean, that's the whole point of a subscription service with auto-renewal: to make you forget that you've committed anything at all. According to one of the few metrics that Netflix was willing to share, watching a movie for just two minutes counted as a "view." *Two minutes?* You spend longer in a drive-thru.

If we chose Warner Bros., the studio would insist that viewers make a commitment before the movie began, in the form of the century-old ritual of moviegoing: the ticket purchase, the walk through the lobby, the popcorn (if you like popcorn), the surge of adrenaline when the lights go down. Each step in the ritual reinforces the sense that the story you are about to see has value, that it deserves your time, your money, your full attention. The link between a ritual and the value of a creative act might be subtle, but I'm not the only one who felt it. As long as Steve Jobs was alive, Apple sold music only one song or album at a time. Its subscription plans came later.

If we made a great movie, and if Warner Bros. marketed it right, we might get the one number that really *did* matter: the box office. No matter what critics think or studios expect, people show up every weekend and use their time and dollars to vote on what they want. Like few facts in this industry built on appearances, spin, and outright bullshit, box office numbers can't be fudged. They are what they are, undeniably. They're a democratizing force—a chance for people to shift the culture in a weekend. If I let my imagination run wild, I could see how the big-screen success of our movie might create new opportunities for Asian America. We could make sure that the next time an Asian filmmaker came along, history would be on their side.

I wanted that to be true. But I also wondered if my romantic vision of Hollywood and its influence belonged to a world that was already gone. Whatever misgivings I had about Netflix, streaming looked like the inevitable next phase in how audiences were going to watch films. Choosing it would be a way of future-proofing the movie, of minimizing the chance that we could lose.

But I decided it was time that we played to win.

In spite of the money, the preference of our advisers, and my Silicon Valley worldview—my lifelong conviction that the new way is the best way—I chose uncertainty, the traditional approach, and Warner Bros. And Kevin was down for all of it.

We were going to risk failure for the chance of success. We were going to bet on ourselves.

A DIRECTOR IS NEVER more popular than on the day when a new movie is announced: so many roles to cast, so many jobs to fill. So when Ken Jeong was the first person to call me after *Crazy Rich Asians* was announced, I figured I knew what was coming.

He invited me to visit him on the set of *Dr. Ken,* the TV series that he'd launched after his enormous success in *The Hangover* and other big movies. When he sat me down, the surprises began.

"Listen, bro, this is the real story," he told me. "What you're doing is not going to be easy. People are going to say all kinds of stuff, and some of it is going to hurt. I want to support you in any way you need. If you want me to tweet stuff or stay quiet, I will." Then he served me Korean barbecue, which is what he'd insisted that the production offer as lunch on the set of his show. Such a power move for one of the few Asian producers in town.

It meant the world to me to know that one of Hollywood's leading Asian actors had my back. And I began to see how much the movie already meant to people in my community. Asian actors *had been* ready, and now they'd finally get a chance to show the world.

It was time for the Asian Avengers to assemble.

THE DROP

About two weeks before every production begins,
something goes wrong. *Very* wrong. A disruption that
could take the whole project down. An actor will quit
or will get cold feet and start agitating for changes to
the script. A location will be lost, or a key member of
the team will melt down because there isn't enough
money in the budget to execute the vision. Having
lived through those crises multiple times, I've realized that they're a natural part of any big, high-stakes
collaboration. I now expect the drop to hit and try to
be ready for it. You should be, too. Our job isn't just to
solve the problem, it's also to take care of the people
we're working with. Be present for them as they face
their obstacles, emotional or otherwise. Help them
find the light amid the darkness of doubt. Those
moments feel chaotic, but remember that creativity
thrives on obstacles. In almost every case, we came
up with better solutions in the end.

I told the casting directors that no matter the role, I was
looking for one quality above all others: confidence. I wanted
actors who were willing to be who they are—funny, outra-
geous, glamorous, sexy—unapologetically.

That meant I wanted Ken, obviously. Everybody knew he
was one of the funniest performers alive, Asian or otherwise.
And we needed Nora Lum, who had built an online following

as the brash rapper/performer Awkwafina. Ronny Chieng had caught my eye when he did a piece on *The Daily Show* that mocked a racist Fox News segment about Chinatown. I loved that he was smart and hilarious and clearly wasn't trying to please anybody. Gemma Chan commanded her space: The world waited on her every move. Her beauty served as cover for the warrior underneath. All of them, plus their costars, such as Nico Santos and Jimmy O. Yang, had different ways of making me feel: *I want to be like that.*

We thought we'd found the perfect Rachel but hit our first big snag. Constance Wu was one of the stars of *Fresh Off the Boat,* the first network TV show in twenty years to have a largely Asian cast. The show's production schedule seemed to make it impossible for her to accept the role. But she wrote me a letter arguing that we should delay the entire movie until she was available. Talk about confidence!

She convinced me. And I'm so glad she did. It was worth the wait for everything she brought to the movie. Plus we would need all the time we could get to cast our leading man.

For Nick, we had to find the most charming Asian actor in the whole world. He also needed to have a totally authentic English accent. And—rarer still—he needed an intangible quality that was exemplified by our model for the role: JFK Jr. in New York. He needed class and style, but he also had to be so grounded that you'd want to have a beer with him. In other words, we didn't just need a great actor, we needed *a movie star,* which is not the same thing.

Movie stars are not like other people. They're not even like other actors. They have an aura, a charisma, that can't be learned or bought. Asian actors, who had been locked out of big studio roles on big screens for pretty much the entire history of Hollywood, hadn't gotten enough chances to show their star power. And by 2016, stars of every background were a disappearing breed. Some people blamed Netflix: It's hard to seem larger than life on a smartphone screen. But to me, the real culprit is social media. Twitter and Instagram can make you famous, but they're so relentlessly intimate that they upset the delicate ecosystem that creates stars, reducing the mystique they need to thrive.

So we searched for Nick everywhere. Not just in the usual spots: movies, TV, Broadway. We scoured drama schools. We explored four continents. I got pitched many, many actors who had talent and charisma but still didn't feel quite right. After months of looking, with a few days left, we had a handful of good candidates but not a single great one. That's when Lisa-Kim Kuan, an accountant in our production office in Malaysia, suggested a guy she remembered from an awards show a few years back. I was skeptical. Then I learned that he'd never acted, or even wanted to act, but only hosted travel programs on TV. I was even more skeptical. But I was also desperate.

I looked him up online and couldn't believe what I saw. Henry Golding was the Asian Cary Grant: handsome, charming, funny, great on camera. After a little cajoling, he agreed to fly to Los Angeles, and I liked him even more. We all felt: *If he's not the guy, it has to be somebody exactly like him.* But there *wasn't* anybody like him. Later, we'd be criticized for hiring somebody who wasn't fully Asian for the role. (Henry's father was from Britain, where he'd lived for a while when he was young.) That hurt him, and it hurt me, but after all that searching, I knew that finding even one actor who fit our profile was a miracle.

The leader of the cast, even if she wasn't playing the lead role, was Michelle Yeoh—a legend even then. She was the only person we considered for the role of Eleanor, Nick's mother. But she wasn't an automatic yes. In the story, Eleanor poses the biggest threat to Nick and Rachel's happiness. She disapproves of this young American and tries to drive her away. To Michelle, the role looked like a trap.

"If you want me to play the villain in this movie, I can't do that," she told me. She wanted to show what people in her generation stand for, what they bring to the table.

I told her that's exactly what we needed. Eleanor would embody the older generation's values of family, authority, and tradition, which would be set against Rachel's youth and independence, but the point wasn't to say that one was right and the other wrong. I wanted to show how Eleanor's and Rachel's experiences in different generations and different societies had led them to different views about responsibility and community. Young Asian Americans had to make up their own minds about which values to live by. That would be the point of our movie.

Over the course of a few conversations, Michelle got comfortable with me and how I thought about the role. And I found a new reason to believe she was the perfect person to play it: She reminded me so much of my parents.

From the day I started work on *Crazy Rich Asians,* Mom and Dad were more involved in this project than in anything else I'd done. I asked them endless questions. After all, this story was set in Asia, which was their world much more than mine. I compiled a playlist of songs from China in the '60s, the kind that might have been in a Hollywood musical back then. When I played them for my mom, her eyes got wide, like a teenager's, which was shocking. "Your dad and I used to do the jitterbug to this music," she told me. She even knew the words.

When I told Michelle that I respected Eleanor's views on family and sacrifice, I was being honest. It's because my dad said those things too, and lived by them. I understood how Eleanor could command a room, because it's the same way my mom had trained herself to do it: not by being big and loud, but knowing exactly what she stood for, which gave her a quiet force that compelled everybody's attention.

No sooner had we finished casting and moved to Malaysia to start shooting than the echoes between Eleanor and my parents began to shape the movie.

In the book, Nick introduces Rachel to his mother at the welcome-home party Eleanor throws for him. But I wanted their first encounter to be more active. How could we establish the Eleanor-Rachel dynamic more vividly? The answer came from memories of my parents.

Eleanor would still meet Rachel at the party, but it would be *in the kitchen*. Eleanor would stride around the room the way my dad did (and does), as if she were walking the deck of a pirate ship. She would put Rachel in her place the way I'd seen my mother put many, many people in their places: subtly but unequivocally. We dressed Michelle in a cape to enhance the regal effect, even though she's so naturally regal, on-screen and off, that the cape is implied.

"You shouldn't have MSG on this table," she told me as we rehearsed on set. "Eleanor would not have MSG on this table."

After all my years in kitchens, I didn't know what a bag of MSG looked like. But somehow she did.

"I think it's okay," I said. "It's way in the background."

"No. Everyone will recognize that."

I moved the MSG.

Once the extras took their places, the kitchen (which was really a library that we'd transformed) started to remind me of home: the flickering light from the burners, the smell of rice steam as it entered my lungs. Only the sound didn't seem right. The *thunk-thunk-thunk* of knives on cutting boards wasn't fast enough. Since none of the extras could match my dad's speed, we asked our on-set caterer to get into costume and do it.

Action.

Nick led Rachel into the kitchen and greeted his mother. "You need a haircut," she told him (which is what my mother would say to me).

He introduced Rachel, who committed a typically American faux pas: She went for a hug, a move so presumptuous it was disrespectful. But Eleanor stayed cool. She just kept on making her rounds, issuing orders, paying little attention to this overeager Western girl.

That day set up the relationships among the three characters perfectly. It also put me on notice: My family life was going to overlap with the movie in ways I couldn't anticipate.

Before we left the set, I asked Michelle if we could take a photo. I texted it to my dad, who's a big fan, and said, "Hey, I'm working with Michelle Yeoh."

He wrote back right away. "Why is there MSG on that table?"

WHEN KEVIN WROTE HIS NOVEL, he kept a Post-it note that said "JOY" on his computer. So during production, first in Malaysia, then in Singapore, we stuck little signs that said "JOY" on the monitors. We even sprinkled some of them around the movie itself, like the ad on the taxi that brings Nick and Rachel to the airport. And it's lucky we did, because I would need the reminders.

Every day on that set was so much pressure. The monsoon

rains, the monkeys stalking us in the trees, and, above all, the pace. I wanted the production to feel lavish, like Old Hollywood, but we didn't have that kind of budget. When we finished at a location, there was no going back. It meant that when we filmed Colin and Araminta's wedding, we had only one take to get the shot of water gently spreading across the floor, an elegant touch I'd seen in a hotel lobby while scouting locations. (The scene's other fanciful moment—people waving little artificial fireflies—was inspired by the butterfly puppets at Jim Henson's memorial.) For the sake of everybody's morale, I was prepared to declare victory no matter what happened. But then, somehow, the movie gods gave us what we needed—with a little bonus. Sonoya Mizuno, who played Araminta, had trained as a ballerina. When she stepped into the water, she did it with a perfectly arched foot.

As filming went on, I noticed a paradox. I'd stopped trying to control everything, and it was making me the director I'd always wanted to be. If Kevin said to replace somebody's watch because the current model wasn't expensive enough, I trusted that he was right. If the producers said we needed to accommodate a couple of extras because they let us use their private jet, I made room. My experience with all those legends in *Now You See Me 2* had changed the way I worked with actors. Instead of playing puppeteer and telling them exactly what to do, I helped them understand where the characters needed to be at a certain moment in the story, then let them decide how to get there.

This newly collaborative approach faced its toughest test on the day Ken arrived. We'd cast him as Mr. Goh, the father of Rachel's friend Peik Lin, who was played by Nora. He told me that he wanted to punch up his first scene, when Rachel joins the family for a rowdy dinner. But our only chance to do it was immediately before we filmed it, while the other actors were getting into costume. I've never been a great improv guy, but I did my best to riff with him, which really meant trying to keep up with him.

Soon—much too soon—the other actors were ready. Then the improv *really* began.

Everybody made stuff up. Calvin Wong, the actor who played Peik Lin's brother, wasn't supposed to have any lines— I just liked his look—but then Ken and Nora kept throwing to him. They convinced me he was comic gold. When they asked him a question, they said I should let him answer, "I love you." The twin kids farther down the table didn't speak English, so as the scene changed, we had to keep feeding them the phonetic versions of what to say.

Dinner scenes are trickier to shoot than they look, because you have to keep repositioning the camera to get the different characters' points of view. But I'd gained enough experience on movie sets over the years, and built enough trust with the actors that day, to get everything we needed—even amid the endless hilarious improvisation. On and on we went, making discoveries, laughing constantly.

DAY BY DAY, SCENE BY SCENE, I could feel the pieces of Rachel and Nick's story clicking into place. But considering how much of my motivation had come from raw personal need—to be more truthful, to make myself vulnerable—I wouldn't be satisfied if we just found a stylish way to answer the big rom-com question *Will they or won't they?* In fact, I didn't think we were telling the story of Rachel and Nick at all.

The longer we worked on reshaping Kevin's book for the screen, the more clearly I could see that it was really about Rachel's self-journey. Her trials in Singapore force her to confront hard questions about who she is and where she belongs. They were the same painful questions I'd faced, or refused to face, my entire life.

A young Asian American facing a cultural identity crisis: *That's* the story I needed to tell.

Pretty late in the process, we still hadn't figured out how the final steps in that story should go. I asked Adele Lim, a gifted Malaysian-born writer, to work with me to develop Peter Chiarelli's screenplay. We realized that it was going to require a whole new third act, the part of the story when Rachel must climb back from her lowest point. To pull it off, we would need to create three scenes that weren't in the book.

That would be the easy part. The hard part would be me reaching deep inside myself to find out what I actually had to say about Rachel's cultural identity crisis—and my own. I remembered all too vividly what happened the last time I'd ventured down this road. How humiliated I'd been by *Gwai Lo,* which had sat in a box for fifteen years and counting. I was scared to go back there, but I knew this was the moment to do it, if I was ever going to do it.

In the first of our three new scenes, we needed to raise the stakes for Rachel. The real question to be decided in her story isn't who she's dating, it's what kind of life she's going to lead and where she feels she belongs. But how do you dramatize a feeling of belonging?

Once again, I found the answer in memories of home. I thought back to how I used to make wontons with my grandmother after school. We'd talk, she'd tell me stories, and I'd feel so loved and heard. So Adele and I proposed a scene in which Nick brings Rachel to his grandmother's house. They'd make dumplings with the entire family.

In Malaysia, in a vast old mansion, a large part of our cast gathered around a table: stars, kids, and Lisa Lu, the amazing ninety-year-old veteran of movies and TV who played Nick's grandmother. (She's the rare actor who had enough gravitas to criticize someone as formidable as Eleanor for making bad dumplings—a little moment that gave Eleanor vulnerability, like seeing Meryl Streep without her makeup in *The Devil Wears Prada*.) The vibe you see on-screen—the jokes, the warm memories—is the same vibe we felt on set. The actors had been taking dumpling-making lessons to prepare for this day. They wanted to show off what they'd learned, though let's just say that some had learned more than others.

When the camera started rolling, Rachel savored every moment. As the only child of a single mother, she'd never been part of something like this, three generations laughing together. She was already in love with Nick; now she was falling in love with his family—just like my dad did with my mom and *her* family. But that warm feeling only set up Rachel for the second scene, the most important scene in the movie: her big crisis, when Eleanor would try to drive her away.

The original plan was to shoot Eleanor and Rachel's confrontation in a hallway. But on set that day, I couldn't stop thinking about the mansion's grand staircase. It was immense, iconic. It made me think of *The Jungle Book*. Eleanor could be like a serpent—she would wear green—and Rachel would be this unsuspecting little mouse caught on a tree branch. Eleanor would wrap her up in a cozy embrace, then crush her.

What should Eleanor say? Adele and the producers and I

had spent a long time trying to figure out the worst thing you could say to someone who was trying to join your family that wouldn't be "mustache twirly." She'd come up with a line that seemed promising, but we wouldn't know if it worked until we filmed it.

As Michelle, Constance, and I rehearsed on the staircase, it felt like we were onstage. Many of the actors who had just filmed the dumpling scene had stuck around to watch.

Eleanor walked up the stairs. She adjusted a photo of her family (which was actually Kevin's family). She talked about her engagement ring (which was actually Michelle's own ring—she liked it better than the one the prop department gave her). She told Rachel about the years of work and sacrifice it had taken for her to be accepted by her mother-in-law.

Then she made her move.

Eleanor approached Rachel, forcing her to back down one step. From the high ground, she delivered the line we had worked so hard to find.

"You will never be enough."

She said it with such contempt, in a way that cut so deep, that Constance immediately burst into tears. Dozens of people silently went, *Oh shit*. We could see how much it hurt. We could *feel* it.

We reset to film a few more takes, but before we got very far, Constance turned to me. "How many times do we have to shoot this? Because I can't stop crying."

We'd gotten what we needed. In fact, I felt while watching it: *This is why we made the movie.*

Eleanor's line and Rachel's reaction expressed what I hadn't been willing to express before and had rarely seen expressed by anybody else. When you grow up the way I did—torn between Asia and America, trying to shed what you are, trying to be what you're not—the world can make you feel worthless. You're not Asian enough. You're not American enough. You're not smart enough. You're not talented enough. If you're an Asian man, you're not attractive enough. And then, louder than all the rest: *You don't belong here.* You hear that one all the time. Everywhere.

Eleanor's line sent shock waves across the set that day because we all worked in Hollywood, where the feeling that you'll never be enough is the very air you breathe. You're not young enough. You're not pretty enough. You need to find a bigger star—or to become one. That constant anxiety, the need to climb, can be fuel when you're starting out. But in time, it breaks all of us.

Eleanor had aimed at Rachel's most vulnerable spot, at her most vulnerable moment. Our third scene needed to show how she could come back from that. It meant I would need to find a resolution to Rachel's cultural identity crisis—and maybe my own.

After her confrontation with Eleanor, she appeared to have two options, both of them bad. If she stayed with Nick, it would blow up his life and his family. If she left, it would seem to confirm that Eleanor was right about her—that she wasn't good enough. How could she get out of this jam in a dramatically satisfying way? As an economics professor, she taught game theory. So what if she and Eleanor played an actual game—like mah-jongg?

I loved the idea, at least until we discovered how unbelievably complicated mah-jongg can be, especially when you're trying to layer the dramatic climax of a movie on top of it. The scene demanded lots of consulting with experts, lots of rewrites, and lots of rehearsal, even on the day we filmed. Then it was time for the cameras to roll. All of us would find out together how Rachel's endgame would unfold.

Eleanor, sitting in the game's "East" seat, tried to win by finding tiles that matched, that belonged together, in much the same way that she tried to find family members who belonged together—that is, not Rachel. But Rachel, in the "West" seat, drew the eight of bamboo, the tile that both of them needed to win. The game was hers if she wanted it.

Instead, she let the tile go—just as she had decided to let Nick go. Not because she thought Eleanor was right about her, but because she had come to see that Eleanor was wrong.

Defying the stereotype of the selfish young Westerner, Rachel sacrificed her own happiness for the sake of someone else's. She loved Nick so much that she refused to see him wreck his life with his family. It wasn't because she felt inferior or undeserving. It was because she knew she was enough.

Rachel did something that Eleanor never thought possible: combine the values of East and West—of family and sacrifice, of independence and self-assertion—to forge her own path. She had discovered her self-worth. She didn't need Nick or anybody else.

Rachel showed everybody her tiles, so Eleanor understood that she could have won if she'd tried. Then she walked away, off to start living her new definition of what it means to be Asian American. One based not on choosing one side or the other but on mixing both to form an identity that's genuinely new.

The movie could have ended right there, and maybe it should have. We kept the story going so Nick could propose to her because, hey, it's a movie. But once she turned her back on

Eleanor, the movie had expressed everything I wanted it to express and that I was *proud* for it to express—which is so different from how I felt after *Gwai Lo*.

If you embrace all the parts of yourself, you can create your own path. I didn't get that message growing up, but I wanted the next generation of Asian Americans to hear it, so they wouldn't feel as isolated or invisible as my generation did.

My thinking about the next generation wasn't hypothetical. Two weeks after we finished shooting, my daughter was born.

FROM THE TIME THAT Kristin and I started dating, I told her I didn't want to get married. At least not until I was old, like in my forties. She was willing to look past this obnoxious statement, probably because of the other thing I started saying before too long: that I couldn't imagine my life without her.

While we were dating, I had my first experiences getting high. My mom had been so terrifyingly opposed to drugs that I'd barely touched them. So THC hit me hard. *Very* hard. The first time I smoked weed, I had an exceptionally vivid flashback to being in my childhood closet, playing with toys. It made me so sad, because I felt that the past was gone and never coming back. Kristin, watching me sob, suggested maybe I shouldn't do drugs again. But I did, and this time I had a kind of flash-forward. It seemed to me that we'd had children, and two of them were coming home from college to have dinner with us.

That vision brought me more joy than anything I'd ever experienced in my entire life. It helped me see that the best days of my life weren't behind me, in my childhood or college days, but in front of me—a theme I'd draw on when I directed *In the Heights*. I suddenly had a new way of viewing my life. A new dream. I wanted that scene to become real as fast as I could have it.

Kristin and I began to talk about starting a family, wedding ring or not. Soon, and in dramatic circumstances, we found out she was pregnant. (She took the test on a night when friends were at our house watching TV. We ducked upstairs, got the results, celebrated for a moment, then rejoined the party—only to learn that Donald Trump had been elected president while we were gone. It was November 8, 2016.)

We didn't know if I'd return from shooting *Crazy Rich Asians* in time for the baby's birth. So before I left L.A., I got dressed up, set up a camera, and recorded a video to our yet-to-be-born daughter. I told her how excited I was to share the adventure of life with her. Then, camera still rolling, I proposed to Kristin.

I hated to be half a world away from my fiancée, especially while she was pregnant. Much as I loved to spend time with the cast, especially on a set where nobody felt like "the one"—the only Asian—I was lonely. On weekends, I'd sometimes go by myself to a random Chili's in Kuala Lumpur just because it felt like America. I caught a lot of shit from my friends and family for those meals.

I got home just in time for Willow's birth. Her eyes were open from the moment she was born. She didn't cry; she just looked around the room as if she'd been there before. Then her gaze met mine. Before she was born, I had turned on a Stevie Wonder playlist. It had landed on "You Are the Sunshine of My Life." When he sang, "I feel like this is the beginning / Though I've loved you for a million years," it seemed like he'd written it just for us. Here was the most beautiful creation I had ever seen.

Bringing her home was like waking up from a dream. All at once I realized my crazy new predicament. Kristin and I would be figuring out how to be parents at the same time Myron Kerstein, the film's editor, and I would be figuring out how to assemble the movie—the biggest bet of my professional life. Look closely and you can see a crossover event early in the film: The baby in the montage of text messages is Willow.

A year later, in the summer of 2018, Kristin's family, my family, and our closest friends gathered in Napa Valley to watch us get married. I know people get stressed about their weddings, but for me, that day was a beautiful respite. The scars of *Jem*'s opening weekend hadn't healed, and the premiere of *Crazy Rich Asians* was only a few weeks away.

I'd arranged a surprise for the reception. Along with my brother Larry and some friends, I performed a tap routine, my first public performance in twenty years. But Kristin one-upped me. She too had planned a surprise dance routine, only she was *backed by the* LXD *crew*. We found out later that we'd just missed running into each other on our way to and from rehearsals with Chris Scott, who turned out to be as good at keeping secrets as he was at choreographing dance steps.

But Willow topped us all. She wore a white dress and made her entrance in a little wagon to the sound of her theme song, "You Are the Sunshine of My Life." It was even more beautiful than Araminta making ripples as she glided down the aisle. Having shot so many weddings in my high school days, I thought I was prepared for how mine would feel. But I wasn't. Everything that I thought would seem like a formality or mere ceremony or just a ritual was the opposite: It all felt so alive. It felt *true*. An affirmation of the love that Kristin and I felt for each other and for our daughter. A celebration of the life together that we had already begun to lead.

Normally, newlyweds make it through the stress of their wedding, then go unwind, enjoying their new married life together. For me it was the opposite. Instead of jetting off on a honeymoon with Kristin, I left for a press junket with Henry. We were about to find out if our big-screen bet had paid off.

THE WORST DAY OF the moviemaking process is when you see the film fully assembled for the first time. Usually you discover that it's not what you thought you were making and you realize how much work you'll need to do to fix it. But the rough assembly of *Crazy Rich Asians* was different. Watching it was like an out-of-body experience.

Though I knew every inch of every scene and every nuance of every performance, it felt totally new, as if I hadn't known a thing about it. I found it moving and hilarious—if also really long (the first cut ran nearly three hours). We clearly had trimming to do, but I could tell that the feeling I wanted to capture, my reflection on what it was like to be me, was alive and well in the movie. I was happy I'd fought for certain moments, like ending the movie with a Mandarin version of Coldplay's hit "Yellow." (Studio execs had worried about the color's associations with anti-Asian bigotry. *That's why we need to do it,* I replied. Then Coldplay turned us down. So, like Constance, I mustered my courage and wrote a heartfelt letter: a personal plea to the guys in the band. They said yes the same day.) I knew we'd made something special, unlike any film that people would have encountered before.

Now we just had to get them to come see it.

Ominously, the studio had a hard time attracting people to the test screenings, even though tickets were free. The comments that accompanied the refusals suggested that non-Asians didn't think the movie was for them and Asians were offended by the title. Once we got people into a theater, we tested very high. But could we actually get people into a theater?

The press began to pay attention because of how big a gamble we were making. The fact that there hadn't been a movie like ours in more than a generation made it feel like a cultural event. It helped that Asian journalists had risen to the kinds of positions where they could convey why all this mattered. And just when we needed it, we started gaining traction within the Asian community, which made the marketing push feel a lot more personal for me.

My friend Bing Chen, who had recently founded the Asian American advocacy organization Gold House, told me he wanted to help the movie however he could. A few weeks before the world premiere, he organized a dinner that brought together influential Asian Americans from media, tech, and finance, plus marketing folks from Warner Bros. Inspired by a similar effort in support of *Black Panther* a few months earlier, we wanted to create ways for people to buy out theaters to get more people to see the movie. But—thinking back to my younger days and the promise of a networked world—it seemed to me that we needed to create a digital infrastructure that would make that process quick, easy, seamless, and replicable. That way, anyone anywhere could support our movement by helping people to see the movie. The big shots assembled in that room had the collective resources and know-how to make it happen, and they did.

In other words: Although I'd decided to release *Crazy Rich Asians* the old-fashioned way (on big screens in theaters) because of the limitations of streaming, we still used newfangled Silicon Valley tools and community ties to help build its audience. As ever, I was trying to combine technology and creativity to make something new. But the stakes had never been as high as this. If the movie failed, it might be a decade or more before Asian storytellers got another chance like this one. Which isn't fair—but *is* life in Hollywood.

My parents tried to do their part, too. We held that Gold House dinner in the private dining room of Chef Chu's. Later, we hosted a media event there. Mom, going all out, put my middle school trophies on a table where everybody could see them. That was stressful, but not as stressful as when I waited to find out what she and Dad thought of the movie.

I knew I didn't need their approval, but the child in me was sort of still seeking it. I wanted them to love it. I wanted them not to be disappointed in me.

I could tell, as they watched a prerelease screening in San Francisco, that they weren't really thinking about the characters. They were thinking about our family. When my dad heard Eleanor talk about sacrifice, he thought it came from him. When my mom saw Eleanor's elegance and style—right down to the pantsuit—she thought it came from her. Both of them thought that I chose "Can't Help Falling in Love" (which was performed at the wedding by Kina Grannis, an Asian American singer I'd found on YouTube) because it was their song. They were right every time.

They also got to see how everybody else experienced the movie: laughing and cheering and getting teary, then wanting to talk about it afterward. Mom and Dad don't tend to unpack how they're feeling, but I think they sensed that something was changing. That instead of being a cultural sidekick, they—we—were becoming the main event. As cliché as it sounds now, I think they felt seen.

What they *actually* said is that they loved it. They hugged me with tears in their eyes. I could tell they were proud—not of what I'd achieved, but of what *we*'d achieved. Because the movie was something we had done together. The work of a lifetime. Or maybe several lifetimes.

ON THE MOVIE'S OPENING weekend, the box office tally was $26 million. Very respectable, but not the big cultural phenomenon we had dreamed of, one that would change all the rules. I tried to put a positive spin on the news, calling it a step forward for Asian American stories.

The numbers for our second weekend reached me in Thailand, where Kristin and I had finally gone for our honeymoon. They were a surprise. The grosses had decreased by only 6 percent—an unusually tiny decline. The next weekend, the numbers defied gravity yet again. And for the third time in a row, we had the number one movie in the country. Exhibitors started *adding* screens. That's when we knew something strange was going on.

That's when we realized the movie had caught fire in exactly the way we dreamed it could.

I'll be honest: When I made the case to the studios that this movie could be a big hit, and when we made the case to ourselves that we should choose Warner Bros. over Netflix in hopes of creating a breakthrough for Asian American stories, part of me never truly believed it. I was so happy I listened to the part of me that always trusted it would work, because the theatrical experience turned out to have all the power that we said it would. By the time the movie left theaters, after a run longer than anybody anticipated, *Crazy Rich Asians* had become the biggest romantic comedy in more than a decade.

The movie's success turned the actors into stars, just as we'd hoped. I'm sure that a streaming release wouldn't have gotten Henry onto the cover of *GQ* or Constance onto the cover of *Time*. A few months after the premiere, Awkwafina would host *SNL*. Then Gemma played a lead role in a Marvel movie. Even now, years later, their triumphs make me incredibly proud.

More broadly, the movie sparked a wave of thoughtful coverage: think pieces about Asian American culture, feature stories about Asian family roles, explainers about mah-jongg (which would've been a big help when we shot the scene). Not all of it was positive. The movie was called unfair to South Asians, particularly in how it depicted Singaporean life. The insular world of the characters, the exclusive bubble created by their wealth, played differently on-screen than it had in the pages of the novel. I wish I'd found ways to foreground South Asians in our adaptation, and I would change it if I could. Other critics said we'd sugarcoated the culture we claimed to depict, that it was an outsider's version of Asian life. There's some truth to that too, but in this case I wouldn't change a thing.

Of course we simplified some complexities of Asian culture. This story was about an Asian American going to Asia for the first time, so we would see the world through her newcomer eyes. We also were inviting a whole world of moviegoers along with us. That's the only way a big-screen romantic-comedy version of this story could work. We had to make something so delicious that everybody would want to be a part of it. For some viewers, it might seem like Asia 101. But without 101, you don't get to the deeper layers—the true change that comes from broader awareness.

That complaint gave me a strange feeling of déjà vu. Finally it hit me. It was word for word what people had said about my parents' restaurant. It made me feel a new kinship with my mom and dad. It made me want to talk. We had the kind of conversation we couldn't have had when I was younger, when I didn't understand what they'd gone through.

"This is how you grew up," my dad told me. "Respecting two worlds because we are of two worlds. People who aren't of those two worlds can't see that's what we're trying to resolve."

To make a life in this country, they had needed to find a way to integrate Asia and America. By doing it at the restaurant—through the food they served, the stories they told, even the cooking classes my dad taught—they had shown me how to do it in my work. I know this sounds like a Hollywood movie, but it also happens to be the truth of my life: After so many years of trying to be like Spielberg and Lucas, I came into my own as a filmmaker only once I started trying to be like my parents—when I started thinking of myself as an ambassador, treating my position between two cultures as something to cherish, not something to hide or resent. They showed me how to tell stories that would open the door for other stories.

And those stories are coming. Lots of them.

The years since 2018 have brought a stream of breakthroughs for Asian American cinema: *The Farewell, Minari, Shang-Chi, Everything Everywhere All at Once.* I'm not claiming a direct line of cause and effect between our movie and any of them (although it did mean the world to hear Ke Huy Quan say that *Crazy Rich Asians* is what convinced him to come back to Hollywood, just in time to win an Oscar). But there is definitely a before and after.

My collaborators and I didn't have some secret recipe. The truth is everybody was ready. The success of Kevin's novel had shown there was an audience for these characters' adventures. The industry was ripe for change. Asian actors had the skills to bring the story to life. I had the experience and clout to get it made. A new generation of reporters could write the articles we needed. Social media could spread the word. Decades of agitating and laying groundwork created a moment of opportunity, and Asian storytellers seized it.

I'll always be proud of the movie, but I know that it has done its work. It has nothing to do with the next phase of the fight to change the way that people see Asian Americans. In this phase, the challenge isn't about representation, about how people depict us. It's about *self*-presentation—the way we choose to depict ourselves.

That's what Rachel is really announcing when she leaves the mah-jongg game, ready to walk a path all her own: *I am not you, Eleanor. But I'm also not the person you've made me out to be. I am me. And this new me is what we are going to define. We're not going to do it in this movie. We're not going to give you the answer all at once. But don't look away. Because in the next ten years, now that we have a place at the table, we are going to tell you who we are.*

Before the release of *Crazy Rich Asians,* I'd been, for the most part, an invisible director, which had its advantages. Since I didn't have much of a public profile, directing had let me continue feeling how I'd felt as my high school mascot. I could put on my panther mask and entertain everybody while staying safely out of sight. All of the fun, none of the danger.

Those days of semi-anonymity were over. I was so closely associated with *Crazy Rich Asians,* and it was so much a reflection of my life, that I was now, in a very literal sense, *seen.* In fact, the way people saw me began to change how I saw myself. Like when audience members told me, "It made me feel proud."

I'd never heard that about one of my movies. And to be painfully honest, with the exception of my mom, I didn't expect that I ever would.

From the beginning of my life in Hollywood, I'd known that I could show audiences a good time: take them on an adventure, let them escape the world for a while, then return them to reality. But I never thought I was the kind of filmmaker who could affect them more deeply than that. I felt that I lacked the kind of life experiences—or wounds, for that matter—that would let me offer any profound insight beyond the spectacle.

When people started looking at my work differently, it gave me a new sense of my self-worth. Maybe my movies could be more than I'd allowed them to be. Maybe I could be, too.

Or, to put it another way: Maybe it was time that I finally grew up.

To be clear, I'd already done that according to most of the standard metrics. I was thirty-nine years old. I was a husband and father. I had a house, a car, and a sore back. But for somebody who thought of himself as a storyteller, I was realizing that my work had lacked a certain courage, a willingness to engage with the world. For the most part, my movies had been intended as steps on the flowchart of Hollywood success.

After *Crazy Rich Asians,* I was free from all that. I no longer needed to worry about becoming a Hollywood director. I'd said what I needed to say about my cultural identity crisis. I'd drawn my family and our history into my work. Viewed that way, the movie felt like a leave-taking from the entire first part of my life—the one I was always meant to make. So what should I make now?

With a fresh sense of conviction, I charted a plan for the next part of my life. I would use my voice in ways that could help other voices be heard, especially the voices of people that gatekeepers have too often overlooked. In the telling of *my* stories, I would aim to inspire other people to tell theirs. I would devote my time and energy to projects that challenged the way Hollywood looks and sounds, as *Crazy Rich Asians* had. That's how I would draw on all my experiences and put together everything I'd learned to contribute to the communities that had embraced and supported me. That's how I would reach the goal that now mattered most: becoming a better husband, father, son, friend, citizen.

My first attempt to live up to this sense of purpose came almost immediately, when I directed the film adaptation of *In the Heights,* the radiant Broadway musical by Lin-Manuel Miranda and Quiara Alegría Hudes. Their story about Washington Heights, the Latino neighborhood in Upper Manhattan, depicted a culture that was very different from my Asian upbringing, but I still recognized the generational clashes, the big immigrant dreams, everybody trying to figure out what home means. I thought that by putting the musical on a big screen, we could elevate those lives and stories and open a new lane for more Latinx storytellers, just as *Crazy Rich Asians* had for Asians.

Since no backlot could capture the beauty and energy of Washington Heights, we decided to shoot on location. The result was the happiest summer of my life. I'd never felt so much love around a set. I had two of my closest friends with me: Alice Brooks, the director of photography, and Chris Scott, the choreographer. In song after song, we applied lessons from our *LXD* experiments a decade earlier. "96,000" was a splashy Busby Berkeley number in a public pool; "When the Sun Goes Down" sent two of the movie's stars, Leslie Grace and Corey Hawkins, dancing up the side of a building. The love and joy extended to my home life, too. When Kristin and I welcomed a new baby that summer, we named him Jonathan Heights Chu.

During production, I couldn't help but dream ahead to how the world might respond to our movie. Plenty of moments during our actual premiere week in New York surpassed those dreams. A prerelease screening for the dancers—a hundred performers screaming with pride, a hundred cell phones recording the closing credits as they scrolled by—was a pure expression of why I love making movies and was one of the proudest nights of my career. The reviews were so glowing it was like we'd written them ourselves. *The Atlantic* called me "Hollywood's New Crown Prince of Musicals." It sounded just like the hype I'd gotten twenty years earlier, when my twenty-three-year-old face was on the cover of *Variety* and I was set to direct *Bye Bye Birdie*. Except this time, it was praise for something I'd actually done.

On the morning of our premiere, I got one last bit of affirmation about the new path I was traveling. I sat for an interview with Harry Smith of NBC News, someone I'd grown up watching on TV. Off camera, he told me that he'd cried and cried while watching the movie.

"Thank you for your artistry," he said.

I remember it so vividly because it was the first time anybody outside my family had called me an artist.

At long last, I felt like I'd lived up to my potential. I'd made the best movie of my career for the best reasons I could imagine. Unfortunately, having an accurate picture of yourself doesn't do you much good if your picture of the rest of the world is wrong. And at this turning point in my life, I was discovering that the picture was very, very wrong.

Our premiere and all its celebrations had been scheduled for June 2020. It ultimately happened a full year after that, because a pandemic convulsed the planet. Before, during, and after that premiere, my work and my life would be shaken by changes in the world around me. Many of my deepest beliefs, including my understanding of the world and my place in it, would be tested in ways I hadn't imagined possible. The plan I'd made for the next phase of my life would come to seem a little foolish.

I'm guessing that you can relate to the feeling, that you remember the scary sense of upheaval—the vertigo of spinning away from the world you'd known. Those couple of years were so messy and chaotic, with so many crises and disruptions, that even telling the story is a challenge. It was hard to know when the next blow might fall or from which direction it might come.

At least I'd been right about one thing: that it was time for me to grow up. Because that's exactly what happened. I had to do it in the most challenging way of all: learning to see the world for what it really is and not what I'd like it to be. Then using that new knowledge to decide, after all my trials and adventures, who I was ultimately going to become.

WE WERE IN POSTPRODUCTION in early 2020, spending long hours in our New York office rushing to finish editing the movie, when the world came undone. COVID-19 wreaked havoc on the city. At night, I listened to ambulances screaming up and down the avenues.

Executives at Warner Bros., the studio releasing *In the Heights,* said the commotion would last only a few days, so I should sit tight for a while, then keep editing. Anyway, they said, it was too risky to fly back to Los Angeles with so many people getting sick. But I could feel more trouble coming. And Kristin and the kids had already gone home. There was no way I was going to spend a pandemic lockdown with a continent between us. I told my assistant to stop answering calls from the studio, then headed to JFK.

In the months that followed, COVID remade societies all over the world, claiming millions of lives, devastating families, and emptying cities. But it brought a special terror for Asian Americans. Once the president started talking about the "China virus" at political rallies, we knew what was coming. And it came.

According to a Pew poll, 14 percent of Asian Americans had someone blame them personally for COVID-19. Relatives of mine were harassed and assaulted. A cousin told me that home didn't feel like home anymore. I knew what she meant. I'd begun to feel unsafe walking around L.A. in a way I'd never felt unsafe before. This wasn't what I thought America could be.

As the anti-Asian rhetoric got louder and stories about sidewalk attacks spread, I worried more and more about my parents. My dad had long ago learned to brush off the occasional rude or racist comment from a customer. But how long can you keep doing that when the world has gone crazy?

The nightmare that we'd all been fearing finally happened. Eight people died in a rampage at three spas around Atlanta. Six of the dead were women of Asian descent. Even in a country that was routinely terrorized by mass shootings, the news was monstrous, sickening. Especially once I saw the photos of the women who'd been killed. They could have been members of my own family.

Gold House helped to launch the #StopAsianHate movement. Using the infrastructure it had created to support *Crazy Rich Asians,* the organization raised millions of dollars for AAPI-led causes. I helped to spread the word about them, but I was uneasy. My new sense of purpose made me feel a deeper responsibility for the well-being of our Asian brothers and sisters, our mothers and fathers and grandparents. It was hard to know how to fulfill it. I've never felt comfortable as an activist. I've never felt that I knew the right things to say, so I always feel an impulse to defer to the people who do and let my movies speak for me. But I knew that with the new visibility I'd received after *Crazy Rich Asians,* I needed to speak out in spite of my self-doubt.

I accepted an invitation to go on CNN. My anger and sadness, which were still raw, found their way on camera. Among other things, I said that Hollywood bore some of the blame for what had happened because of the constant demeaning stereotypes of Asian women in movies. At the end of the interview, the host, Ana Cabrera, thanked me for doing my part, but I cut her off.

"I haven't done enough," I said. "We have not done enough. So this is just the beginning."

I meant what I'd said. I knew that I had more to do. It was one of the essential ways in which I needed to grow up. In the meantime, some basic confidence I'd always had in this country, about the welcome it extended to people like my family—about the fact of our belonging here—was being tested more each day. Had I been a fool to believe it?

WHEN THE PANDEMIC CLOSED movie theaters, leaving viewers endless hours trapped at home with their TVs, it accelerated changes already under way in Hollywood. The digital technology that had started to arrive from Silicon Valley around the time that I did suddenly played a larger and larger role in the industry. Especially now that the "streaming wars" were in full swing.

Those wars had begun when legacy media companies looked at the success of Netflix and decided the only way to compete with the endlessly growing tech company was to copy it. The corporate parents of virtually every studio concluded that they needed their own direct-to-consumer streaming services, even if building them meant adding billions of dollars in expenses and forsaking billions of dollars in licensing revenue.

Our studio, Warner Bros., was one of the war's chief combatants. Its parent company, WarnerMedia, had launched HBO Max to compete with Netflix, Disney+, and other streamers. Now it needed fresh content to attract subscribers. So when the pandemic forced us to cancel the premiere of *In the Heights,* the studio gave us a choice: We could keep our original premiere date and release the movie on HBO Max, or we could stick with a theatrical release—but it would mean waiting a full year.

I had a feeling of déjà vu: It was like being back on that high-stakes phone call when Kevin Kwan and I had to decide whether to make *Crazy Rich Asians* with Netflix or Warner Bros. This time, like last time, I felt sure that we needed the power of the big screen to achieve our goals. We wanted the scale and visibility of a cinematic event to elevate those Latinx lives and stories, to make new stars. So Lin, Quiara, the producers, and I decided to hold out for a theatrical release.

In the "before times," that would have settled the matter. But one day during postproduction, in December 2020, I received a call from an executive at Warner Bros. She informed me that in forty-five minutes, the studio was going to announce that *In the Heights* would be released on HBO Max on the same day as the movie's theatrical premiere. It was going to happen even though we had all agreed on a big-screen release, not a streaming release.

And no, there was nothing we could do about it.

This plan, internally called Project Popcorn, was WarnerMedia's attempt to salvage the botched launch of HBO Max. It had failed because the service didn't offer enough original content. But then (I imagine) somebody remembered that Warner Bros. had *In the Heights* and sixteen other movies slated for cinematic release in 2021. For decades, studios and theater owners had battled over the proper length of the release window, the number of days that a movie appears on a big screen and nowhere else. Project Popcorn was WarnerMedia's way of unilaterally dropping that number to zero, then doing it sixteen more times.

I'll be honest: In the early part of my career, with my Silicon Valley upbringing, I probably would have supported that change. A movie is a movie, so why not let customers choose where they want to watch it? If the release window has been getting squeezed for years, why not finish it off? But in light of the new way I'd started to think about movies after *Crazy Rich Asians,* I changed my mind. I'd seen proof that a movie in a theater has a power that doesn't transfer to any other situation. The immense scale of the images, the sound so big you can feel it, the energy generated when hundreds of strangers focus their attention on a single point: Movies can elevate lives and shift perceptions like no other form of storytelling. *In the Heights* needed that power even more than *Crazy Rich Asians* had. I felt that Project Popcorn was surrendering it much too quickly.

I also felt, more generally, that it was a shitty thing to do.

Ask anybody: Until that morning, Warner Bros. seemed like the last studio that would pull something like this. A unilateral decision, without consultation, with barely any warning to its filmmakers. I'd enjoyed long, close relationships with a lot of people there. They'd promised that they'd always be up-front with us. I didn't blame them for what happened, because I could tell they weren't calling the shots anymore. In 2018, Warner Bros. had become part of AT&T. Ironically, the acquisition had happened because Jeff Bewkes, coiner of the famous "Albanian army" metaphor for Netflix, had decided that Time Warner, then the parent of Warner Bros., couldn't survive on its own. (One analyst called the merger "a Hail Mary pass" for Warner Bros. to survive in a field shaken up by Netflix.)

The move seemed even shittier once I saw the public announcement. WarnerMedia had made an elaborate trailer to accompany the press release, which told me that studio execs had known about the decision for weeks—the same weeks when they'd gotten suddenly and unexpectedly generous with me. They'd offered me the chance to direct a DC Comics movie of my choice. They'd also fast-tracked negotiations to close a deal for *Crazy Rich Asians 2*. Had it all been a ploy to reel me in closer before I heard what was coming? I didn't know. I still don't know. But once I saw that trailer, I shut down those conversations.

There's a lesson here. If you're going to compete against a tech company, it's not enough to hire a bunch of programmers and rent a server farm. You'll also need to embrace their world-view, the Silicon Valley philosophy that Netflix had deployed with such sensational results: Grow. Grow at any cost. Grow no matter what you've promised. That approach had made so much sense to me when I was younger. I'd believed it—I'd acted on it. But with my new understanding of what movies could do and my sense of purpose about why I should be making them, I had a different point of view. This was no way to run an industry. Not one where artists and businesspeople need to work together, which means they need to trust each other.

On opening weekend, after all the accolades and interviews and parties, it took an unusually, excruciatingly long time for us to learn how *In the Heights* had fared. We'd hoped that the weekend box office total would surpass $20 million. A number that high would mean unequivocal victory. It would open the lane for Latinx artists and stories that all of us wanted to open. Based on the reviews and the buzz, and our underlying belief that moviegoers were ready to return to theaters, we were confident we'd reach it. In fact, I nursed a quiet hope that people might be so hungry to come back to the movies that we'd blow past that projection. But the actual number turned out to be $11.5 million, lower than I'd thought possible.

It was crushing. It was bewildering. What had happened? There's probably no single answer, only a bunch of contributing factors. First, it's always a stretch to turn a movie that doesn't have huge stars and isn't a sequel into a hit, even one that had gotten some of the best reviews of the year. Second, musicals tend to do best in the winter, but we thought that for a summer story like ours, June would be our safest bet. A third factor, compounding the other two, was the pandemic. We'd believed that after people had gotten vaccinated, they'd rush back to the theaters. We were wrong. COVID was turning out to have a more lasting and more destructive impact on movie-going than we'd realized. A few months later, Bob Iger would say that the pandemic had inflicted "a severe injury that maybe doesn't heal." *In the Heights* caught more of the blast than a lot of other movies. The audiences for musicals tend to be older, but older moviegoers were turning out to be the last demographic group to come back.

Finally, there was Project Popcorn. Giving viewers an alternate way to see the movie had muddled the messaging—you should either rush out to see it right away or catch it for free sometime from your couch—which diminished the sense of urgency that marketing campaigns need. It seems that the movie didn't draw a huge streaming audience either, so the effect might not have been huge, but it was big enough to matter. We had counted on opening at number one that weekend, so we could declare victory no matter how many tickets we sold. But we missed number one by half a million dollars, a tiny gap that would likely have disappeared if home viewers had gone to the theater instead. Hollywood, obsessed as ever with numbers and rankings, would have viewed it differently over the long term.

I was confused—and not just about the fate of the movie. For half a lifetime, I'd felt certain that I understood technology and could make the right choices about how to use it. But now who even got to choose? Suddenly technology didn't feel like a set of tools for me to deploy; it felt like a system being imposed on me—and the rest of us.

It's strange: You can grow up in Silicon Valley, and spend decades watching it disrupt one industry after another, and still not be ready when the industry being disrupted is yours.

I packed my bags and headed for JFK, once again bound for home. But more upheaval waited for me when I landed. The movie was being criticized for not featuring dark-skinned Afro-Latinx actors prominently enough in a story set in a predominantly Dominican neighborhood. We'd had a lot of conversations during preproduction about casting, about finding the right way to reflect the makeup of the neighborhood and—our ultimate aim—to capture the breadth of Latinidad. We thought we'd done it right, representing as many different sizes, shapes, home countries, and skin tones as we could. And we were proud that the movie had a virtually all-Latinx cast, after a year in which only 4 percent of speaking roles in Hollywood movies had gone to Latinx actors. The response told us that no matter what we thought or what our intentions had been, we'd missed crucial nuances in our representation. It was a painful message to absorb. After we'd made something in the name of love and inclusion, a movie about hopes and dreams instead of the stereotypes that Hollywood traditionally spreads about Latinx lives, it was soul-crushing to hear anyone say they felt left out.

Instead of trying to defend ourselves, we chose to respect the concerns that people had raised. We decided that we would do what we wished people would have done when we'd brought up our own examples of insufficient representation in the past: Shut up and listen. Lin wrote a post on our behalf that offered an acknowledgment of the criticism, an apology, and a vow to do better in the future.

Meantime, social media had begun doing what social media does. I knew from experience that it was time to log off and stay off. But the damage to my sense of myself, and the kind of positive impact that I thought my work could have, had been done.

In the sudden silence that followed premiere week, I tried to understand what had happened. I'd wanted to engage with the world, then discovered that the world was not what I thought it was, in all sorts of ways: the status of Asians in this country, the relationship between Silicon Valley and Hollywood, the appeal of the stories I wanted to tell and my ability to tell them. I missed the days when I'd felt so much confidence in my picture of the world and my place in it. But there was no going back to the euphoric reception of *Crazy Rich Asians* or our joyous summer in Washington Heights. There was only this new world, with no clear path through it that I could see.

WEEKS PASSED. THE FESTIVITY around our premiere—hugs for friends, raucous parties, Lin's parents teaching my parents how to salsa dance—began to seem like a little window of communal joy that had immediately slammed shut. Because in spite of our vaccines, the Delta variant started driving people back into their homes. Case counts climbed higher than before. Then the Omicron wave pushed them higher still. Was this ever going to end?

From a distance, I tried to keep in touch with friends from

the movie, but it was hard to know what to say. The heartbreak was too sudden and too severe. In my disappointment and confusion, I could feel depression very close by, as I had after the collapse of *Bye Bye Birdie* and again after *Jem*. Memories of surviving those ordeals gave me strength this time around. So did a feeling of pride that lived alongside the disappointment: With *In the Heights,* we'd made something radical—truly radical—telling stories that wouldn't have been told, showcasing actors who finally got to prove what they could do.

I also drew resilience from my kids. A week after the opening of *In the Heights,* and two years after we'd welcomed our son, he and Willow got a baby sister, Ruby. I wanted all three of them to see that the world was beautiful, even though at the moment it didn't seem beautiful to me. I wanted them to feel that it was a joy to create, even though I'd rarely felt less of that joy. In teaching them, I was inadvertently teaching myself.

All the while, I tried to make sense of how Hollywood had changed. That wasn't easy, because the changes hadn't stopped. In fact, the more I looked, the more confounding they seemed. By some amazing cosmic coincidence, twenty years after Steven Spielberg and I had bonded over wanting to direct a musical, we'd gotten our wish in the same year and even in the same neighborhood: While I was filming *In the Heights,* he was right around the corner filming *West Side Story*. His movie got great reviews. It had the makings of a big hit. Then it opened with a lower box office total than *In the Heights* had.

If Steven Spielberg himself couldn't open a movie in this confusing new reality, what hope did the rest of us have?

In the newly tech-dominated Hollywood, it seemed that the only storytellers positioned for sustained success were industry-spanning multihyphenates, the people who constantly generated new material for multiple platforms. If I wanted to play that game, I would need to work even harder than I'd been working. Much harder. Exponentially harder. My adolescent dream of running a company, always hovering in the background of whichever movie I happened to be directing, now seemed like a necessity. Of course, with the ground having shifted so profoundly under my feet, I wasn't sure what my prospective company would actually make. All I knew was that with big-screen movies seemingly endangered, I would need to think of myself as somebody who made content for any and every platform I could. Man, I hate the word "content."

Except then the landscape convulsed yet again—and more violently than before. Netflix announced that after a decade of relentless growth, it had, for the first time, lost subscribers. Its stock price plunged 35 percent in a day; its market value fell by $50 billion. You didn't have to grow up in Silicon Valley to hear echoes of the dot-com crash. An era of high hopes and astronomical spending ended in a flash—and not just for Netflix. With precious few exceptions, everybody in Hollywood had chased Netflix's model and everybody had lost. Wall Street decided that it now cared about profits, not growth. But the legacy media companies had just torn apart a business model that had generated a century's worth of profits so they could make a headlong pursuit of growth.

In 2010, the year I met Steve Jobs, I felt sure that there was limitless possibility in the union of Hollywood and Silicon Valley—the union that he embodied. Now the two worlds had smashed together, leaving Hollywood in shambles. None of the industry's leaders seemed to know a way out of the mess. I certainly didn't have any answers. But I also couldn't just sit around, hoping that one day everything would make sense again.

So it was time for one last shift of vision. I had to make one more attempt to see myself and my place in this disordered world clearly. I felt that I had some advantages, like the fact that I'd seen both Silicon Valley and Hollywood from the inside. And I'd begun to understand my family history, which meant that the deep background of my worldview had finally come into focus. Somehow I had to see it all in the new light of the last few years, with the dislocations in society and technology and the industry and my life.

This book that you've been reading is a record of that search. The story I've been telling you is a story I first had to tell myself. And at the end of it, I found what I was looking for—some insights to reorient myself in a changing world and to keep moving.

WHEN I REFLECTED ON the movies I'd made, I noticed a pattern. The moments that I was proudest of, that audiences had responded to the most, tended to be the moments that my collaborators and I had worked out together: the *LXD* experiments with Alice and Chris, the cliff fight with action figures in *G.I. Joe,* Ken Jeong's freewheeling lunch scene in *Crazy Rich Asians*. Those moments had worked because the *process* had worked. I had carved out space and allowed time for creative breakthroughs to happen—for all of us to make one another smarter and more inventive. The moments that didn't work as well tended to be when I came up with some idea, then pursued it without leaving any room for deviation.

The lesson, it seemed to me, was that I needed to spend more time and energy getting my process right, day by day, and less time stressing about how much progress I was making toward some far-off destination I'd chosen. That required a lot of trust, both in my collaborators and in myself: a confidence that if you get today right, you'll be able to get tomorrow right, too.

This wasn't just a lesson about creative work. When my kids would get upset, I didn't just soothe them and send them on their way. I tried to help them understand why they felt the way they did. Instead of waving their pain away, I urged them to acknowledge that it was real. I showed them how to be calm, to breathe. It might be a good thing for all of us to have in our toolbox: a process for getting our joy back.

I started wondering where I'd picked up this habit of fixating on a spot far down the road and not being mindful of what was right in front of me. Why had I been so unprepared for all the changes the world threw at me? In large part, I learned it in—and from—Silicon Valley. Its worldview encourages you to keep your eyes on the horizon, looking past today in favor of the dreamy tomorrow that's going to rise into view. Experience had taught me that if you indulge that habit, you can end up looking in the wrong places for the wrong things.

In other words, you can end up like a movie studio.

One way to understand how the industry fell apart is that the leaders of Hollywood's legacy media companies didn't grasp the difference between getting a process right and obsessing about progress toward some goal. These legendary studios, some of which have been around for a century, didn't understand the strengths they were sacrificing in their quest to turn themselves into Netflix. They didn't know who they were.

Looking back along the paths I'd traveled, I could see lots of examples of people and organizations not knowing who they were, myself included. But one institution had always known: Chef Chu's. Within months of opening the restaurant, my dad had figured out its identity. He saw a need in his community and he filled it. Then he went on filling it for the next fifty years.

Very belatedly, I began to appreciate his decision not to expand to lots of new locations. It might have brought him money and attention, but he already had a successful restaurant. So what value would he be serving? He was right to defy the Silicon Valley logic of endless growth and to brush aside the son who argued on its behalf. The same son who, many years later, would extract from this story a lesson that would change his life.

Dad's example helped me to realize that Silicon Valley's obsession with growth and Hollywood's obsession with success—the flowchart that keeps you moving from hit to hit—are two versions of the same disorder. Neither of them considers values, or a lasting sense of worth. They don't ask *why,* they care only about *how many* and *how much.*

That realization made me think differently about the dream I'd harbored since high school of building my own creative company. At the time, it seemed like a way to extend my reach and maximize my impact. I began to see that it hadn't grown out of a creative impulse; it was just an expression of the worldview that Silicon Valley had planted in me and that

Hollywood had nurtured: that more is always more. Dad had wanted me to see that the opposite is true: that enough can be enough.

I'd finally gotten the message. So I let go of my adolescent dream of building a sprawling enterprise, just as my dad had. I want to save my creative energy for the stories I choose to tell. I want to spend my time with my family, preparing my kids for what's coming. That's the work that matters most.

When I thought back to how I was raised in Silicon Valley in the '80s and '90s, and contemplated the very different world in which my kids were growing up, I realized I couldn't follow my dad's lead—or my mom's. In some important ways, I needed to do the opposite.

Now that I truly knew my parents' story, I understood that they'd wanted to spare me the ordeals they'd faced when they got here. So they had encouraged my desire to be an all-American boy, someone fully assimilated into the mainstream culture. I loved them for wanting that for me. And their choices did help me to reach some new places in my life: to get into the college I'd wanted to attend and the industry of my dreams. But an impulse to be like everybody else couldn't bring me any lasting sense of fulfillment.

The whole point of *Crazy Rich Asians*—the element of the movie that made Asian Americans tell me they felt proud—is that we need to create our own identity on our own terms. My children won't grow up thinking that there's safety or value or beauty in trying to be like somebody else. If I can help it, they'll learn to embrace all the traditions that make them who they are and to do it a lot more quickly than I have. They'll know that they are enough.

Above all, they won't ever hear the phrase "Never complain." That might have helped my parents' generation to survive, but it's holding us back. In light of the Asian hate attacks, it's past time for us to stop accepting other people's ideas of who we are or absorbing comments that we used to let slide. Hollywood has made progress since I got here. The stuff people routinely said in meetings twenty years ago would get them all canceled today. But there's still plenty of unacceptable stuff being said and done, and I've gotten a lot quicker to call bullshit on it. Recently, when an Asian American executive told me he didn't have the power to protect a role for an Asian American actor, and I thought that he did, I challenged him. When a line producer on a project said he would strive for diversity in hiring but of course it wouldn't be possible in a certain crucial department, I let him know that if he didn't find it in that department, he was out.

Speaking up in meetings will help. I know it's one of the ways that I need to use the visibility—and live up to the responsibility—that came my way after *Crazy Rich Asians*. But my best chance of making a positive contribution in this world will always be through the stories I tell. My confusion and sadness after *In the Heights* led me to question a lot of things about my life, but I never really questioned that. So how do I go about it?

Considering what I've seen of Silicon Valley and Hollywood, I don't feel hugely optimistic about the future of that relationship. I can imagine the famous old studios ending up as minor divisions of tech companies. Movies would act as the little bit of sugar that gets you to part with your data for the benefit of advertisers. Not just your credit card number, but your taste, your sense of humor—qualities that lie so much closer to your soul.

I don't like the look of that future. But if it comes to pass, it becomes more important, not less, that we flood the system with our dreams and visions, that we keep telling new stories about who we are and what we want the world to be.

For me, that means telling the kinds of stories that people used to call me naive or whimsical thinking or weak for wanting to tell: stories about kindness and optimism. That has become a strength to me now, because it's a way of ensuring the system isn't filled with cynicism and division. And I know that no matter what happens to Hollywood, the best way for me to do it will always be making movies.

Not content—*movies*.

The big commercial kind that go on big screens. The kind that excite people and make them eager to sit in the dark and experience together. It could be that movies never again have the cultural prominence they had when I saw *E.T.* with my family or when so many people turned out for *Crazy Rich Asians* that they shifted the culture. But after seeing what I've seen in my years in Hollywood, I wouldn't ever underestimate the power of cinema. No other medium can change the culture as drastically or as quickly. Films offer visions that are too sweeping for a TV to contain, too rich to be absorbed in thirty-second clips on your phone.

Movies are the light in the dark. They take you out of yourself and transport you into another person's experience. They give you a reason to believe that heroes are real, that love can be true, and that America can be what it has promised to be. They spark wonder that transcends your senses. They show you a make-believe land and make it call to you.

After all my doubts, I couldn't wait to make another one. And I couldn't believe the chance that came my way.

KEEP MAKING THE MOVIE
UNTIL THEY SHUT YOU DOWN

This old-school Hollywood advice, which I had the good luck to hear when I was just starting out—and which is really a philosophy of life—doesn't need any explaining. It just needs repeating. And repeating. And repeating . . .

IT STARTED WITH A phone call to my agent. A cryptic one.

An exec at Universal wanted to check my availability for a project—one that he wasn't allowed to name. My agent, being a very good agent, pretty quickly figured out what the movie had to be: *Wicked*.

As you might recall, I'd loved the show since I'd seen its pre-Broadway tryout all the way back in 2003. It had been on my list of dream projects for as long as I'd been a director. The studio was planning to do it as two full movies, so Universal was really asking about my interest in making what would be by far the biggest and most complex undertaking of my career.

All those factors made me want to do it. The question was: Was there a connection between the show and what I had begun to feel about my work and the world?

So I listened to the songs.

I appreciated all over again how cleverly the show relates to *The Wizard of Oz*. Its promise to the audience is: *You weren't told the whole story. There's a different perspective.* This idea spoke to me when I was reconsidering so many of the things I'd been taught, things I'd accepted without questioning. Glinda goes through life in a bubble, and then it pops, and she has to confront some hard realities of life. Elphaba learns that the Wizard isn't what she was led to believe. That's the point of "Defying Gravity"—she acknowledges that everything she's been told is a lie, and out of that anger and feeling of betrayal, she discovers her power and begins to fly.

I thought too about the sense of purpose I'd begun to feel and how reinterpreting stories about Oz would help me to serve it. Those stories occupy a powerful, unique place in our national culture, since they're one of the only truly American myths. They didn't get imported from someplace else: L. Frank Baum dreamed them up right here. And the 1939 movie version, starring Judy Garland, might be the most beloved film of all time. It wasn't lost on me what it would mean to have this iconic American story reimagined by the son of immigrants. Somebody who is, like Elphaba, a child of two worlds.

To make a version of these stories that suits our time, I'd have to find a way to be more precise and more thoughtful about casting than I'd ever been before, across every dimension: race, gender, and also disability, because Elphaba's sister, Nessarose, uses a wheelchair. The result wouldn't look like the vision of America I received from mass culture growing up, a monochrome vision of Main Street, USA. Our job would be to present a more honest depiction of the country as it exists today and to do what past generations of Americans did before us: tell a story that restates the country's ideals, that shows the kind of values we aspire to for the future.

To bring Oz to life on-screen, I'd draw on what I'd learned

in all my adventures about technology's possibilities—and its limits. In spite of all the fantastical elements in the story, I'd want to underscore the reality of the characters' relationships, the messy human dynamics. I'd want to bring the audience to a place beyond the rainbow and make it seem real to them—so real that they could smell the flowers, touch the dirt, feel the wind. Computers would generate some of these effects, but to a great extent—probably a surprising extent, for somebody who grew up obsessed with digital tools—I'd want to really build things, to render them in three solid dimensions.

By finding a balance between cutting-edge technology and old-fashioned craft, I could make a larger point about Silicon Valley and Hollywood. Despite their recent collision, tech isn't the enemy. Nor is it a savior. It's still what it has always been: a series of tools. Steve Jobs, who understood this better than anybody, called computers a "bicycle of the mind," something that can carry us further than we could go on our own.

I took a deep breath and shared all these ideas with the key figures on the project: Stephen Schwartz and Winnie Holzman, who created the musical; Marc Platt, the producer; and Donna Langley, the head of the studio, whom I'd met all the way back on my water-bottle tour after film school, when we bonded over our dance backgrounds. All of them gave me their blessing.

It meant that like Dorothy, Elphaba, and Glinda before me, I could begin to wonder: *What will it be like when I get to the Emerald City?*

I imagined shades of green on green. There would be magic—not the supernatural kind, but the kind that comes from wondrous machines, like the inside of a clock. And it would be *huge,* towering over me. That immense scale meant that I'd finally get to direct the kind of big, inclusive, wonder-inducing spectacle that Steven Spielberg makes, at dimensions that had awed me when I visited him on the set of *The Terminal.*

There's a lesson here about not giving up on yourself that you don't need me to spell out. In fact, I'm glad it took me so long to get to the Emerald City—that I would see it for the first time as an adult. By reaching it after the sudden shocks and commotion of the pandemic years, I'd have an advantage over everybody who had preceded me.

Dorothy, Glinda, and Elphaba arrived thinking that their problems were going to be solved, their questions were going to be answered. Because of the paths that I took to get here, I know better than to expect that. The Emerald City can't deliver a happily-ever-after ending, because no such thing exists. There will always be another question to answer, another story to tell. I will savor every second of my time on that set, then I'll leave. And after I finish making my film about the witches of Oz, I'll make a different one. I don't know what it will be, but I trust that when the time comes, I'll figure it out.

Then I'll do it again. And I'll keep on doing it, always feeling the same sense of purpose, and the same uncertainty about what lies ahead, that I have learned to feel today.

We can't expect any single path to take us all the way to our destination anymore. Even the yellow brick road is only showing you where somebody else thinks you should go. I used to think that Glinda was being friendly when she started Dorothy down the lane that leads to the Emerald City, but when I rewatch *The Wizard of Oz* these days, I'm not so sure. Dorothy starts to ask, "But what happens if I—" and Glinda won't let her finish. It seems a little manipulative, another case of a young person being steered down a predetermined path. Each of us needs to find our *own* path. Doing so will take us through pain and fear, but if we trust in ourselves and listen to one another, we'll get through it.

At one point in L. Frank Baum's original novel about Oz, Dorothy and her friends realize they've gotten lost. She tries to reassure them: "If we walk far enough, we shall sometime come to some place, I am sure."

EPILOGUE

I grew up in the future. But I don't live there anymore.

I still love to get my hands on new technology as soon as it appears: virtual reality headsets, 3D printers, AI software. I'm just as excited to figure out how it works as I ever was. But I no longer feel like I have secret advance knowledge of what's coming. That belongs to an earlier phase of my life, when I was a wide-eyed kid, when the boundaries of my world were set by the edges of Silicon Valley.

I've shed other views from that time and that place. Like the belief that every upgrade or beta release leads to meaningful progress for the world. Or that things that happened yesterday are somehow obsolete and no longer matter. Or that tomorrow will—all by itself, without any special effort from us—turn out to be an improvement on today. Some days, I miss that easy optimism, but I know it's better to be free of it. Because once you see the world as it really is—and really was—you have a chance of helping it to become what it might be.

No matter how much I drift away from the place, Silicon Valley still occupies a big part of my heart and mind. It's in my DNA. Even when I'm on the other side of the world.

The search for soundstages big enough for *Wicked*—that is, absolutely, staggeringly gigantic—led all the way to England. So Kristin, our kids, and I made plans to spend a year in London. After we arrived, I needed to fly back to Los Angeles now and then. One of those trips left me with a little extra time in California. It was less than a day but still enough to do what I really wanted: fly up to Los Altos to visit Mom and Dad.

It's been hard to see much of them lately. In fact, it had been more than a year. You can probably relate to the reasons: the pandemic, the demands of having young children, the pressures of work. Since the trip was happening on very short notice, I decided to have some fun with it. I asked my brother Larry to help me arrange a surprise. He agreed to coax them to the restaurant, then keep them there until I arrived.

The whole family was glad and a little relieved that Chef Chu's made it through the pandemic when so many other businesses didn't. I was happy to see its familiar features rising into view: the sign that my grandfather had designed, the eternal red door. Lately the restaurant seems like even more of an outlier than it used to. Silicon Valley has brought massive changes to Hollywood, but the reverse is also true. There's a showiness, a thirst for celebrity, that didn't exist here when I was a kid—not even in the heyday of Steve Jobs, still the greatest showman I've ever seen. Maybe I've slightly romanticized my memories of the '80s and '90s. Maybe it wasn't as heavily populated by engineers, unflashy men and women who went to work each day genuinely believing they were making the world a better place (and sometimes coming to Chef Chu's for dinner). But having seen Silicon Valley and Hollywood up close over decades, I can't shake the feeling that each has absorbed some of the worst qualities of the other.

My parents and three of my siblings still live around here. Larry and Chrissy help at the restaurant now, and Howard is at home with Mom and Dad. But in spite of family ties and history, Silicon Valley doesn't feel like home to me anymore. Home is wherever Kristin and our children are. There's even a kind of symmetry in my life: I used to be a kid with four older siblings. Since the birth of my son Ignatius (or Iggy)—our little Londoner—I'm a father with four kids of my own. It's not easy to reconcile two sets of traditions: the one I built here with my parents and brothers and sisters, and the one I'm building now with Kristin and our daughters and sons. Sometimes the past and present line up, but usually they don't, and I'm forced to choose. The complexity of directing the biggest movie musical of all time is nothing compared to figuring out our Christmas plans.

I'd reached the parking lot outside the restaurant. It was time for the big surprise. I FaceTimed my parents, pretending that I was in London. When I stepped inside, their reaction was everything I could have dreamed. Mom's mouth dropped open. Dad recoiled in shock. They both burst into tears.

A customer dining at Chef Chu's that afternoon, after not having been there for a decade or two, might have been startled to see how little my parents have aged. They still have health, energy, drive. You need to know them as intimately as my brothers and sisters and I do to notice the changes. We used to tease Dad that the only way he could still have jet-black hair, even as he approached his eighties, was by dyeing it. He always swore he didn't. In the last couple of years, a little bit of gray has finally begun to show. I guess he was telling the truth all along.

Mom remains indomitable, still calling the shots, still golfing (and still winning). But she sounds a little different lately, too. During prep for *Wicked,* we talked about *The Wizard of Oz,* which she'd watched many times as a girl. In both Taiwan and America, she hoped that she would find the Wizard. He would have answers to all her questions; he could make everything good. She's still looking for him, she says. But now she thinks that she'll run out of time.

There's a benefit to reaching your forties, though it's a bittersweet one. From here, you have an up-close view of the entire range of human life, from youth to age and all the points in between. On one side, I see Mom and Dad; on the other, my kids, who are still little but already have a past. With all the moving around we've done lately, we spend a lot of time putting things in boxes, then, weeks or months later, taking them out again. I already see them forgetting their connections to things that used to mean so much.

Being able to see both extremes, and the changes that happen in each, has led me to a final, belated discovery.

It involves the pile. The immovable, indestructible, apparently perpetual mountain of stuff in Mom and Dad's garage. That dumping ground for all the things they refused to throw away—things that I tried, in my younger days, to dispose of as a way of helping them. I remember how my mom cried at the sight of my bulging trash bags, how loudly we argued about why she should get rid of this junk. I was sure that it had no place in our eminently tidy, Polo-wearing lives. And I feel so much shame about it now, because I see how wrong I was.

Though my parents have a strange way of showing it—one that requires a big garage—their impulse was right. The things in the pile were never junk, not if Mom and Dad said they weren't. Each item was a link to a person. In most cases, to me or one of my siblings. Hanging on to those worn-out stuffed animals and disintegrating basketball shoes was really a way of hanging on to us. It was their way of trying to hold on to the disappearing past, even as the present rushes into the future. It was their attempt to hold it all.

There's beauty in the pile. It's the mess that shows we were here.

They helped me to realize that what I've tried to do in this book—looking at my past to see the present more clearly, trying to find a better way into the future—isn't something to do only when I feel lost. It's not something to undertake every couple of decades. It's a constant need, a daily practice. If we really want to know ourselves, each of us has to try to find a vantage point to see all of it: the messy past, the confusing present, the unknowable future.

You were right about the pile, Mom and Dad.

I didn't say it out loud. No matter how much introspection my family has been doing lately, heartfelt declarations are still not how we roll. Anyway, they had too many questions for me. They wanted to know all about our life in London. They wanted to see it. They practically grabbed my phone and its camera roll out of my hand. Do not stand between Bu Bu and pictures of her grandbabies.

I had to get back to the airport soon, so we made the most of the time we had. We sat down in the restaurant's private dining room. It's where I'd had my fifth birthday party, and the *Crazy Rich Asians* dinner that did so much for me, and where my dad hosted the cooking classes that did so much for him and for all of us. But there was no crowd this time. Just me and my mom and my dad, sharing a meal, talking and laughing, looking at pictures.

ACKNOWLEDGMENTS

The authors would like to thank the colleagues and friends whose inspired efforts made this book possible: Ben Greenberg, Susan Corcoran, Ayelet Durantt, London King, Alison Rich, and Leila Tejani of Random House; Allen Fischer and Brian Dobbins of Artists First; Rob Carlson and Jake Rotger of UTA; Bebe Lerner and Elisa Kim of ID; Lacy Lynch, Jan Miller, Dabney Rice, and Haley Reynolds of Dupree Miller; Jennifer Joel, Colin Graham, Jamie Stockton, and Sindhu Vegesana of CAA; Alison Binder of Goodman Genow Schenkman Smelkinson + Christopher LLP; Eric S. Brown of Eric S. Brown Law PLLC; and Jon's assistants, past and present: Jane Lee, Daisy Rodger, Kyle Chin, Reagan Shea, and Ashley Eakin.

We are grateful to Chris Allen for the jacket design; to Barbara Bachman for the interior design (and Stephanie Greenberg for some quick help with the images); to Kelly Chian for managing the process; to Evan Stone, Barbara Jatkola, and Frieda Duggan for the proofreading; to Richard Elman for the production; to Nancy Tan for the copyedit; to Julie Tate for factchecking; and to Jeff Yang for his invaluable feedback on the manuscript.

We also thank the people who generously shared their memories and insights with us in interviews: Alice Brooks, Bing Chen, Brenda Goodman, Christopher Scott, Dave Smith, and members of the Chu family. We are grateful to Dean Elizabeth Daley and Justin Wilson for a tour of The USC School of Cinematic Arts, to Scott Riches for a tour of Pinewood School, to the Polanowski family for their hospitality, and to Chef Lawrence Chu and Ruth Chu for all the dumplings.

For their love and boundless support, Jon thanks Kristin, Willow, Heights, Ruby, and Ignatius; and Jeremy thanks Julie, Sloane, and Alexandra. We love you, too.

JON M. CHU is known for his visually stunning blockbuster films, such as *In the Heights* and *Crazy Rich Asians,* which was nominated for numerous awards, including two Golden Globe Awards, one for Best Motion Picture—Musical or Comedy; a SAG Award for Outstanding Performance by an Ensemble in a Motion Picture; a PGA Award for Outstanding Producer of Theatrical Motion Pictures; and four Critics Choice Awards, winning one for Best Comedy. As the youngest of five children from Los Altos, California, Chu continues to use the influences of his childhood (family, technology, food, music, and movement) to tell personal stories in a variety of mediums that connect with audiences from around the world.

JEREMY MCCARTER is the author of *Young Radicals* and co-author, with Lin-Manuel Miranda, of the *New York Times* bestsellers *Hamilton: The Revolution* and *In the Heights: Finding Home* (also with Quiara Alegría Hudes). He is the founder and executive producer of Make-Believe Association, a Chicago-based audio storytelling company. He spent five years on the artistic staff of the Public Theater and serves as the literary executor of the novelist and playwright Thornton Wilder. He has written about culture and politics for *New York* magazine, *The New York Times,* *The Wall Street Journal,* and other publications. He lives in Chicago with his family.

ABOUT THE TYPE

This book was set in Bembo, a typeface based on an old-style Roman face that was used for Cardinal Pietro Bembo's tract *De Aetna* in 1495. Bembo was cut by Francesco Griffo (1450–1518) in the early sixteenth century for Italian Renaissance printer and publisher Aldus Manutius (1449–1515). The Lanston Monotype Company of Philadelphia brought the well-proportioned letterforms of Bembo to the United States in the 1930s.